D0078732

JULIA M. WATKINS, Ph.D., A.C.S.W., Associate Professor of Social Welfare and Coordinator of the Social Welfare Program at the University of Maine at Orono, received her M.S.W. and Ph.D. from the University of Utah. She is a member of the Publications Committee and the Task Force on Recruitment of Students to Social Work Education Programs of the Council on Social Work Education. She has served as a member of the Executive Committee of the Association of Baccalaureate Program Directors. With Dennis A. Watkins she has co-authored articles and reports focusing on the planning and delivery of rural social and health care services.

DENNIS A. WATKINS, Ph.D., Associate Professor of Community Development at the University of Maine at Orono, received his Ph.D. from the University of Utah. He is a member of the American Public Health Association and the National Association of Housing Redevelopment Officials. He has authored publications and reports in the areas of rural health, community services, and community economic development.

Springer Series on Social Work

Albert R. Roberts, D.S.W., Series Editor

Advisory Board: Joseph D. Anderson, D.S.W., Barbara Berkman, D.S.W., Paul H. Ephross, Ph.D., Sheldon R. Gelman, Ph.D., Nancy A. Humphreys, D.S.W., Louise P. Shoemaker, D.S.W., and Julia Watkins, Ph.D.

361.973
W335w

Social Policy and the Rural Setting

Julia M. Watkins, Ph.D., A.C.S.W.
Dennis A. Watkins, Ph.D.

Epilogue by Nancy A. Humphreys, D.S.W.

Springer Publishing Company
New York

TABOR COLLEGE LIBRARY
HILLSBORO, KANSAS 67063

870097

Copyright © 1984 by Springer Publishing Company, Inc.

All rights reserved

No part of this publication may be reproduced, stored in a retrieval system, or transmitted in any form or by any means, electronic, mechanical, photocopying, recording, or otherwise, without the prior permission of Springer Publishing Company, Inc.

Springer Publishing Company, Inc.
200 Park Avenue South
New York, New York 10003

84 85 86 87 / 10 9 8 7 6 5 4 3 2 1

Library of Congress Cataloging in Publication Data

Watkins, Julia M.
   Social policy and the rural setting.
   (Springer series on social work; v. 3)
   Includes bibliographies and index.
   1. Social service, Rural—United States. 2. United States—Social policy—1980–
3. United States—Rural conditions. I. Watkins, Dennis A. II. Title. III. Series.
HV95.W34 1984   361'.973   83-20358
ISBN 0-8261-4240-0

Printed in the United States of America

Contents

Preface and Acknowledgments

The purpose of this book is to introduce the reader to the study of social policy within the setting of an advanced industrial society and a changing rural environment. It is the major premise of the book that social policy, generally formulated from an urban perspective, impacts rural areas differently than it does urban centers. The impact, if viewed by examining the goals of a particular policy statement, is more often than not only marginal in addressing the needs of rural America. This book recognizes the interdependence of rural and urban settings yet shows the reader that urban solutions are not transportable to rural environments with similarly expected outcomes. This means that rural populations should be equal participants in emerging goals for all Americans but the implementation of those goals must recognize the differences between rural and urban settings.

It is not always clear to a general audience what constitutes rural. For social workers who live and work in sparsely populated areas, the characteristics that define rural are self-evident: professional isolation, long distances to travel, severe proverty and deprivation, and social service systems that do not fit our vision or expectation of how we can best work with people to improve their standard of living and give them encouragement for their own vision of the future. We also know that rural interior Maine with its bitter cold winters has little in common with Ocotillo, California, a desert retirement community 30 miles from the Imperial Valley. Rural America is characterized by immense diversity which must be emphasized in the social policy arena. Just as urban-designed policy performs a disservice in rural America, we likewise must be careful not to make policy responses based on a stereotype of rural America.

In part, the diversity characteristic of rural America is based on some relatively recent population changes—the in-migration or population turnaround in some rural areas. The setting of advanced industrial society coupled with the in-migration of populations leads to tensions between expectations of growth and a better quality of life and the desire to preserve the best of rural America. The social policy arena therefore becomes increasingly complex.

For the student, this book serves as an introduction to social policy analysis and formulation. Throughout, examples are used which highlight the rural environment and link it with contemporary social policy. The reader will find an integrated view of social policy rather than an examination of such specific policy arenas as health or children and families. The integration is achieved by analyzing the themes characteristic of contemporary social policy decisions and using specific pieces of social policy from several substantive areas as examples. In addition to the analysis according to prevailing philosophies of the welfare state, the implications for rural settings are underscored making the focus of the book on the interface of social policy and rural environments.

In writing this book several important issues became increasingly clear to us. First, it was necessary to supply the reader with a sufficient general base of traditional knowledge regarding social policy. At the same time we felt it important for the reader to have a sense of appreciation for the historical context of some of the contemporary social policy themes and then be able to begin applying the understanding to one's own social work practice. Issues of balance were most important. Second, to be most useful to the student, the study of policy must be anchored in an analytic perspective. We have chosen to present the setting and the basis for analysis and allow the student to construct the important analytic questions. To accomplish this purpose we have chosen to include extensive references. Moreover, we have chosen not to guide the reader in a preset direction with the inclusion of discussion questions and exercises.

A third issue that has become abundantly clear to us is the challenge of articulating a rural perspective from a wide range of literature found in numerous locations. Much literature in social work with a rural focus is descriptive and impressionistic. This literature base, while important, does not easily lend itself to documentation as is usually necessary in the formulation of social policy. The difficulty in finding much needed documentation was confirmed by the National Research Council in its report *Rural America in Passage* (1981), which cited the problems of insufficient and inappropriate data on rural populations, problems, and needs. Adding to our frustrations in trying to include for the reader the most recent sociodemographic data was the fact that detailed 1980 census data were not yet available. Where such specific program statistics as benefit levels are presented as part of case examples, it is done to provide a perspective on a particular principle. We are aware that specific figures quickly become outdated, but the principles do remain applicable.

A fourth observation, perhaps an issue, we want to convey to the reader is how we experienced firsthand the turbulence of the advanced industrial society. As we attempted to follow the development of social policy under a new federal administration, vast changes occurred quickly, and documentation became a process of reviewing numbers of professional newsletters and political reports that captured change in a timely fashion. We have attempted to convey these changes but one can only speculate about their full impact on rural areas at this time.

Although this work is not intended as a book in social work practice, it does, through an extensive list of references, familiarize the reader with some basic resources that will make interactions with social policy more productive. It can be seen as the analytic bridge between an introductory course in social services and a later course in macro or indirect methods—those methods frequently found highly useful in a rural community. As such it is assumed that the reader has a basic familiarity with the historical roots of the social welfare institution and social work practice.

To more fully acquaint the reader with the setting, Chapter 1 examines the characteristics of advanced industrial society, characteristics of rural environments, and the potential as well as actual interaction of the two. A definition of social policy and its importance as an area of study and action provide content for the first part of Chapter 2. This is followed by an examination of the generic policy choices from which the policy themes are developed. The policy choices—allocation, provision, delivery system, and funding—have provided the analytic framework for several policy books. To provide the base for the chapters which follow, the translation of the generic policy choices to the rural setting is presented in a brief, descriptive way.

Chapter 3 examines policy responses to income inadequacy

by briefly describing the present social insurance and public assistance programs and suggesting how each impacts rural populations. Current policy themes, derived from the advanced industrial society, provide the substance for Chapters 4 and 5. First, in Chapter 4, themes relevant to service delivery and organization are elucidated. Those themes more clearly oriented toward management and fiscal concerns are examined in Chapter 5. In our opinion, the policy themes we have chosen to examine are those having major implications for social work practice. Their understanding by the social work practitioner in a rural environment will facilitate the development of sound policy and agency level policy with a positive impact on rural people and their quality of life.

Chapter 6 serves to integrate and link social work practice in the rural setting with social policy and its formulation. To accomplish this goal we have chosen to articulate a strategic perspective of planning and program development as a way of responding to change, transitions, and resource scarcity. By using examples of services to the elderly and child welfare, applications are suggested which draw from material presented in previous chapters.

As learning outcomes, we expect that the reader will be more aware of the complexities of the policy process and be able to participate conceptually and analytically in that process, understand and anticipate the implications of social policy for social work practice, and, in a more limited way, know how to begin to impact social policy decisions directly to the benefit of rural populations.

No book is the sole product of its authors. To many people we express gratitude and appreciation: To Professor Milton I. Roemer for his exceptional insights and commitment to a just society, and to Edward O. Moe for his understanding of rural settings we are deeply appreciative; to Albert R. Roberts who provided encouragement and guidance, and to Florence Bubar whose steadfast commitment sustained us; and finally, to our children, Matthew, Christopher, and Andrew who busied themselves many weekends trying not to disturb.

Social Policy and
the Rural Setting

1 The Setting

Introduction

While rural populations should have equal participation with their urban counterparts in the development of national goals (Powers & Moe, 1982), the ways in which the two populations are affected by social policy differ. Therefore, before the interface can be addressed adequately, it is necessary to understand the broader societal forces and issues that constrain social policy in the rural setting. For purposes of discussion, these forces are presented as the challenges to the formulation of social policy, the setting of post-industrial society, and characteristics of the rural environment, including changing migration patterns. It is to a discussion of these forces that this chapter is directed.

Challenges to Social Policy

As the decade of the 1980s unfolds, the profession of Social Work finds itself in an increasingly turbulent and uncertain environment. During this period and during that of the next few decades, the future of social work may be, in the words of Beck (1981, p. 367), "triumph or disaster." Although there is disagreement as to the permanence of the neoconservative movement and its effect on social programs, there is growing concern that the programs and a political constituency carefully built and developed over the past 50 years are in danger of being abruptly dismantled during the early months of a newly elected, conservative administration (Stoesz, 1981).

The undercurrent and pressures of what has been identified as the "conservative revolution" (Stewart, 1981) are forcing a re-examination of the fundamental values and belief structures of the Social Work profession as it seeks to chart its direction for the future. Minahan (1981, p. 363) suggests that social workers have the responsibility to help people adjust to or shape their future as well as to act in ways that will shape a broader future of which the profession is part. In the words of Beck (1981):

> Adherence to the interest in social issues and social action that characterized our forebears and still characterizes social work leadership is the right direction and the only direction that can ultimately bring about a world order characterized by peace and justice.

The policy issues being raised are challenges to the mission of social work. How the profession and its individual members respond will have far-reaching implications. Policy questions include the following:

1. Will the traditional commitment to the poor and disadvantaged as a client system continue or will there be an increasing emphasis on a more middle-class client system?
2. Will social policy be directed in the liberal tradition toward enhancing the ability of institutions to address human problems of a post-industrial society or will social control prevail as a guiding philosophy (Rochefort, 1981)?
3. What will be the funding base for social programs as the federal government decreases its financial role in the area of social program funding?
4. Under whose auspice will the majority of social programs be delivered? Will there be a demise of the public sector? What role will the private sector be willing/able to perform?
5. What will be the form a social provision takes? Will cash and vouchers exchangeable in the open market prevail over public in-kind provisions or will new mixes of the two develop?
6. Will there be a retrenchment of service diversification, that is, a return to services aimed primarily at reducing poverty and dependency (Gilbert, 1977)?
7. To what degree will an intensified integration of informal and formal support networks be able to reinforce sepa-

rately functioning systems without sacrifice in the quality of services under conditions of resource scarcity (Froland, 1980)?

An eighth policy question related specifically to the profession is:

8. Will the profession turn increasingly inward to issues of self-interest or will it maintain a broad vision true to its historical base and take a proactive stance to shape the future?

The answers to these questions are both difficult and complex. On the one hand, there are certain structural developments in society which tend to indicate that the current resurgence of a conservative view toward social policy is something more than a swing of the pendulum. With the growing proportion of the population at 65 years and over; declining productivity in the economy; high unemployment; and unpredictable inflationary pressures, a structural scarcity must be acknowledged that will require a fundamental reexamination of our current social policies. On the other hand, if the commitment to the traditional mission of social work is to be maintained, nothing short of vigorous advocacy and social action will be required to diminish the impact of the current changes, maintain the historical focus of social work, and intensify the participation of social workers in shaping the future as equitable and just.

Post-industrial Society

Understanding social policy and its formulation and impact requires a knowledge and appreciation of the characteristics of a setting in historical perspective—that is, the broader social, political, and economic context (Sarason, 1973). Social policy is developed as a response to the environment, and in a reciprocal way it is impacted by the environment. According to Rein and Peattie (1981), policy is shaped by the actions taken or those viewed as possible.[1] This arena of action is shaped by the institutional and

[1]The position taken by Rein and Peattie is that social policy is developed from actions taken and those thought possible. This is in contrast to the prevailing view expressed in Chapter 2, that social policy develops and serves as a guide to action. Aside from academic abstractions, the policy development process probably involves both parameters interacting reciprocally.

programmatic responses of the social, political, and economic spheres of activity. Failing to recognize the interplay of social policy and the setting, policy analysis, formulation, and implementation become static concepts, void of the dynamic forces of change and development.

Bell (1967 a, b; 1973) characterizes the transformation of society as one changing from an industrial base or goods-producing economy to one of a service economy. This post-industrial era is characterized by changes in occupation from agriculture and blue collar to professional and technical; the importance and use of theoretical knowledge with new information technologies as the basis of decision making; the scarcity of resources—food supplies, energy resources, and land availability; and the growing interdependence of economic and political environments with the political realm becoming increasingly important as a decision-making arena.

For social policy and social work practice the essence of the transformation is in the structural changes occurring in individual relationships and their interactions with the broader social and economic institutions. The implications of the post-industrial society for social policy can be reviewed according to three major emerging structural developments.

The Changing National Economy

The shift from a goods-producing to a service economy has resulted in dramatic changes in the occupational structure of the United States. In 1920, 53 percent of the workforce was engaged in manufacturing activity, 28 percent in agriculture and extractive industries—mining, forest products, and so on—and 19 percent in the service sector—education, knowledge, information, and other service-oriented occupations. By 1976, agriculture represented 4 percent of the workforce, 29 percent was in manufacturing, 50 percent in information, and 17 percent in other services. It is predicted that by the year 2000 only 2 percent of the workforce will be engaged in agriculture and 22 percent in manufacturing, while 66 percent will be working in information technologies, and 10 percent will be engaged in other services (Molitor, 1981).

There is an increasing danger that this trend will contribute to the development of a permanent underclass of people, those who were once blue-collar workers but who now have limited access to education and technical knowledge needed for employment in the highly specialized information and service sectors. The entry of more women in the workforce as well as the abolition of mandatory retirement and proposals to increase the age of retirement necessary for receipt of income-entitlement benefits, create a crowded labor market in which younger and less-skilled workers and minorities and women find entry into the labor force increasingly difficult. (Bluestone and Harrison, 1982, p. 12).

Industrial firms are no longer tied to urban centers. Location decisions favoring nonmetropolitan areas have been stimulated by increased access to supplies and markets, less expensive land and labor costs, and the environmental amenities found in less populated areas (Smith, Deaton, & Kelch, 1978).

Within the service sector with its dramatic expansion, other changes have occurred. Whereas personal services, that is services characterized by personal interaction or performed by individuals, were the predominant category of employment, the change has been to professional services demanding highly technical and sophisticated equipment for performing the service. The airline industry is an example. In addition, service employment in small organizations or independent, self-employment have given way to professional employment in large, highly bureaucratized organizations, of which government is a primary example (Bradshaw & Blakely, 1979; Urquhart, 1981).

The Changing Demographic Profile

The United States is changing from a population of younger to one of older people. This is the result of lower fertility rates combined with increasing longevity of the adult population. Following the postwar baby boom, the annual fertility rate, that is, the number of births per 1,000 women 15 to 44 years old, has steadily declined to an all-time low in 1976. The fertility rate in 1980 was 1,875 children per 1,000 women which represented a decrease of 25 percent over the 1970 rate of 2,480 children per 1,000 women. The fertility rate for 1980 represents 1.9 children per woman. The actual numbers of births declined little during the years 1970 to 1980, primarily because of the increased numbers of women of childbearing age (U.S. Bureau of the Census, 1981b).

While the population under age 14 decreased by 11.5 percent in the decade 1970 to 1980, the population aged 65 and over increased almost 28 percent during the same period. Those persons over age 65 represent approximately 10.5 percent of the total population. It is projected that this group will be 11.7 percent of the total population in the year 2000 and between 17 and 20 percent by the year 2030 (Benedict, 1977; Brehm, 1978). This older group of people has significant numbers over age 75 (approximately 40 percent). In addition, the older population has a ratio of 146 women per 100 men which increases to 217 women per 100 men in the 85 and over age group (Brotman, 1978). Although the median age of the population in 1980 was 30 years, minority groups had a lower median age: Blacks 24.9, American Indians 23, Asian Americans 28.6, and Hispanics 23.2 years (Robey, 1981). In 1975 the overall mortality rate for minorities was greater than for the white population by one third, a fact which has not been adequately addressed in social policy decisions (*Health Status of Minorities and Low Income Groups*, 1979).

This shifting demographic profile results in greater demands on retirement income systems, leisure time and recreational activities, and an unprecedented strain on health care resources. Older people, in part because of reimbursement policies, place the greatest demand on the most costly type of health services— hospitalization and nursing home care (Hudson, 1978a).

Increasing Competition for Scarce Resources

The retrenchment of the federal government as a provider of substantial fiscal resources for social provisions, increasing demands for public sector accountability, and cost containment policies have resulted in an atmosphere of restraint and pressure on local services. As public attitudes harden toward continued increases in the tax burden reflected in Proposition 13 (California), Proposition $2\frac{1}{2}$ (Massachusetts), and the repeated defeats of bond issues to finance needed public services, the fiscal pressures on nonprofit community and social services are exacerbated, adding to the already inadequate existing funding mechanisms (Florestano, 1980; Hudson, 1978b). Moreover, traditionally low-priority social services must not only compete among themselves for reduced levels of block grant funding but must also continue to compete with other public sector demands of higher priority in an environment of increasing turbulence and uncertainty. The search for such new funding mechanisms as public/private partnerships for community-based nonprofit organizations will gain increasing importance as the level of unmet need intensifies (Urban Land Institute, 1980).

Rural America in an Advanced Industrial Society

Given the developments of a post-industrial society, it is appropriate to ask, as did Warner (1974), what is the place of rural society in a post-industrial age or, more important, what will be the impact of post-industrialism on rural society? The latter question implies the interdependence of rural and urban settings and the importance of examining ". . . how the fundamental structures and processes of national society differentially involve, represent, and affect rural people" (p. 307). This view is underlined in a recent publication of the National Research Council (1981) which states, "The growing interdependence of rural and urban people causes the problems of each group to affect the other, and policies designed to meet the needs of either group will affect the other" (p. 193).

A more detailed examination of post-industrial society shows, according to Bradshaw and Blakely (1979), that although the shift in economic activity from goods-producing to service industries and the subsequent shift from blue-collar to white-collar technical and professional occupations has occurred, a further point of clarification is needed. Rather than a substantial decline in goods-producing industries, the shift to the service sector has occurred at the expense of agriculture, which has experienced a steady decline over the past 75 years. In 1920 the farm population accounted for almost one third of the total population of 106 million. In 1980 this number had decreased to 6 million farm population, representing only 2.7 percent of the total population of 218 million or a total decline to about one eighth of its previous level (U.S. Bureau of the Census, 1981c). The decline in manufacturing for the same time period was to approximately one half of its previous level. Furthermore, as described by Deaton (1976), agriculture itself has been transformed from small farms to fewer, larger farms; from an average of 138 acres in 1910 to 383 acres in 1970.

It is Bradshaw and Blakely's preference (1979), ". . . to use the term 'advanced industrial society,' which reflects the increasing importance of new and advanced technology in creating social changes of vast proportions and to reserve the term 'post-industrial' for possible future developments" (p. 13). The implications of advanced industrial society for rural areas are substantial. While urban industrial development eroded the economic and human energy of rural America, advanced industrial developments, including rural industrialization, may contribute to a revitalization of many areas of rural America, yet at the same time exacerbate the differential between growth and declining areas (Bradshaw & Blakely, 1979; Deaton, 1976).

The increased reliance on technology and the importance of knowledge in the advanced industrial society cannot be ignored in social work practice. Impacts are experienced in the diffusion of technology in our public institutions and community social structures. Social systems, as pointed out by Bradshaw and Blakely, become appropriate arenas for management and coordination skills, and employment is increasingly in large-scale, highly bureaucratized institutions. New professions are created, demanding high degrees of specialization and technical skill and knowledge. As technology heightens expectations about what can be accomplished in society, it also contributes to consequences of an unintended nature in the form of waste, pollution, regulations, and job displacement (Bradshaw and Blakely, 1979). In the rural setting technology can be, as Deaton (1976) suggests, "a mixed blessing." While increasing the conditions of poverty and alienation, resources that stimulate hope for a different future have also been increased.

Rapid social change and the concomitant expansion in white-collar occupations where information processing, as opposed to production of goods, is the valued skill places persons of minority background with traditionally less access to technology and knowledge in a position of continuing discrimination, thus in an underclass. This is particularly relevant to rural populations that have historically experienced a lower standard of living and social status as compared with more affluent urban and suburban populations (Hoppe, 1980).

Increasing interdependence of units of government, economic activity, and social relations, both horizontally and vertically, and the technological modernization of rural areas have reduced geographic isolation. Rural and urban environments must be viewed as interacting with one another in substantially more influential ways than they have been. Regulatory processes, hence litigation, are more important in defining not only relationships between institutions but also relationships among individuals.

The Changing Rural Environment

In order to understand, participate in, and initiate the policy making process with appropriate impacts on the rural environment, a knowledge of the rural setting is essential. This includes a description of the social, economic, and political dimensions of rurality, the changes occurring in rural settings, and the translation of these factors into social needs.

Determinants of Rurality

To the social worker who practices in a rural community and most likely also lives there, the description of rural is often made by noting the qualitative social and environmental conditions experienced by a population, generally in contrast to those which predominate in more urban areas. A review of the literature leads one to conclude that no single, agreed-upon definition of rural exists. As a "vague, sensitizing concept" (Ecosometrics, 1981, p. 1) the lack of an explicit definition is not problematic. However, multiple definitions contribute to the vague concept and reduce its efficacy as a policy perspective.

Often ruralness is described as constituting a continuum which allows inclusion of a wide variety of communities as rural (Hines, Brown, & Zimmer, 1975). A further delineation of rural which implies the characteristics of isolation, small population, low population density, and an economy that depends on the land in terms of agriculture and extractive industries is found in Bealer, Willits, and Kuvlesky (1965). This discussion leads to three types of criteria which operationalize the rural definition: ecological, occupational, and sociocultural. Ecological criteria are the frequently used quantitative descriptors of population numbers, density, and geographic isolation. Occupational criteria describe the economic organization of an area. Usually these criteria relate to agriculture, but increasingly in an advanced industrial society the economic base may attract other industries and become more populated, with greater transportation and telecommunication access. The sociocultural criteria emphasize rural as homogeneity of population and interaction based on face to face, informal relationships (Bealer et al., 1965).

From a quantitative point of view, rural is defined by the U.S. Bureau of the Census as areas (open country or towns) having fewer than 2,500 people. Nonmetropolitan, a more inclusive distinction, of no more than 50,000 people, is considered a more or less urbanized area, depending on the area's proximity to a more populous Standard Metropolitan Statistical Area (SMSA). In an attempt to assess the policy implications of rural, Ecosometrics (1981) found that definitions of rural differed widely between federal agencies as well as for differing programs within a single agency. Furthermore, it was found that discussion frequently focused on the interdependence of rural and urban and suggested that a convergence exists.

Nevertheless, it is our position, in agreement with Ecosometrics (1981) and the National Research Council (1981), that rural areas differ from urban settings most importantly in their small population size and density, and in space and distance characteristics. This results in a different scale of life with different responses of institutions (Ecosometrics, 1981). Such issues of scale include a lack of employment options available to young people entering the work force; less population diversity; more informal communication; and local governments run by the local power structure often to the detriment of the poor, minorities, and the elderly (Ginsberg, 1976, pp. 3–5; Steinberg, 1978). As in much of the literature, we will use the terms rural and nonmetropolitan interchangeably throughout this book.

Recognizing the difficulties in definition, some general observations on population trends are in order. The percent of rural population in the United States has decreased dramatically in the past two centuries. Figures for the first census in 1790 show that 95 percent of the total U.S. population of 3.9 million people was considered rural. This percent decreased continually over the years to 30 percent in 1960 and 27 percent rural in a total population of 203 million in 1970. During the twentieth century the actual number of people in rural areas has remained fairly stable with a high of 57 million in 1940 and a low of 45.8 million in 1900. The Census listed 53.9 million rural residents in 1970. The decade of the 1970s witnessed a turnaround in this pattern with 28 percent of the total population of 226 million considered rural in the 1980 census or a 15.4 percent rate of growth. This represents a net in-migration to rural areas of approximately 4 million people (Beale, 1981).

Characteristics of Rural Environments

Considering the consistent decrease in the rural population, until the 1970s, it is not difficult to understand the stereotypic views of rural America. A homogeneous view has predominated in which one rural setting is considered to be very much like another rural setting. The similarity has been described as a declining status which is the direct result of urban industrialization and the mechanization of agriculture. Decline has been pervasive and has included population and economic decline with an attendant decline in standard of living and indicators of well-being. A sensitive examination of rural settings, however, dispels the myth of homogeneity and suggests that greater differences now exist among rural environments than at any time in the recent past; in fact, great diversity exists within any single rural community (Coward, 1979; Ginsberg, 1976; National Research Council, 1981; Taietz & Milton, 1979).

Recognition of diversity among rural settings suggests that they may be viewed on the one hand as seriously deprived and on the other hand as idyllic places in which to live with an inherently good quality of life (Dillman & Tremblay, Jr., 1977). While neither view is totally correct, each suggests concerns which social policy must address and to which social workers must direct their attention. Attention in this book is first directed to the well-documented problems of much of rural America, resulting in large part from the isolation and economic and population decline discussed earlier in this chapter. Second, the emerging problems reflective of the growth occurring in some rural areas as people exert preferences for living in rural settings will be briefly examined.

Poverty and Income

It is no secret to those who live in many rural areas that poverty and its attendant problems affect a major portion of that population. In 1967 the President's National Advisory Commission on Rural Poverty created by President Lyndon Johnson, submitted its final report, *The People Left Behind*. This report contained 158 recommendations that were considered important to the betterment of rural life. Although changes in policy have resulted in some improvement in quality of life, much still needs to be accomplished.

In 1960, prior to the rediscovery of poverty in America and the publication of *The Other America* by Harrington (1962), 22.2

percent of the population was considered poor, that is, had incomes below a nationally determined standard. By the year 1980, after 15 years of antipoverty programs, 13 percent of the population remained in poverty.[2] This represented 29.3 million persons. In that same year, 1980, rural (nonmetropolitan) areas with 27 percent of the population, had 33 percent of the nation's poor (U.S. Bureau of the Census, 1981a). This disproportionate number of poor people in rural areas is thought to be in part the result of a more economically dependent population of elderly and young people, minorities and farmers, who have remained in rural areas often with substandard wages and sporadic work histories. According to Tweeten and Brinkman (1976), "The high dependency rates (ratios of the young and old to working age people) make it extremely difficult to maintain enough people to keep a community economically viable in providing services for the young and old" (p. 14).

From the U.S. Bureau of the Census (1976), poor families in America in 1975 were characterized as shown in Table 1.1.

Table 1.1. Characteristics of Poor Families in 1975, by Residence*

Residence	Families with male heads	Children in families with male heads	Male family heads who worked	Female family heads who worked
Urban	43.6%	39.0%	57.6%	32.9%
Rural	69.5%	63.6%	63.0%	42.3%

*U.S. Bureau of the Census. Current Population Reports, Series P-60, No. 110, 1976.

Sixty-nine and one-half percent of rural families were headed by a male (43.6 percent, urban); 63.6 percent of children in rural families were headed by a male (39 percent, urban); 63 percent of rural male family heads worked (57.6 percent, urban); and 42.3

[2]The relative contribution of antipoverty programs to the reduction in the number of people below the poverty level (1965 to 1975) is a complex subject of continuing controversy. To what degree cyclic economic movements, changing definitions of poverty, differential inflationary impacts on working and nonworking poor interact to significantly affect the number of poor people is simply not known. For a review of the relevance of assumptions underlying antipoverty programs see Martin Rein, "Community Action Programs: A Critical Assessment," in Social Policy: Issues of Choice and Change. New York: Random House, 1970, Chapter 8, 153–164.

percent of rural female family heads worked (32.9 percent, urban) (U.S. Bureau of the Census, 1976).

The rural poor live dispersed throughout the United States. However, rural poverty is more prevalent in the South where approximately 20 percent of rural people are poor. This compares with 10 percent in the North Central states, 9 percent in the Northeast, and 10 percent in the West. Statistics tell only part of the story. In terms of income level, the data indicate that substantial numbers of rural poor people, approximately 12 million in 1976, have insufficient income to purchase necessary food, clothing, and shelter, Furthermore, the widely dispersed population and geographic isolation place an additional burden in procuring employment and social services (Bluestone, 1980).

Poverty in the United States has not been addressed from a comprehensive policy perspective. Furthermore, despite the high incidence of poverty in rural America, federal funds expended for income and other welfare programs in rural areas were one quarter the amount received by metropolitan areas (Osgood, 1977). According to Osgood this can be attributed to the structure of programs with a bias toward urban participation as well as to the attitudes of rural people that are principally conservative on issues related to social policy. Other government programs in recent years have substantially increased funding levels to small communities (Sullivan, Collins & Reid, 1981), as will be explored in later chapters.

Education

In rural areas with the greatest incidence of poverty a pattern of lower educational achievement has been documented (Chadwick & Bahr, 1978). Tweeten (1980) reported that for 1975, the median number of years of school completed was 12.6 for metropolitan persons, 12.2 for rural nonfarm, and 11.4 for rural farm residents. Although this difference exists, the gap has narrowed considerably since 1970 when the reported median years of schooling for rural residents was 11.2 and 12.2 for urban residents. At that same time—1970—the median level of education for most rural counties was 9.9 (Hines, Brown, & Zimmer, 1975). These same counties had the highest dropout rate among 16 and 17 year old children; 15.2 percent versus 13.6 percent for all rural counties. For persons of minority status the educational gap is even more serious. As a comparison, black male urban residents in 1975 had completed a median of 11.6 years of school while their rural nonfarm counterparts had completed 8.1 years and rural farm blacks had completed 5.9 years of school (Tweeten, 1980).

The United States has historically espoused a policy of public education as a right for all children, to be funded primarily from local revenues raised through the property tax. It is assumed that education will improve one's employment success and thus have long-term effects on diminishing poverty and increasing self-sufficiency. Although the assumption of education positively impacting income is frequently expressed, accounting for the total array of issues involved makes this assumption less tenable. For example, the income disparities between white rural and urban populations are shown to be related, as an estimate, more to the factors of age, job opportunities, and gender. Income disparities between black rural and white urban males are thought to be primarily (45%) due to race factors. However, income disparities between black urban and black rural males are due predominately (60 percent) to differences in levels and quality of education (Tweeten, 1980). Policy decisions must, therefore, focus simultaneously on educational gaps and on eradication of gender and racial discrimination as well as in creating job opportunities in rural, depressed communities.

The data showing lower levels of education for rural populations are not easily explained. They result from a combination of factors such as the trend for better-educated youth to leave rural areas, a higher proportion of elderly persons with lower education levels, large numbers of blacks in the rural South, and, not to be dismissed, the lower level of public expenditures on education in rural areas.

The funding of quality education in sufficient quantities in rural areas proves problematic because of a generally lower tax base and a dispersed population (Tweeten, 1980; Dillman & Tremblay, Jr., 1977; Tweeten & Brinkman, 1976). Dispersed populations result in small schools for which economies of scale in many maintenance, educational, and ancillary services cannot be realized. Additional funding problems result from the allocation of state and federal school finance monies that are based on numbers of students or a minimum enrollment. Such mechanisms place small community schools at a decided disadvantage in securing these external monies (Bass & Berman, 1979). Consolidation into school administrative districts has commonly occurred, yet criticism surrounding the centralization of policy decisions is now resulting in many communities advocating for the dissolution of consolidated districts with a return to local control as well as increased efforts to maintain existing community schools (Jelle, 1982).

Funding for public educational programs has recently come under increased scrutiny as the result of taxpayer revolts in several states and what is perceived by many people to be the rapidly escalating costs of public education. It is difficult, as Tweeten (1980) points out, to arrive at an equitable financing system for local schools because of the variation in tax base from one area to another as well as the way in which different types of properties are assessed. The question as to how property is viewed as synonomous with ability to pay is also raised. For example, farm property may be assessed, for tax purposes, at a high level, yet the farm income may be relatively low. The same problem arises for the elderly person on a low, fixed income whose house, through years of appreciation, has a high assessed value for tax purposes. However, in neither of these examples is ability to pay related positively to assessed value of property; each may suggest financing of schools through a tax based on income rather than property. Another positive suggestion for school financing is to earmark general funds at the federal level, perhaps through general revenue sharing, for public education.

In summary, access to high quality education, occupational incentives to stay in school, and solutions to the financing problems of public education must be sought in order to promote and increase the viability of education in rural areas. These educational issues are not discrete but are closely interwoven with the fabric of rural life and demand a comprehensive view toward their solution.

Health Care

The health status of a population is inextricably related to social well-being (Roemer, 1968). Often the idea that it is more healthy to live in a rural as opposed to an urban area is expressed. To the contrary, urban residents have a higher degree of health status than do their rural counterparts (Roemer, 1968). In a study by McCoy and Brown (1978), using information from the Health Interview Survey, it was found that nonmetropolitan residents were more limited by chronic conditions while urban people exhibited more acute conditions (p. 15). Rural residents also experience higher levels of morbidity (illness) and days lost from work due to illness and work-related injuries. Although differences are not as great as they once were, the most rural areas of the United States are far in excess of the general population in morbidity and infant mortality (Ross, 1975). Although the discrepancy in rates of infant mortality between rural and urban areas has decreased substantially in recent years, rates remain considerably higher for the rural nonwhite population at 22.7 infant deaths under one year per 1,000 live births, compared to 12.4 for the rural white population. These data are presented in Table 1.2.

Table 1.2. Rural and Urban Infant Mortality Rates, 1978 by Race

Race	Rural		Urban	
	Under 1 year	Under 28 days	Under 1 year	Under 28 days
White	12.4%	8.5%	11.8%	8.3%
All Other	22.7%	14.0%	20.5%	14.0%
Total (U.S.)	13.9%	9.3%	13.7%	9.6%

U.S. Dept. of Health and Human Services, Public Health Service, National Center for Health Statistics. *Vital Statistics of the U.S.*, Vol. II, Mortality, Part B, 1978.

Adding to the magnitude of the health problems experienced by rural people is the lack of access to health care personnel and facilities. As viewed by Kane, Dean, and Solomon (1979) the basic problem in rural health care is that of personnel, which is directly related to issues of access, financing, and utilization. The supply of health care personnel and resources is, according to Ahearn (1979), unrelated to the degree of need and clearly related to the adequacy of an area's medical system. Therefore, although the health care needs of a rural population are greater because of poverty, more hazardous occupations, greater numbers of elderly people, and lower educational levels, the existing health care system is not adequate to attract new providers who generally locate in urban areas where already adequate medical care systems exist. To what degree new technologies in telecommunications will reduce the net effect of personnel differences is an open question in rural health care.

A recent report by the Bureau of Health Professions, Health Resources Administration, indicated a growth of 159 new health manpower shortage areas in the calendar year 1981. Of the total

43 million Americans living in the 2,033 designated shortage areas, one third are metropolitan residents and two thirds are nonmetropolitan residents (Miller, 1982). In contrast to this evidence and the projected need for an additional 6,000 primary care physicians to change the designations of the shortage areas, a recent study published by the Rand Corporation (Schwartz, Newhouse, Bennett, & Williams, 1980) found that, with a growing surplus of physicians in the United States, more are entering practice in rural areas.

The maldistribution of medical and health personnel is shown in Table 1.3 as the ratio of providers per 100,000 population (Ahearn, 1979, p. 17):

Table 1.3.   Distribution of Health Personnel

	Urban	Rural
Physicians (1975)	157.0	71.0
Dentists (1974)	57.0	35.0
Osteopathic Physicians (1975)	4.7	3.5
Registered Nurses, Active (1972)	380.0	270.0
Licensed Practical Nurses	190.0	198.0

Fewer specialized medical services are available in rural areas and if used as a proxy measure for quality of care, it can be concluded that the quality as well as the quantity of care is less in rural than in urban areas (Ahearn, 1979).

Health care facilities, namely, hospitals, nursing homes, and clinics are also unevenly distributed between rural and urban areas. Community hospitals and nursing homes, while existing in greater numbers in rural areas are smaller, resulting in fewer beds per 100,000 population (Ahearn, 1979). In urban areas there are 460 beds (2 hospitals) as opposed to 428 beds in 5 hospitals in a rural area and similarly 479 beds (5 nursing homes) as opposed to 407 (6 nursing homes) per 100,000 population (Ahearn, 1979, p. 20). Rural hospitals tend to be older, less well equipped, and less likely to be accredited than urban hospitals. In addition, modern ambulatory facilities are lacking in rural areas (Kane, 1978). With the combination of poorer health status and fewer personnel and facilities, rural areas face continued decline in health status.

The health care policy of the United States has been one

based on the philosophy of private, fee-for-service. Although the substantial majority of Americans feel that health care should be available to all people regardless of income, the United States is the only industrialized Western nation without a national health care program.

Rural areas have been particularly disadvantaged in securing health services because of the reimbursement strategies of Medicare and Medicaid. Although several key federal programs (Health Underserved Rural Areas, Rural Health Initiative, Rural Health Clinics, Migrant Health Clinics, and National Health Service Corps) have impacted rural health systems, the basic issue remains that of guaranteeing the availability of quality health care to rural populations who characteristically have a lower health status and lower income levels than do their urban counterparts.

Housing

Housing means more to many Americans than a shelter. It is viewed as an indicator of well-being, a structure that consumes the largest single expenditure in the family budget, and an expression of personality and desire to move ahead economically (Dillman & Tremblay, Jr., 1977).

In reviewing the state of U.S. housing conditions from 1950 to 1975, a recent publication (Bird & Kampe, 1977) cited dramatic improvements, particularly for nonmetropolitan settings. Although the quantity and quality of housing in nonmetropolitan areas has expanded rapidly, one quarter of housing construction in rural areas was federally financed, a reflection of lower per capita income and less availability in the commercial/private credit market in nonmetropolitan areas.

Housing affordability, an increasingly pressing national issue, is a particularly difficult policy issue in nonmetropolitan areas. A substantial proportion of owners (15 percent) and renters (36 percent) spend more than 30 percent of their income to occupy adequate housing. This percentage is in excess of the 25 percent of household income generally recommended as allocated to housing. Although lower incomes of rural households are to some degree offset by lower housing costs, basic income differences between rural and urban areas exceed housing cost differences. In contrast to the twenty year period 1950 to 1970, housing availability in rural areas has not changed significantly during the last decade (Economic Research Service, 1981).

In comparing urban with rural housing for the 25 year period ending in 1975, rural housing expanded more rapidly, owner occupancy increased more quickly with housing inventory increasing faster than the population. Mobile homes appear to be the most popular alternative to conventional housing, with 60 percent of mobile homes located in rural areas. Home ownership is higher in rural areas with one third of the nation's housing. Although the single family house is the most popular dwelling in both rural and urban areas, rural areas hold a significantly higher proportion of single family dwellings, 80 percent versus 60 percent, respectively.

Insignificant differences exist with respect to age of housing between rural and urban areas with 34 percent of rural housing built before 1940. However, significant differences do exist with respect to housing quality. Inadequate sewage systems in rural areas are the most frequent defect distinguishing rural from urban housing quality. Plumbing, kitchen, and heating defects are next in order of frequency.

Although the number of occupied substandard units declined dramatically from 1950 to 1975 with housing units less crowded, central heating being more common, the housing conditions of minorities, particularly blacks improved less rapidly than that of whites; the elderly tended to occupy an increasing proportion of substandard housing.

In contrast to emerging housing policies, there is a growing sentiment that the private housing market will not be able to offer adequate housing for low-income persons without some type of direct federal assistance. The issue revolves around the most politically acceptable type of intervention. Although a limited number of federal programs—for example, Farmers Home Administration (FmHA)—are designed to impact rural areas, the benefits of most housing programs limit rural participation. According to the Economic Research Service (1981) this unequal distribution of housing benefits is the result of a lack of financial institutions in rural areas with the capital and skills to take advantage of the various programs. It is expected that demand for housing in rural areas with little increase in capital availability will further strain the housing picture in rural America.

Housing policy proposals currently being considered for rural areas include consumer housing assistance grants or housing vouchers and individual housing accounts. Housing vouchers differ from existing policies which emphasize federally supported public housing by providing cash supplements to low-income homeowners or renters. At this writing, specific policy details have not been outlined, but several examples of likely programs can be reviewed. If the voucher program were designed to promote homeownership, such a program could provide partial funding of a downpayment, allow eligibility for a market rate mortgage by supplementing a designated percentage of a low income budget for housing. Policies designed to assist low-income renters might well follow the Section 8 approach used predominately in urban areas.[3]

A second approach involves individual housing accounts. The intended beneficiary is the first time home buyer who would be allowed to accumulate savings for a down payment through favorable tax treatment. However, the proposal to tax exempt the first $10,000 of savings tends to give most benefit to the wealthy. In contrast, a tax credit would make the benefit a function of the actual amount of the accumulated savings, not the marginal tax rate (Khadduri & Struyk, 1982).

Rural Attitudes and Values

It is widely recognized that values and attitudes of a population (or those held by the political decision makers representing the population) are a major influence on social policy decisions. Therefore, it is important to call to the attention of the reader the sociocultural descriptors of the rural population as presented in the literature. The difficulty which arises in identifying rural attitudes and values is found in the perceived convergence of rural and urban life (Glenn & Hill, Jr., 1977), and the diversity found among rural people (Larson, 1978). Because of telecommunication and transportation systems, rural populations are not isolated in the same way they once were. However, there are differences in

---

[3]The Section 8 housing program, authorized under the Housing and Community Development Act of 1974, provides housing subsidies to low and moderate income families. This is accomplished in three different ways: 1. rent payment subsidies are provided for eligible families who find units in the private market; 2. guarantees that eligible families will receive a rent subsidy are provided to private developers who are making renovations in multifamily dwellings; and 3. the same guarantee is provided to developers who are building new multifamily dwellings. The subsidy is paid directly to the landlord and makes up the difference between 25 percent of the family's income allocated for rent and an agreed upon rental price for the unit (Weinberg, 1982).

having access to one TV channel versus 8 or 10 channels and one plans quite differently to attend a function in a town 25 miles driving distance over single lane winding road than one does a function 4 miles by bus or car on interstate highway. Nevertheless, the literature at this point is sufficiently inconclusive to adhere to Glenn and Hill's (1977) "massification thesis" which maintains that rural/urban differences become less pronounced in the latter stages of industrialization.

According to Larson (1978), differences between rural and urban populations might be expected based primarily on the factors of income level, occupation, and religious affiliation. These factors which are in contrast to urban populations can be tied to an early piece of work by Dewey (1960) in which rural/urban populations were conceptualized as different but not importantly so on the basis of: (1) homogeneity versus heterogeneity; (2) intimate versus impersonal social relations; (3) simple versus complex division of labor; (4) familiarity versus anonymity; and (5) status which is not symbolized by personal acquaintance.

Building on the work of Dewey, researchers have attempted to isolate the key characteristics of ruralism as reflected in values and attitudes. Glenn and Hill (1977) and Larson (1978) in particular cite differences in that rural people tend to be more conservative, distrustful of outsiders, work-oriented, religious, and more hesitant about change than their more urban counterparts. Furthermore, people living in the open countryside show more prejudice and ethnocentrism when compared with more urban populations.

Political participation among rural residents is higher in rural areas when controlled for income and social status than that found in urban communities (Knoke & Henry, 1977). True to a more conservative political posture, rural residents are more often Republican in their voting preferences while the most urban populations tend to be liberal in political persuasion and to vote in support of Democratic candidates.

This succinct statement of rural values and beliefs serves as a caution to not overstate the differences between rural and urban populations yet to recognize that subtle differences may impact receptivity to particular policy postures and affect the implementation of a variety of social programs. One must also be cognizant that rural America is in transition, a point to be examined in the following section.

To summarize, the statistics given in Table 1.4 are illustrative

of the conditions of poverty and deprivation experienced by many
rural areas.

Table 1.4.   Social Indicators of Rural/Urban Differences

Social Indicators	Percent of the Population (except infant mortality)	
	Urban	Rural
Persons at poverty level, 1980	11.9	15.4
Persons 65+ years, 1980	9.6	13.7
Persons 65+ years below the poverty level, 1979	12.0	20.5
Persons in families below the poverty level with female householder—no husband present, 1979	34.0	36.9
Poverty, by race, 1980		
White	8.8	12.9
Black	30.1	40.6
Spanish origin	25.5	26.3
Substandard housing, 1977	6.8	9.4
Infant mortality per 1000 live births, 1978		
Total, U.S.	13.7	13.9
White	11.8	12.4
All other	20.5	22.7
Persons of 25+ years having high school or greater education, 1979	70.7	61.6

Although the objective conditions show clearcut differences
in the quality of life between rural and urban areas, studies of
subjective attitudes of well-being do not follow such clear, objective distinctions (Lee & Lassey, 1980). That is, rural people con-
sistently report a higher level of satisfaction with their community
than do urban populations, even though they are aware of the
inadequacies that exist. If anything can be deduced from these
findings at this writing, it is the challenge of social policy and
social work practice to more clearly address and articulate this
inconsistency.

Rural In-migration

Substantial population growth in many rural areas during the decade of the 1970s has been the result of broad-based social and
economic changes in society (Brown & Wardwell, 1980; Linge-

man, 1980). This has resulted in the present turnaround in migration patterns with a broad impact on rural America. As reported by the U.S. Bureau of the Census (1981b), preliminary data show a total U.S. population increase of 11 percent for the decade 1970 to 1980. For urban areas the increase was 9.5 percent while nonmetropolitan areas grew by 15 percent. Net migration is now the primary determinant of changes in local population characteristics (Brown & Wardwell, 1980). Economic decentralization, the modernization of rural life, and a stated preference for rural living are perceived as the underlying yet interdependent reasons for what appears to be a striking rural population turnaround (Brown & Wardwell, 1980).

In spite of this trend, the diversity of growth patterns is heightened by differences in economic base among rural areas, for example, manufacturing, extractive industries, and agriculture. Over 400 nonmetropolitan counties of the United States continue to be characterized by social and economic decline. The emerging issues are complex. On the one hand, the return migration to rural areas may exacerbate problems of an already poorly developed service infrastructure. On the other hand it may, according to Deavers and Brown (1980), stimulate a creative optimism that rural America can respond positively to needs and at the same time preserve the prevalent character of the area.

For the rural areas experiencing population growth as a result of in-migration, a range of problems and opportunities exist (Blakely & Bradshaw, 1981). Adjustments in the social fabric exert tensions between the new rural immigrants and the longtime rural residents (Carlson, Lassey, & Lassey, 1981). The in-migrants are more frequently employed in professional and technical occupations. In other words, the decline of a farming and agricultural population is replaced by a more diverse population in terms of occupational structure. The in-migrants are usually by choice, exerting their preference (a preference expressed by most Americans) to live in small communities where it is perceived that pollution, crowding, and crime are less prevalent. While they are disenchanted with urban life, at the same time they desire a rural setting that is modern in terms of services and conveniences.

The in-migration is a direct result of the post-industrial society. Advanced technology and information processing have allowed business and industry to locate outside of urban, metropolitan areas, contributed to the modernization of rural life, and advanced the possibility of people exercising their preferences for living in smaller communities (Brown & Wardwell, 1980). These same factors have resulted in problems of energy availability and land-use policy. Energy resources, much in demand, are located primarily in rural areas. Increased leisure time in all occupations has resulted in increased recreational use of limited land resources. At the same time, the world faces dramatic levels of malnutrition and starvation, creating tensions in land-use decisions. For those rural areas beset by still further declining populations or no-growth patterns, the social problem endemic to rural America persist.

Summary

The major thrust of this chapter has been to introduce the reader to the concept of post-industrial society and its impacts on rural environments. The understanding of social policy requires a knowledge and appreciation of a setting, and the transitions occurring in that setting.

The presentation in this chapter has shown rural America to be more disadvantaged than urban America on many key social and economic indicators. Although in transition, rural areas generally experience lower levels of education, health status, housing quality, and income than that found in urban areas of the United States. Moving into and through a post-industrial era will necessitate policy decisions on behalf of rural communities that will develop and maintain a quality of life responsive to the needs of long-term residents as well as new in-migrants. The remainder of this book is directed toward an examination and understanding of the interface of social policy and rural environments.

References

Ahearn, Mary C. *Health Care in Rural America*. U.S. Department of Agriculture, Washington, D.C.: Bul. No. 428, 1979.

Bass, Gail and Berman, Paul. "Federal Aid to Rural Schools: Current Patterns and Unmet Needs," Washington, D.C.: ERIC ED 184 804, 1979.

Beale, Calvin L. "Rural and Small Town Population Change, 1970–

1980," Economics and Statistics Service, 5, Washington, D.C., USDA, 1981.

Bealer, Robert, Willits, Fern K., and Kuvlesky, William P. "The Meaning of 'Rurality' in American Society: Some Implications of Alternative Definitions," *Rural Sociology*, 1965, 30(3):255–266.

Beck, Bertram M. "Social Work's Future: Triumph or Disaster," *Social Work*, 1981, 25(5):367–372.

Bell, Daniel. "Notes on the Post-Industrial Society," *The Public Interest*, 1967a, Winter(6):24–35.

Bell, Daniel. "Notes on the Post-Industrial Society," *The Public Interest*, 1967b, Spring(7):102–118.

Bell, Daniel. *The Coming of Post-Industrial Society*. New York: Basic Books, 1973.

Benedict, Robert C. "Emerging Trends in Social Policy for Older People." Paper presented at the 1977 National Round Table Conference, American Public Welfare Association, Washington, D.C., Dec. 9, 1977.

Bird, Ronald and Kampe, Ronald. "25 years of Housing Progress in Rural America," Economic Research Service, Agricultural Economic Report No. 373, Washington, D.C.: U.S. Department of Agriculture, 1977.

Blakely, Edward J. and Bradshaw, Ted K. "Implications of Social and Economic Changes on Rural Areas," *Human Services in the Rural Environment*, 1981, 6(2):11–21.

Bluestone, Barry and Harrison, Bennett. *The Deindustrialization of America*. New York: Basic Books, 1982.

Bluestone, Herman. "Rural Income Growing and Changing" in Brown, David L., Steward, Donald D., Ingalsbe, Gene (Eds.), *Rural Development Perspectives: Focus on Rural Poverty*. Washington, D.C.: EDD, ESCS, USDA, 1980, 27–28.

Bradshaw, Ted K. and Blakely, Edward J. *Rural Communities in Advanced Industrial Society*. New York: Praeger Publishers, 1979.

Brehm, Henry P. "The Future of U.S. Health Care Delivery for the Elderly" in Herzog, Barbara (Ed.), *Aging and Income*. New York: Human Sciences Press, 1978, 225–257.

Brotman, Herman B. "The Aging of America: A Demographic Profile," *National Journal*, 1978, 10(40):1622–1627.

Brown, David L. and Wardwell, John M. (Eds.). *New Directions in Urban–Rural Migration*. New York: Academic Press, 1980.

Carlson, John E., Lassey, Marie L., and Lassey, William R. *Rural Society and Environment in America*. New York: McGraw-Hill, 1981.

Chadwick, Bruce A. and Bahr, Howard M. "Rural Poverty" in Ford, Thomas R. (Ed.), *Rural USA: Persistence and Change*. Ames: Iowa State University Press, 1978, 182–195.

Coward, Raymond T. "Planning Services for the Rural Elderly: Implications from Research," *The Gerontologist*, 1979, 19(3):275–282.

Deaton, Brady J. "The Impact of Altered Economic Conditions on Rural Community Development" in Green, Ronald K. and Webster, Stephen A. (Eds.), *Social Work in Rural Areas*. Proceedings, First National Institute on Social Work in Rural Areas, University of Tenn., Knoxville, Tenn. 1976, 24–35.

Deavers, Kenneth L. and Brown, David L. "The Rural Population Turnaround Research and National Public Policy" in Brown, David L. and Wardwell, John M. (Eds.), *New Directions in Urban–Rural Migration*. New York: Academic Press, 1980, 51–65.

Dewey, Richard. "The Rural–Urban Continuum: Real but Relatively Unimportant," *American Journal of Sociology*, 1960, 66(1):60–66.

Dillman, Don A. and Tremblay, Kenneth R., Jr. "The Quality of Life in Rural America," *The Annals of the American Academy of Political and Social Science*, 1977, 429:115–129.

Economic Research Service. "Housing Rural America." Prepared by the Housing Program Area Economic Development Division, Washington, D.C., U.S. Department of Agriculture, 1981.

Ecosometrics, Inc. *Review of Reported Differences Between the Rural and Urban Elderly: Status, Needs, Services, and Service Costs*. Draft report for Administration on Aging, July 10, 1981.

Florestano, Patricia S. "Revenue Raising Limitations on Local Government: A Focus on Alternative Resources," *Public Administration Review*, 1980, 40(2):122–131.

Froland, Charles. "Formal and Informal Care: Discontinuities in a Continuum," *Social Service Review*, 1980, 54(4):572–587.

Gilbert, Neil, "The Transformation of Social Services, *Social Service Review*, 1977, 51(4):624–641.

Ginsberg, Leon (Ed.). *Social Work in Rural Communities*. New York: Council on Social Work Education, 1976.

Glenn, N.D. and Hill, L., Jr. "Rural–Urban Differences in Attitudes and Behavior in the United States," *The Annals of the American Academy of Political and Social Science*, 1977, 429:36–50.

Harrington, Michael. *The Other America: Poverty in the United States*. Baltimore, Md.: Penguin Books, Inc., 1962.

Health Status of Minorities and Low Income Groups, Health Resources Administration. Washington, D.C.: U.S. Government Printing Office, 1979.

Hines, Fred, Brown, David, and Zimmer, John. *Social and Economic Characteristics of Population in Metro and Non-Metropolitan Counties*, Washington, D.C.: USDA, ERS-272, 1975.

Hoppe, Bob. "Despite Progress, Rural Poverty Demands Attention" in Brown, David, Steward, Donald D., and Ingalsbe, Gene (Eds.),

Rural Development Perspectives, Washington, D.C.: Economic Development Division, ESCS, USDA, 1980.

Hudson, Robert B. "The 'Graying' of the Federal Budget and its Consequences for Old-Age Policy," *The Gerontologist*, 1978a, 18(5):428–440.

Hudson, Robert B. "Political and Budgetary Consequences of an Aging Population," *National Journal*, 1978b, 10(42):1699–1705.

Jelle, Dianne L. "The Disappearance of the Community School in Rural America," in Morris, Lynne Clemmons (Ed.), *Dignity, Diversity, and Opportunity in Changing Rural Areas*. Paper presented at the Sixth National Institute on Social Work in Rural Areas, University of South Carolina, 1982, 37–51.

Kane, William J. "Rural Health Care," *Journal of the American Medical Association*, 1978, 240(24):2647–2650.

Kane, Robert, Dean, Marilyn, and Soloman, Marian. "An Evaluation of Rural Health Care Research," *Evaluation Quarterly*, 1979, 3(2):139–189.

Khadduri, Jill and Struyk, Raymond J. "Housing Vouchers for the Poor," *Journal of Policy Analysis and Management*, 1982, 1(2):196–201.

Knoke, David and Henry, Constance. "Political Structure of Rural America," *The Annals of the American Academy of Political and Social Science*, 1977, 429:51–62.

Larson, Olaf F. "Values and Beliefs of Rural People" in Ford, T.R. (Ed.), *Rural USA: Perspective and Change*. Ames, Iowa: Iowa State University Press, 1978, 91–112.

Lee, Gary and Lassey, Marie L. "Rural–Urban Residence and Aging: Directions for Future Research," in Lassey, William R., Lassey, Marie L., Lee, Gary R., and Lee, Naomi (Eds.), *Research and Public Service with the Rural Elderly*, WRDC Pub. No. 4, 1980, 77–87.

Lingeman, Richard. *Small Town America*. New York: G.P. Putman's Sons, 1980.

McCoy, John L. and Brown, David L. "Health Status Among Low Income Elderly Persons: Rural–Urban Differences," *Social Security Bulletin*, 1978, 41(6):14–16.

Miller, Adele M. "Bureau of Health Professions Designates Shortage Areas," *Public Health Reports*, 1982, 97(4):388–389.

Minahan, Anne. "Social Workers and the Future," (editorial), *Social Work*, 1981, 26(5):363–364.

Molitor, Graham, T.T. "The Information Society: The Path to Post-Industrial Growth," *The Futurist*, 1981, 15(2):23–30.

National Research Council. *Rural America in Passage: Statistics for Policy*. Washington, D.C.: National Academy Press, 1981.

Osgood, Mary H. "Rural and Urban Attitudes Toward Welfare," *Social Work*, 1977, 22(1):41–47.

Powers, Ronald C. and Moe, Edward O. "The Policy Context for Rural-Oriented Research" in Dillman, Don A. and Hobbs, Daryl J. (Eds.), *Rural Society in the U.S.—Issues for the 1980s*. Boulder Colorado: Westview Press, 1982, 10–20.

President's National Advisory Commission on Rural Poverty. *The People Left Behind*. Washington, D.C.: Government Printing Office, 1967.

Rein, Martin. "Community Action Programs: A Critical Assessment," in *Social Policy: Issues of Choice and Change*. New York: Random House, 1970, Chapter 8, 153–164.

Rein, Martin and Peattie, Lisa. "Knowledge for Policy," *Social Service Review*, 1981, 55(4):524–543.

Robey, Bryant. "Age in America," *American Demographics*, 1981, 3(7):14–19.

Rochefort, David A. "Progressive and Social Control Perspectives on Social Welfare," *Social Service Review*, 1981, 55(4):568–592.

Roemer, Milton I. "Health Needs and Services of the Rural Poor," in *Rural Poverty in the United States*. A Report by the President's National Advisory Commission on Rural Poverty, Washington, D.C., 1968, 311–332.

Ross, M.H. "Rural Health Care: Is Pre-Payment a Solution?" *Public Health Reports*, 1975, 90(4):298–302.

Sarason, Seymour B. *The Creation of Settings and the Future Societies*. San Francisco: Jossey-Bass, Inc., 1973.

Schwartz, W.B., Newhouse, J.P., Bennett, B.W., and Williams, A.P., Jr. *The Changing Geographic Distribution of Board-Certified Physicians—Facts, Theory and Implications*. Santa Monica, Calif.: The Rand Corporation, 1980.

Smith, Eldon D., Deaton, Brady, and Kelch, David R. "Location Determinants of Manufacturing Industry in Rural Areas," *Southern Journal of Agricultural Economics*, 1978, 10(1):23–32.

Steinberg, Raymond M. "Functional Components and Organizational Issues in Rural Service Systems for the Aged: A Framework for Discussion," in Watkins, Dennis A. and Crawford, Charles O. (Eds.), *The Proceedings of the Workshop on Rural Gerontology Research in the Northeast*. Ithaca, N.Y.: Northeast Regional Center for Rural Development Pub. 14, Cornell University, 1978, 74–99.

Stewart, Robert P. "Watershed Days: How Will Social Work Respond to the Conservative Revolution?," *Social Work*, 1981, 26(4):271–273.

Stoesz, David. "A Wake for the Welfare State: Social Welfare and the Neo-conservative Challenge," *Social Service Review*, 1981, 55(3):398–410.

Sullivan, Patrick J., Collins, Judith N., and Reid, J. Norman. "Local Government Trends and Prospects" in Steward, D. and Dickson, Don (Eds.), *Rural Development Perspectives*. Washington, D.C.: Economic Development Division, ESCS, USDA, 1981, 4–11.

Taietz, Philip and Milton, Sande. "Rural–Urban Differences in the Structure of Services for the Elderly in Upstate New York Counties," *Journal of Gerontology*, 1979, 34(3):429–437.

Tweeten, Luther. "Education Has Role in Rural Development" in Steward, Donald D., Ross, Peggy J., and Ingalsbe, Gene (Eds.), *Rural Development Perspectives: Focus on Youth*. Washington, D.C.: Economic Development Division, ESCS, USDA, 1980, 9–12.

Tweeten, Luther and Brinkman, George L. *Micropolitan Development*. Ames, Iowa: Iowa State University Press, 1976.

Urban Land Institute. *UDAG Partnerships: Nine Case Studies*. Washington, D.C., 1980.

Urquhart, Michael. "The Services Industry: Is It Recession Proof?," *Monthly Labor Review*, 1981, 104(10):12–18.

U.S. Bureau of the Census. "Characteristics of the Population Below the Poverty Level: 1975," *Current Population Reports*, Series P-60, No. 110. Washington, D.C.: U.S. Government Printing Office, 1976.

U.S. Bureau of the Census. "Farm Population of the United States: 1980," *Current Population Reports*, Series P-27, No. 54, Washington, D.C., U.S. Government Printing Office, 1981c.

U.S. Bureau of the Census. "Money Income and Poverty Status of Families and Persons in the United States: 1980," *Current Population Reports*, Series P-60, No. 127. Washington, D.C.: U.S. Government Printing Office, 1981a.

U.S. Bureau of the Census. "Population Profile of the United States: 1980," *Current Population Reports*, Series P-20, No. 363. Washington, D.C.: U.S. Government Printing Office, 1981b.

U.S. Department of Health and Human Services, Public Health Service, National Center for Health Statistics. *Vital Statistics of the U.S.*, Vol. II, Mortality, Part B. Washington, D.C., 1978.

Warner, W. Keith. "Rural Society in a Post-Industrial Age," *Rural Sociology*, 1974, 39(3):306–317.

Weinberg, Daniel H. "Housing Benefits from the Section 8 Housing Program," *Evaluation Review*, 1982, 6(1):5–24.

2 Components of Social Policy

Social Policy:
Toward a Definition and Purpose

The concept of social policy is often ill-defined and, at best, broad in scope. At a general level of understanding some agreement exists, but as pointed analytic questions are raised, consensus dissipates into a variety of definitions and applications. In large part, the concept becomes a function of the specific setting and the professional actors involved in its definition.

A significant group of policy analysts has struggled to define the concept of social policy by explicating its goals, examining its product, relating to its process, and focusing on its boundaries (Boulding, 1967; Burns, 1956; Freeman & Sherwood, 1970: Marshall, 1965; Rein, 1970; Schorr, 1968). Without going into finite detail, as this would only reiterate the information in the aforementioned works, the most salient definitions will be brought to focus and a boundary that has most applicability to the rural setting in an advanced industrial era will be suggested.

At an action-oriented level of explication, social policy is often described as any course of action followed by a government in relation to its citizenry. The inclusive nature of this definition becomes problematic to social workers in their efforts to somehow impact quality of life of a target population. Yet, depending on the developing nature of a policy process, there are merits in a general, nonprescriptive approach to definition in the latitude allowed for restructuring and targeting more specific policy objec-

31

tives within a broader goal statement. The work of Gil (1970; 1976), with much the same general focus as that of the previous action-oriented description, broadly includes all aspects of relationships between individuals and social units as the subject matter for social policy.

Social policy represents organized efforts (Burns, 1961) that provide some degree of order to what Morris (1979) and Baumheier and Schorr (1977) characterize as randomly occurring social phenomena. As a definition of social policy this is stated clearly by Baumheier and Schorr (1977) as:

> . . . those principles and procedures that guide any course of action related to individual and aggregate relationships in society and are used to intervene in and regulate an otherwise random social system. Established social policy is a settled course of action with respect to selected social phenomena that govern social relationships in the distribution of resources in a society. (p. 1453)

The National Association of Social Workers (NASW) through its biannual meeting of the Delegate Assembly acts on numerous social policy goals. A definition suggested by the profession, which shares much in common with that of Burns (1961) and Baumheier and Schorr (1977), is stated as consisting ". . . of those laws, policies, and practices of government that affect the social relationships of individuals and their relationship to the society of which they are a part" (NASW, 1963, p. 7).

On a continuum of definition, moving from broad policy goals to more specific objectives are other definitions of social policy which are action directed toward a certain problem. This view, according to Morris (1979) ". . . simply identifies an area of human relationships in which advocates of action want society, through its mechanisms of government, to respond to a need although the details of action are not specified" (p. 10). As an example, The Older Americans Act of 1965, as amended, contains such an action statement in the preface to a declaration of objectives in Title I.

> Sec. 101. The Congress hereby finds and declares that, in keeping with the traditional American concept of the inherent dignity of the individual in our democratic society, the older people of our Nation are entitled to, and it is the joint and several duty and responsibility of the governments of the United States and of the several States and their political subdivisions to assist our older people to

secure equal opportunity to the full and free enjoyment. . . .
[Older Americans Act of 1965, §101, 42 U.S.C. §3001 (1978)]

Policy definitions with a narrow and highly circumscribed perspective represent yet another view of social policy. However, they fail to address with sufficient recognition the greater issues that have traditionally provided the raison d'être of social policy, that is, economic, social, and political discrimination leading to the stigmatization and vulnerability of specific population groups in American society (Titmuss, 1963). According to Morris (1979), narrowness of definition has as its setting the day-to-day functions of program and service operations. These operational policies affect and influence how a more broadly articulated policy is implemented. However, it is not the purpose of this book to call attention to this narrower policy parameter.

Approaching the issue from another perspective, policy is sometimes defined as a program. This inductive approach to definition assumes that because there is a program, a well-developed policy underpins its existence. Similarly, it is sometimes assumed that policies do not exist simply because programs are not reflective of what particular advocates believe to be the proper course of action (Morris, 1979). Approaching the definitional issue from this perspective has major limitations. First, if adequately formulated, policy is designed to determine the base of program existence and action. Second, to ignore the existence of policy actions with which one does not agree risks the error of incorrect assessment and strategy formulation directed toward change. In a recent article Rein and Peattie (1981) suggest that policy, rather than defining the action taken to remedy a problem situation, evolves from the actions taken and defined as possible. The relationship of policy to action is not linear but is reciprocal; one dimension legitimates and refines the other.

Not to be dismissed from discussion of policy definition are the attempts to suggest an appropriate arena of action that social policy should encompass (Boulding, 1967; Gilbert & Specht, 1974; Rein, 1970). It is assumed that social policy is in some way different from public policy, economic policy, or social welfare policy. Public policy is the arena of concern to the public at large. As such it includes such foci as the public defense (military) and environmental protection. Economic policy, according to Boulding (1967), includes monetary, price, and tax policy. Gilbert and Specht (1974) suggest that the arena of focus for social welfare

policy is the social welfare institution, which, through a pattern-
ing of relationships, performs mutual support functions in the
absence of or in support of such other need satisfying institutions
as the family, church, and the marketplace. Included in this policy arena is a wide range of programs, for example, social insurance, public assistance, and social services with a variety of target
groups: the elderly; minorities; families; and children. From Morris' (1979) point of view, ". . . social policies are identified as
those through which government seeks to correct inequities, to
improve the condition of the disadvantaged, and to provide assistance to the less powerful" (p. 1).

An understanding of the setting—the advanced industrial
society—suggests that to confine discussion to social welfare
policy ignores the dynamic interdependence of the social, political, and economic institutions. To the social worker in a rural
environment where a high degree of interdependence of institutions and less professional specialization exists, the policy perspective must be broadened beyond the social welfare institution
to include education, employment, housing, health, and politics
(Marshall, 1965). This points to the usefulness of the broader
perspective—that of social policy. The goal then of social policy
is, according to Boulding (1967), ". . . to build the identity of a
person around some community with which he is associated" (p.
7). In Boulding's view, the thread of commonality woven in
social policy statements is social integration and identification as
a way of addressing problems of social devisiveness and alienation. Conflicts and disagreements arise in the process of policy
formulation because those involved disagree about which course
of action promotes divisiveness and alienation and which will
best promote integration and identification with the larger social
system. In one sense Boulding's view raises the concern that
social policy serves not as a mechanism for integration but ultimately as a mechanism for social control (Piven & Cloward,
1971; Rochefort, 1981).

In addressing the goal of social integration, social policy becomes not only a series of statements which determine the relationship between governments and individuals or social units, but
it is viewed, and appropriately so, by Kahn (1979) and Morris
(1979) as a standing plan or guide to decision making or action
around currently identified problems and unanticipated future
problems. Therefore, social policy is reflective of an overarching
principle or set of principles exercised in making choices by one

group relative to decisions affecting another group. It is formulated at both a macro- and microlevel of individual/social unit interaction. In other words, it includes the broad guidelines, both legislative and regulatory, enacted at the federal and state levels of government as well as the more specific guidelines promulgated at the local and agency level. However, operational policies which encompass the day-to-day operations of an agency are not the focus of this discussion; in addition, the regulatory function— the rules governing the implementation of broader social policy mandates—is not a focus of this book.

Social policy decisions in an advanced industrial society are, in part, a reflection of the growing interdependence of social, economic, and political institutions (Rein, 1977; Rein & Peattie, 1981). With increasing specialization of occupation and heightened scarcity of resources, policy decisions that more fully govern the interactions of individuals and institutions as well as the relationships among institutions are made routinely.

Defining social policy as a guide to action in response to currently identified problems and unanticipated future problems, emphasizes the importance of social policy and its impact on social work practice, particularly if social work is to have a role, as suggested by Minahan (1981), in shaping the future. The social worker, whether in a community or institutional setting, dealing with clients on a direct practice level or negotiating a purchase-of-service contract with a state agency, participates in the policy process and is affected by policy decisions. To the social worker in a rural setting where the practice skills related to community assessment, program design, implementation, evaluation, negotiation, and advocacy are particularly important, considerable influence can be exerted on the formulation of policy. Likewise, policy decisions can have an immediate impact on social work practice. This is underlined by the fact that social workers in rural settings are more clearly a part of the community; they work actively in the community and often live in that community (Sherman & Rowley, 1977). The practice setting is the community. This requires a generalist perspective and a holistic view of the social policy process.

From past experience it is apparent that major policy decisions made at the federal level have a decidedly urban bias. That is, the decisions reflect an urbanized post-industrial society and either exclude attention to the problems of rural America or view those problems as similar to those of urban settings. However, in recent years a heightened sensitivity to rural issues has occurred on the part of policy decision makers (Brown, Steward, & Ingalsbe, 1980; President's National Advisory Commission on Rural Poverty, 1967; Samuels, 1978). If indeed, social policy goals should be directed toward improving the quality of life of a community and its individual members, thereby reducing frustration and alienation from the community, it is crucial that social workers serving small communities participate actively in policy decision making and ensure that decisions made external to the community reflect the directions and priorities desired by the total community, including the more vulnerable and less vocal members.

Framework for Analysis

It is not sufficient to explore social policy with a rural perspective by simply describing in detail the various programs resulting from policy directives. Rather, as in Burns' (1956) work, the student is encouraged to apply an analytic framework to social policy. In other words, a series of questions may be raised about a number of pieces of social policy. One can examine the end product according to specific choices made as applicable to the majority of policy decisions. The choices will be anchored in both knowledge and values (Gilbert & Specht, 1974). To view analytically the product also involves some understanding of what Freeman and Sherwood (1970) refer to as social policy as a framework for action. Social policy involves a product, but furthermore it is a process wherein social policy is continually developing ". . . by which enduring organizations maintain an element of stability and at the same time seek to improve conditions for their members" (p. 3).

For the rural setting, a focus of analysis on action which is a combination of process and product (Freeman & Sherwood, 1970) reinforces the view of the dynamic nature of the rural environment and social work practice. It is recognized, in addition, that many "process" issues, some of which are included in Chapter 6, may be more appropriately addressed in a course on social work practice in a rural setting. Thus, the more productive point at which to begin is understanding the policy choices related to a policy product. This understanding will generate a position for isolating social policy themes which emerge and, in later chapters in this volume, developing the themes as they have implications for rural areas.

The critical substance of policy decisions is viewed by Gilbert and Specht (1974) and Burns (1956), as "dimensions of choice" in the decision-making process. The choices made are directed by values and cultural base, theories and assumptions about social and individual change, and the range of alternatives thought possible. Across the four dimensions of choice, which are thought to be generic, that is, applicable to a wide range of social policy decisions, a range of possible responses is generated. The response may be underpinned on the one hand by a discussion of such fairly general values and belief systems as the individual right to self-determination or, on the other hand, more specific ideologies reflective of decisions emphasizing the capitalist marketplace economy, government ownership and management, or group associations at the neighborhood level (Gilbert & Specht, 1974). The four dimensions of choice discussed by Gilbert and Specht and based on the earlier work of Burns (1956), are as follows:

1.   What are the bases of social allocations?
2.   What are the types of social provisions to be allocated?
3.   What are the strategies for the delivery of these provisions?
4.   What are the methods of financing these provisions?

These questions suggest a schema for the allocation of benefits that addresses who receives what and how, and furthermore at whose or what expense. The question of who is answered by eligibility criteria; the question of what is determined by the form a provision or benefit takes; how involves questions about the delivery mechanism; financing questions reflect on the source of funds and their flow to an appropriate provider or beneficiary. Although Burns applied these dimensions of choice to the social security system, Gilbert and Specht extended the framework's application beyond social security. The approach taken by Gilbert and Specht corresponds with the broader focus on social policy and covers policy directed toward either a services or an income ideology.

In all social policy decisions, the four dimensions of choice are substantially influenced, regardless of ideological perspective, by an overarching reality that the present economic system func-

TABOR COLLEGE LIBRARY
HILLSBORO KANSAS

tions so that as one sector (or individual) gains, another loses. This translates into what Thurow (1980, p. 18) views as a "zero sum society," in which the realities of slowed economic growth and the subsequent need to make decisions about income equity are producing tensions and strains of *ourselves* against *ourselves* that previously have been ignored. So long as we were convinced of a growing economy we were equally convinced that incomes would rise and the provision of benefits to the few in need would not be a difficult adjustment or a sacrifice for anyone.

The Basis of Social Allocations

As a dimension of choice in social policy decisions, the basis of allocation responds to the question of who is eligible to receive a particular benefit or provision. According to Burns (1956) this translates into questions concerning the receipt of benefits by whom and the types of risks for which society accepts responsibility. This means, in the systems language of social work practice, who will constitute the target population for a benefit? Again, drawing from Burns' work on social security, choices are made to allocate benefits according to need, as in the case of public assistance, or according to contributions as related to previous earnings, exemplified by the social security retirement system. Further decisions about social responsibility for risk involve choices concerning provisions to cover the risks of unemployment, disability (physical and mental), and old age. The choices made can relate to both income security and the provision of services broadly defined (Burns, 1956).

Such decisions are terribly complex and susceptible to political manipulation and negotiation. In one currently prominent position, adhering to the principles of the free market economy in which less government is viewed as good government and in which it is thought, or at least assumed, that employment is available to anyone who wants to work, social programs are targeted, in a general sense, to the "truly needy." With social program resources increasingly scarce, eligibility criteria become more categorical and narrow; for example, they apply to the vulnerable or frail elderly and are means-tested—that is, income is related by placing the burden of proof of poverty on the potential recipient. This approach to eligibility is viewed by Wilensky and Lebeaux (1965) as representing a residual view of the social welfare institution, that is, a system that "should come into play only when the normal structures of supply, the family and the market break down" (p. 138).

Critics of this position argue that the net result of such beliefs translated into social policy is stigmatization of the recipient. Furthermore, inherent in the means-tested criterion, the target group is perceived as being privileged to receive, the social distance between "giver" and "receiver" is increased, and the need being addressed is the result of individual deficiency and viewed as temporary in its manifestation.

Although the means-tested approach to eligibility has a long history, its current emphasis is viewed by many as an economically sound way to cut government expenditures. Targeting a narrow group eligible to receive benefits and insisting on a rigid means-test process may discourage applicants by making the potential benefit not worth the loss of personal freedom, pride, and integrity (Piven & Cloward, 1971). In Gilbert and Specht's view (1974), policy makers operate under the assumption of receptivity, that is, potential recipients of a benefit will be receptive to it. The conditions surrounding receipt of the benefit, however, may mitigate against it.

The thrust toward a more universal approach to eligibility recognizes the dysfunctions of a free market economy in which women, minorities, children, the elderly, and to a large extent, rural populations, have less access to the perceived benefits of the market economy. Universal criteria generally reflect the policy choice that *all* persons within a particular group or community are to benefit from a service or provision as a social right. Public education and social security retirement benefits reflect this general stance toward universality. In the view of Wilensky and Lebeaux (1965), this approach represents an institutional or developmental view of the social welfare institution, that is, welfare services are a normal function in an industrialized economy.

Proponents of universality of eligibility maintain that the approach is less costly in social terms. Obscuring the differences between those who receive a benefit and those who do not diminishes social divisiveness. Although the pool of people to benefit is substantially broadened under universal criteria, the costs are thought to be less because fraud and abuse are diminished and the need for an entrenched bureaucratic structure to administer and monitor the neediness of the beneficiaries is lessened. Furthermore, as pointed out by Garfinkel (1978), "Subjecting rich and poor alike to the same set of rules reduces the likelihood of differential treatment." This occurs because upper-class people voice disapproval when an organization treats them in an objectionable way, and given the propensity for a bureaucratic organization to routinize procedures, ". . . poor people are almost certain to be treated with more dignity in universal than in income-tested programs" (p. 188).

An additional advantage cited by proponents of universal benefits is the relative political stability a universally based program enjoys. When the constituency group is broadly based, threats to a program can be countered by widespread political pressure. The continuing attacks on the Social Security system have been held in check by the strong political lobby of a broadly based group of elderly people. The policy choice of universal allocation is more realistic in its assessment of the current interdependencies of social, economic, and political structures characteristic of an advanced industrial society.

The reality of decision making on the basis of allocation (eligibility criteria) reflects a process of negotiation and compromise among a pluralistic set of actors, seldom resulting in the dichotomies portrayed in the examination of concepts. Rather, the decisions reached reflect a mix of selective (means-tested) and universal criteria. Although Social Security retirement benefits (OASDHI) are viewed as universal, there are idiosyncracies to the provision that exemplify well the processes of negotiation and compromise. Viewed as a social right which recognizes the social and economic exigencies of advancing age, the amount of the benefit is indexed to the individual's contribution during the working years. Furthermore, age at receipt of the benefit influences not only the benefit amount—for example, less than full benefit to one who retires earlier than 65 years—but also the amount of additional earnings one may garner without a subsequent reduction in benefit amount—after age 72 one receives full benefits regardless of the amount of additional earnings. The "earnings test" was first included in the 1939 Amendments to the Social Security Act. In 1982 the earnings test will not apply to those age 70 and over (Ozawa, 1979).

For rural areas the implications of allocation decisions based on universal or selective criteria are noteworthy. First, the distinctions between those who receive a benefit and those who do not are painfully evident in a small community where confidentiality and anonymity are not the same as in urban settings (Sherman & Rowley, 1977). Second, in rural settings, where it is presumed there is greater extended family and community support, the means-tested criteria may be differentially applied with the expectation that the informal network will provide a sufficient quantity of a social provision or service. Third, problems associated with already low incomes in rural areas are evident in the levels of benefit associated with universal programs (OASDHI) in the United States. Finally, the heightened visibility of townspeople to one another in small communities increases the risk of subjective judgments based on personal animosities and experiences entering the means-test process. This philosophy was recently exemplified by the following case example:

> In the discussion of a town council of a small community the salary of the welfare official was being increased substantially. Commenting on what one council member thought to be a high salary, another council member suggested that it was going to be worth paying more money because she (the welfare director) would in turn save the community a good deal of money by making it difficult to get welfare assistance. In another small, rural town of 496 people the most recent annual town report indicated $1,000 allocated for the "town poor" but totally unspent at years end.

Is one to assume that there are no poor people in this town, that federal and state programs fully meet the needs, or that persons will not subject themselves to the scrutiny of town officials and suffer discrimination by the townspeople? Further discussion of these issues is included in Chapter 3 in an examination of income security programs.

Form of Provision

A second major question of importance to social policy decisions is that of the form a provision will take. Such decisions are related to the degree of transferability the provision has in the open marketplace to procure valued goods and services. A continuum of transferability is conceptualized with social control constituting the basis of choice at one end and autonomy of decision making characterizing choices at the opposite end of the continuum (Gilbert & Specht, 1974). Translated into "form of provision," in-kind provisions are viewed as coercive and controlling and cash benefits as more in the progressive tradition (Burns, 1956; Rochefort, 1981).

American history is replete with examples of provisions that dictate and control the behavior of the recipient (Piven & Cloward, 1971; Rein, 1977). Historically, in-kind benefits have been the backbone of philanthropy and charitable giving. To collect food and clothing for the family whose home is destroyed by a chimney fire is an example familiar to rural residents. Food baskets at Thanksgiving and secondhand toys at Christmas are familiar responses to need which have enjoyed the support of church groups, civic, and fraternal organizations. These provisions dictate the behavior of the recipient and assure the giver that the provision will be used as was intended. The provision may have some transferability on the open market, that is, it can be sold for cash, but this is not easily done within the normal market exchange networks.

The decision to provide in-kind benefits makes some rather unsettling assumptions about the recipient. First, it assumes that the recipient does not have sufficient knowledge to make a socially determined appropriate choice; second, if the recipient is knowledgeable, other needs will interfere with what society considers to be the better choice. One is reminded of the charitable thrift shop where money is exchanged for goods but control is exercised by underpricing children's clothing and substantially overpricing women's dress shoes, jewelry, and cosmetics.

Furthermore, providing in-kind benefits makes certain assumptions about need. Viewing need as residually based, that is, temporary and the result of individual deficiency, makes justification of the in-kind benefit less difficult. It is expected that the beneficiary will not have to rely on the receipt of charitable, secondhand clothing (or other in-kind provisions) for long. Once again the complexities of the advanced industrial society have been ignored.

At an intermediate point on a continuum of transferability is the voucher as a form of provision. While less controlling than in-kind benefits, the receiver is still directed to use the voucher within a certain economic sector. For example, an emergency voucher may be issued for groceries or fuel oil, a student loan may be procured for tuition only and further circumscribed for use at a particular educational institution. At this writing it is being suggested that public housing will soon be available through a voucher system as opposed to the present in-kind system wherein housing built and maintained by public entities is available to eligible recipients (Khadduri & Struyk, 1982). The use of a voucher, like cash, assumes the availability of a benefit in the marketplace.

Cash as a form of provision allows for the most consumer choice and is least controlling of behavior in the economic marketplace. It is also most supportive of the concept of a free market economy. The recipient is free to make choices, limited primarily by the amount of the cash benefit and somewhat by the goods available. Cash, as is known, can buy power, control over resources which may be goods, services, or access to political and economic structures. Cash benefits make assumptions about the integrity and sovereignty of the recipient and acknowledge that choices may be appropriate or inappropriate according to some predefined, socially acceptable standard. However, it is accepted that people make both kinds of choices and furthermore, that the risks of inappropriate choices at the point of consumption are not as troublesome as the risk of social control through the form a provision takes. As pointed out by Burns (1956), cash payments became the predominant form of provision in the United States following the Depression because of the widespread unemployment of previously independent people.

The policy decision to provide a cash payment is complicated by the recognition that the benefit is usually not adequate to meet a standard of need. To address this concern, programs of an in-kind nature have been enacted as supplementary to the cash benefit. Examples of this approach are free milk and/or lunch in the schools, nutritional supplements for children and pregnant women (WIC Program), and subsidized, in-kind housing assistance. Another difficulty associated with the low level of the cash benefit is that the recipient does not have sufficient latitude in exercising choices, and the cash therefore becomes primarily a way of supporting the market economy.

Once again, dichotomous positions have been used as a way of conceptualizing views which more often than not resist being so clearcut. Other forms of provision that exemplify a blending of positions are opportunities, services, and power. Opportunities are viewed, according to Gilbert and Specht (1974), as vague provisions with least transferability. Opportunities, frequently in the form of equal employment opportunity, affirmative action, or some type of preference based on one's status, for example as a woman, minority, veteran, or handicapped person, are viewed as means to an end which includes increased autonomy and rewards within the market system. Such services provided to/for the client as counseling, family planning, homemaking, and education, have no equivalent of exchange in the marketplace. However, one s future ability to use the marketplace and its monetary basis of exchange may increase as a result of the service. For example, as the result of an educational program one may later obtain a higher paying job with discretionary cash to use in the marketplace.

Although power can be purchased by cash, it can also be gained through mandated requirements for the participation of clients/consumers in decision making that will ultimately affect them, an example being consumer participation on Boards of Area Agencies on Aging (AAAs). The goal of redistributing decision-making power and authority will be discussed in Chapter 5. Power, then, cannot be used to purchase goods in the marketplace, but it can lead to a command over choices in the social and economic structures of society.

Adding to the complexity of decision making are situations in which one form of provision, for example, cash, carries with it the expectation of participation in another form of provision, for example, services. Such was the expectation for receipt of public assistance before a separation of services was mandated in 1967. Sometimes the expectation governing the receipt of a provision is not so clear; it is, nevertheless, present. Most economic market transactions involve the exchange of money, that is, a bilateral exchange. However, social provisions, although appearing to be freely given involving unilateral exchange (Boulding, 1967), carry vague, ambiguous reciprocal expectations that have the result of controlling recipient behavior. The use of a cash benefit to purchase an automobile for transportation to work may be sanctioned by society. However, as the recipient of a public benefit, one is admonished not to buy a large car which is probably older, less fuel efficient, and less costly; buy instead an "economy" car (even if one cannot afford it).

The form a provision takes has implications for rural settings that differ from urban environments, if not in form, then certainly in degree. Although the principle of in-kind giving is viewed as stigmatizing and controlling, what does this mean in a rural setting? Do rural people, accustomed to bartering and trading with one another, attach the same meaning to the Thanksgiving basket (social control) as might their urban counterparts? Do we risk destroying a system of less transferable provisions and the care expressed by the giver by imposing a highly transferable (cash) provision as a substitute? Cash provisions are underpinned by the assumption of availability of a good or service, an assumption that may not be correct in a rural setting. These are questions not easily answered. However, it would seem prudent to advocate for rural power as a form of provision, from which other choices may be exerted—clearly as a choice not as the only possibility.

The Delivery System

Generic social policy choices about who and what are followed conceptually by decisions as to how a provision will reach the intended beneficiary. Questions of service delivery are preceded by an understanding of what constitutes the system. Hearn (1979) states "A system is defined as a set of objects together with relationships between the objects and their attributes (p. 346). Gilbert and Specht (1974) state that the delivery system "refers to the organizational arrangements among distributors and consumers of social welfare benefits in the context of the local community" (p. 108). To further refine the concept of a system with the primary function of the delivery of social benefits, Boettcher (1974) suggests that the delivery system can be conceptualized at an institutional (macro) level or an organizational (micro) level.

At the macro level the delivery system is equated with the entire institution of social welfare or, more specifically, a network of organizations that are interrelated with commonality of goals and functions. Boettcher states that the institutional construct ". . . refers to general public social policy, programs, and practices which are national in scope. Moreover, the construct refers to developments and trends which affect the network of organizations responsible for the provision of benefits and services to particular populations of citizens" (p. 48). The organizational or micro view of the delivery system refers to an agency setting in terms of a program or a program component. The components of the delivery system at the organizational level are the following:

1. Agency policy consisting of the goals and objectives as well as the operational policies that facilitate attainment of agency purpose.
2. Agency structure designating the responsibilities and tasks incumbent upon the various positions in the structure.

3. Agency personnel identified with the positions in the structure, both formal and informal.
4. Agency service consumers utilizing the benefits provided through the agency.

Consumers are those individuals or groups and third parties who represent consumer groups, who are users of the agency provision. According to Boettcher, "Presumably, the policy, formal structure, and personnel of the agency have been developed and selected on the basis of certain information and predictions about the clientele" (p. 48). This indicates a reciprocal process of interaction and exchange.

Both the institutional and the organizational levels of abstraction are important from a social policy perspective. Choices made about the delivery of a service or provision at the institutional level impact the organizational level. Depending on the degree of reciprocity operating in the policy decision-making process, the reverse is also true. However, it is at the micro level, the point of consumption, that organizations in interaction with service consumers feel most dramatically the impact of social policy.

The community setting provides the external environment in which the provider–consumer interaction takes place as well as the interaction between provider organizations. The community can be conceptualized at several levels—federal, state, local— each reflecting beliefs and traditions about social and economic organizations. It is the community setting that most closely represents Boettcher's reference to the institutional system. The organizational abstraction is represented by providers and consumers. In the delivery of services and allocation of provisions the community setting is viewed as the local level since it is at this point that the majority of provider–consumer interactions take place.

As providers and consumers interact and as one provider interacts with another, the opportunity for dysfunction occurs. At any point in the interaction process that the provider takes steps to deliver a benefit and consumers acquire the benefit, the process may be interrupted and the agency may fail to carry out its function in an appropriate manner. The frequently cited major failures of the delivery system (Gilbert & Specht, 1974; Rein, 1970) are:

1. Fragmentation: organizational characteristics and relationships resulting from specialization, location, and communication barriers.

2. Discontinuity: obstacles to moving through the delivery system and the potential gaps in services as agencies attempt to reconcile client needs with available resources.

3. Inaccessibility: obstacles exist that prevent client movement into the service network. These may be organizational characteristics or attitudinal or knowledge barriers that interfere with access to a service or provision.

4. Unaccountability: a lack of responsiveness on the part of the agency to external influence, particularly consumer input in decisions that will affect him or her.

Social policy decisions made at the institutional and organizational levels may, in actuality, either contribute to failures or seek to address the basic failures within the delivery system. Policy decisions, seeking to promote an intended outcome, may produce unintended consequences of a magnitude greater than those anticipated consequences. Although it is not the intent of this book to examine why delivery systems fail, it is appropriate to point out some underlying concerns.

Bernard (1975), in a critique of service delivery programs, points to the "grandiosity of their goals" as contributing to failure to achieve goals of social change. An example of this concern is expressed by proponents advocating home-based care for the elderly. Using the argument that a system of home-based care will be less costly than the present system of institutional care ignores the reality that providing adequate home-based care will increase the numbers of individuals who, out of personal choice, will then have access to the delivery system and therefore costs will increase. Furthermore, empirical evidence suggests that home-based care is usually used in conjunction with other services, for example, day care and boarding care, and is therefore not a full substitute for institutional care (Weissert, 1980).

Following the continuum presentation used in examining allocation and form of benefit, the questions to be addressed about the delivery system relate to all components—policy, structure, personnel, consumer, and community. The structural questions relate to issues as wide ranging as those highly bureaucratic and formalized structures to those more informal in character. Personnel questions address the issues of types of personnel, their training and experience and the role of consumers in the actual delivery of service. Community questions address the very important issues of location of service and the point at which agency authority and control (policy) decisions are made. From the perspective of the total delivery system, and given the current political environment, there is particular value in examining the decision for a centralized or decentralized delivery system. Broadly speaking, centralization refers to administrative centralization or centralization of decision making. It also refers to the location of a service in terms of consumer access. Decentralization suggests more local autonomy in service decisions and service access in close proximity to the consumer group.

Two benefits which exemplify the concepts of centralization and decentralization are Social Security retirement benefits and rural health clinics. Social Security (OASDHI) is administered centrally by the federal government, with policy decisions (basis of allocation, form, delivery, and funding) legislatively mandated—with intended equal impact on all recipients. However, local and/or regional offices exist, and these offices, in a decentralized fashion, interpret the policy decisions to local residents. Due to the idiosyncracies characteristic of each Social Security office, the four failures of the delivery system, cited above, can occur. This is not meant to imply that failures occur only at the more local level, but rather to maintain a focus at the point of interaction between provider and consumer.

A rural health clinic represents decentralization of the health care system in terms of location, services provided, and consumer group. Although a clinic may receive federal funding that will determine, in part, its operating policies, it is primarily freestanding and answerable to the local community. In some instances, the clinic may function as the satellite operation of a larger, more distantly located medical facility and may, therefore, exercise more or less decision-making autonomy. In either case, the clinic is subject to the failures of the delivery system.

Although the concept of the delivery system is generic, that is, applicable to most settings, there are subtleties that differentiate rural delivery systems from those systems generally represented in the literature as urban-based models. The literature suggests, for example, much more reliance on an informal delivery system in rural areas (Johnson, 1980). The provider entity represents a greater mix of formal organizations interacting with friends, family, neighbors, and community groups (Bertsche & Clark, 1981; Clark, Bertsche, & Bates, 1980; Coward, 1978; Froland, 1980; Wylie, 1976). This suggests a more decentralized delivery system; one in which, as suggested by Oates (1977), the success or failure of the social worker is dependent in no small part on an understanding of the community (the setting for the delivery system), and the ability to use the community structure (informal) to connect people with programs or other resource systems. In addition, the social worker mobilizes the informal structure to be part of the delivery system and thus expand its available resources.

Another characteristic of rural delivery systems is the small size of organizations and the fewer numbers of them. This difference of scale was discussed in Chapter 1 and translates into fewer professionally trained people to deliver all services—not simply fewer social work services, less expertise available to deal with larger bureaucratic organizations at the state and federal level, and fewer resources to address pressing social issues (Hamilton & Reid, 1977; Watkins and Watkins, 1976; 1981). Some view small size as a virtue (Schumacher, 1973). On the one hand, small size may increase caring among persons in a community in which face-to-face interaction is more prevalent. On the other hand, it may increase the ostracism faced by people who do not measure up to community norms. Receipt of a social benefit may have a price tag associated with it in terms of social (community) control of the recipient.

Smallness also suggests that most of what happens in the delivery process occurs in a fishbowl. Little goes on without the awareness of the general community (Sherman & Rowley, 1977). At the base of this "knowing" network are the extended family and friendship relationships. According to Sherman and Rowley:

> Worker–client roles are not separate from the fabric of this life but are the functional transmission links of change within it. Hence in the rural area lifestyle, almost all information is personal and personalized. Much is public, accessible either from public records or from personalized inference based on observation, rumor, or gossip. What remains private, therefore, seems entirely debatable. . . . (p. 19)

Although dysfunctions may occur in the delivery of services, the use of services by the consumer is related to receptivity as the following exemplifies:

> Based on a community needs assessment, indicators pointed to the need for day care services in one small Eastern mill

town. Town officials, responding to the assessment and the availability of some one-time monies from the state submitted a proposal for project funding.

The opening of the day care center was greeted with enthusiasm by town officials. However, 70 percent of the day care slots were vacant at the opening of the center.

A closer look at the development process brought out several important and neglected considerations: (1) The day care facility was a building that had been used previously as a sheltered workshop for the mentally retarded; (2) The facility was located two miles from the center of town where most people were employed by a textile firm; (3) Staff members for the center were hired from a larger community 50 miles away and were unknown to the community members.

Even though all indicators pointed to the need for a day care center in the example cited above, attitudinal and value considerations precluded use of the center by many town residents. The stigma of mental retardation, the distance from work with no transportation service, and the distrust and apprehension of leaving one's children with strangers mitigated against service utilization. The difficulty of this situation lies in the possible interpretation that the 70 percent vacancy rate means there is not a need for day care in this rural community; this reinforces the urban perception that rural people do not need or want this service perhaps because of extended families and informal care giving patterns.

Funding Decisions

A fourth dimension of the decision-making process and that which completes the major components in the framework for social policy analysis is that of funding (Burns, 1956; Gilbert & Specht, 1974). Funding decisions for purposes of this discussion revolve around issues related to the source of funds, for example, public versus private, and the transfer of funds to a provider source, for example, block grants versus categorical grants-in-aid.

The underpinning of social program funding beginning with the New Deal and the Social Security Act of 1935 has been public expenditures originating from public tax monies at federal, state, and local levels.

the private sector will increase their participation in providing funds for essential services. This expectation assumes a sufficient tax base built on an expanding economy, and/or a willingness of taxpayers to increase their tax load. Both assumptions are problematic. In declining rural areas, for example, the tax base is insufficient to generate the needed dollars. Furthermore, low-income rural people already pay a disproportionate share of their income in sales, excise, and property taxes. Finally, the American economy is not in an expansionary period.

Whereas the federal strategy is to minimize its participation in funding programs, it has been suggested that states maximize funding capabilities. From the point of view of the state this strategy means seeking ". . . for itself, for its human service programs, and for its citizens all of the entitlements available under existing Federal law and regulation" (Copeland & Iversen, 1981, p. 19).

Funding issues in rural areas are closely related to the often used funding formulae based on population numbers, for example, the Older Americans Act, which results in the distribution of lower amounts of money combined with the relatively greater costs of providing services to isolated populations. Furthermore, although program funds may be available, the proper or required organizational context may not be in place to use the funds. As a result, municipalities that in the past have not dealt with provision of social benefits will increasingly be called upon to do so. Findings indicate that they are often ill-equipped and ill-prepared to peform this function (Watkins & Watkins, 1976).

Dynamic Tensions: The Policy Themes

As a result of interaction between advanced industrial society, the rural environment, and the nature of policy choices, a series of dynamic tensions emerge influencing the action outcomes of policy decisions. The dynamic tensions are represented as challenges to our traditional belief systems or ways of thinking about the provision of social benefits. Tensions exist as social policy decisions are made based on the precepts of social justice and equity while being confronted with a shifting political and economic environment that views past social policy decisions as ineffective, wasteful, and destructive to our traditional institutions. The task of social policy in general is to address the challenges to our belief systems by elucidating policy actions that reflect a commitment to a just society within the constraints of advanced industrial society. In particular, we are concerned that rural America, with its differentiating characteristics, be equal with urban America in its participation toward elucidating the policy actions. Those formulating social policy and those who implement social programs must acknowledge and grapple with the following challenges:

1. the provision of adequate and high quality services in a political environment overwhelmingly concerned with cost containment and reduction of public expenditures;
2. the renewed thrust toward decentralized decision making at the state and local levels in an environment requiring institutional interdependence that contrasts sharply with a growing passive federal involvement unprecedented in recent times;
3. the growing social inequities in a society increasingly reliant on highly technical and theoretical knowledge as the base of reward systems, with a loss of manufacturing and blue-collar employment enlarging the composition of a permanent underclass;
4. increasing turbulence in the environment and large, bureaucratic organizations unable to respond appropriately to not only the external environment but to internal organizational needs;
5. the growing importance of the political arena as the center for problem resolution and the zero-sum character of the adversary relationship resulting in a paralysis of the decision-making process.

    In response to the tensions generated by the characteristics of advanced industrial society and the need to develop appropriate social policy responses, actions or themes emerge which provide the substantive content for further analysis of social policy in rural environments.

Summary

In this chapter a framework for policy analysis as introduced by Burns (1956) and later expanded by Gilbert and Specht (1974) has been discussed. That is, a series of questions have been articulated with importance in guiding the choices made by policy decision makers. It has been the intent of this discussion to prepare the reader for the subsequent analysis of income security programs, the organization and delivery of services, and fiscal, management, and development themes which constitute the parameters for rural policy analysis.

Although the dimensions have been presented conceptually as discrete entities in the decision-making process, in actuality this is rarely the case. A constant flow and interaction among the dimensions develops a variety of forms of benefits and results in the identification of themes characteristic of the policy product. Using the four dimensions of choice, the student of social policy can raise issues appropriate to a variety of social programs. In addition, a series of tensions was articulated which has implications for programs of income security or social services. Both, considered strategies for fulfilling the social responsibility of government to people who are vulnerable in the setting of an advanced industrial society, form the substantive content for the remainder of this book.

Chapter 3 will examine income strategies while Chapters 4 and 5 will look at the policy themes developing around the service strategies. The reader is alerted that themes are also applicable to income strategies, and the outcome in terms of income strategies will have a bearing on the services strategies. Neither, in the present system, can be viewed separately within a context meaningful to social work practice or the rural setting.

References

Baumheier, Edward C. and Schorr, Alvin L. "Social Policy" in Turner, John B. (Ed.), *Encyclopedia of Social Work*, Washington, D.C.: NASW, 1977, 1453–1463.

Bernard, Sydney E. "Why Service Delivery Systems Fail," *Social Work*, 1975, 29(3):206–211.

Bertsche, J. and Clark, F. "Improving the Utilization of Informal Helping Systems," *Sharing*, 1981, 5:2–3.

Bixby, Ann Kallman. "Social Welfare Expenditures, Fiscal Year, 1979," *Social Security Bulletin*, 1981, 44(11):3–12.

Boettcher, Richard E. "The 'Service Delivery System' What is it?" *Public Welfare*, 1974, 32(1):45–50.

Boulding, Kenneth. "The Boundaries of Social Policy," *Social Work*, 1967, 12(1):3–11.

Brown, David L., Steward, Donald D., and Ingalsbe, Gene (Eds.). *Rural Development Perspectives: Focus on Rural Poverty*. Washington, D.C.: Economic Development Division of ESCS, U.S. Department of Agriculture, 1980.

Burns, Eveline M. *Social Security and Public Policy*. New York: McGraw Hill Book Co., 1956.

Burns, Eveline M. "Social Policy: The Stepchild of the Curriculum" in *Proceedings*, Ninth Annual Program Meeting of the Council on Social Work Education. New York: CSWE, 1961.

Clark, F.W., Bertsche, J.W., and Bates, V.E. "Informal Helping in a Rural Boom Town," *Human Services in the Rural Environment*, 1980, 5:19–24.

Copeland, William C. and Iversen, Iver A. "Refinancing and Reorganizing Human Services," *Human Services*, Monograph Series No. 20, 1981.

Coward, Raymond T. "Considering an Alternative for the Rural Delivery of Human Services: Natural Helping Networks." Paper presented at the Annual Meetings of the Rural Sociological Society, San Francisco, 1978.

Freeman, Howard E. and Sherwood, Clarence C. *Social Research and Social Policy*. Englewood Cliffs: Prentice-Hall, Inc., 1970.

Froland, Charles. "Formal and Informal Care: Discontinuities in a Continuum," *Social Service Review*, 1980, 54(4):572–587.

Garfinkel, Irwin. "What's Wrong With Welfare?," *Social Work*, 1978, 23(3):185–191.

Gil, David G. "A Systematic Approach to Social Policy Analysis," *Social Service Review*, 1970, 44(4):411–426.

Gil, David G. *Unravelling Social Policy*. Cambridge: Schenkman Publishing Co., 1976.

Gilbert, Neil and Specht, Harry. *Dimensions of Social Welfare Policy*. Englewood Cliffs, N.J.: Prentice-Hall, Inc., 1974.

Hamilton, Joel R. and Reid, Richard. "Rural Communities: Diseconomies of Small Size and Costs of Migration," *Growth and Change*, 1977, 8(1):39–44.

Hearn, Gordon. "General Systems Theory and Social Work," in Turner, Francis (Ed.), *Social Work Treatment*. New York: The Free Press, 1979, 333–359.

Johnson, Louise. "Human Service Delivery Patterns in Nonmetropolitan Communities," in Johnson, Wayne (Ed.), *Rural Human Services*. Itasca, Ill.: Peacock Publishers, 1980, 65–74.

Kahn, Alfred J. *Social Policy and Social Services*, (2nd ed.). New York: Random House, 1979.

Khadduri, Jill and Struyk, Raymond J. "Housing Vouchers for the Poor," *Journal of Policy Analysis and Management*, 1982, 1(2):196–201.

Marshall, T.H. *Social Policy*. London: Hutchinson University Press, 1965.

Minahan, Anne. "Social Workers and the Future," (editorial), *Social Work*, 1981, 26(5):363–364.

Morris, Robert. *Social Policy of the American Welfare State*. New York: Harper and Row, 1979.

National Association of Social Workers. *Goals of Public Social Policy*. New York: NASW, 1963.

Oates, Janice. "A Systems Approach to Rural Communities" in Bast, David (Ed.), *Human Services in the Rural Environment*. Madison: University of Wisconsin, 1977, 67–74.

Older Americans Act of 1965 as Amended. (Public Law 89–73, as amended). Washington, D.C.: Administration on Aging, U.S. Department of Health and Human Services, 1978.

Ozawa, Martha N. "The Earnings Test in Social Security," *The Social Welfare Forum*, 1978. New York: Columbia University Press, 1979.

Piven, Frances-Fox and Cloward, Richard A. *Regulating the Poor: The Functions of Public Welfare*. New York: Pantheon Books, 1971.

President's National Advisory Commission on Rural Poverty. *The People Left Behind*. Washington, D.C.: U.S. Government Printing Office, 1967.

Rein, Martin. *Social Policy: Issues of Choice and Change*. New York: Random House, 1970.

Rein, Martin. "Equality and Social Policy," *Social Service Review*, 1977, 51(4):565–585.

Rein, Martin and Peattie, Lisa. "Knowledge for Policy," *Social Service Review*, 1981, 55(4):524–543.

Rochefort, David A. "Progressive and Social Control Perspectives on Social Welfare," *Social Service Review*, 1981, 55(4):568–592.

Samuels, Michael. "The Federal Initiative in Rural Health" in Watkins, Dennis A. and Watkins, Julia M. (Eds.), *Rural Health Care and the Land Grant Institution Emerging Roles and Responsibilities for the 1980s*. Orono, Me.: Life Sciences and Agriculture Experiment Station, University of Maine at Orono, Expt. Sta. Misc. Report 210, 1978, 26–32.

Schorr, Alvin. *Explorations in Social Policy*. New York: Basic Books, 1968.

Schumacher, E.T. *Small is Beautiful*. New York: Harper and Row, 1973.

Sherman, Joanna and Rowley, Lucy. "Confidentiality: What is Private in a Rural Area" in Bast, David and Schmidt, Julie (Eds.), *2nd Annual Human Services in the Rural Environment Reader*. Madison: Center for Social Service, University of Wisconsin Extension, 1977, 10–19.

Thurow, Lester C. *The Zero-Sum Society: Distribution and the Possibilities for Economic Change*. New York: Basic Books, Inc., 1980.

Titmuss, Richard. *Essays on the Welfare State,* 2nd ed. London: George
    Allen and Unwin Ltd., 1963.
Watkins, Dennis A. and Watkins, Julia M. *Community Services Plan-
    ning and the Small Municipality: A Quality of Life Framework for
    the Development of Rural Human Services.* University of Maine at
    Orono, Life Sciences and Agriculture Experiment Station Bulletin
    726, 1976.
Watkins, Julia M. and Watkins, Dennis A. *Toward a Continuum of
    Care Policy Framework for Decision Making by State Units on
    Aging and Area Agencies on Aging: Issues and Opportunities in
    Rural Service Provision.* Final Report AOA Grant #90-AR-2073/01.
    University of Maine at Orono, 1981.
Weissert, William G. "Toward a Continuum of Care for the Elderly: A
    Note of Caution." Paper presented at the 108th Annual Meeting of
    APHA, Detroit, Mich., 1980.
Wilensky, Harold L. and Lebeaux, Charles N. *Industrial Society and
    Social Welfare.* New York: Russell Sage Foundation, 1965.
Wylie, M.L. "Nonmetropolitan Social Planning" in Ginsberg, Leon H.
    (Ed.), *Social Work in Rural Communities.* New York: Council on
    Social Education, 1976, 47–55.

3 Income Security: Response and Reflection on Rural America

Introduction

The focus of this chapter is on income strategies as a way of dealing with economic vulnerability in an advanced industrial society. In Chapter 1 the parameters of poverty in rural America were introduced. Thus, the stage has been set for a more extended look at rural poverty, government expenditures in rural areas, and an examination of the American system of income security and how it differentially affects rural and urban populations. For purposes of discussion, the income security system is dichotomized into programs of social insurance and those of public assistance.

The Face of Rural Poverty

To define poverty is no easy task. It is generally agreed, however, that poverty can be defined in an absolute or in a relative sense. However defined, poverty implies the inadequate consumption of both goods and services believed necessary to maintain a socially defined adequate living standard. The definition most commonly reflected in the formulation of social policy is that developed by the Social Security Administration in 1964 (Orshansky, 1965) and later modified by the Federal Interagency Committee in 1969 (U.S. Bureau of the Census, 1969). The "poverty index" relates to the ability of a family to meet a predetermined standard of food consumption. The standard set in 1964 was based on research into the recommended dietary allowances (RDA) of specified nutrients and used by the Department of Agriculture to establish in 1961, an "economy food plan" for families of differing sizes, composition, and location (Orshansky, 1965). Other family expenditures were related to the cost of food, based on research in the early 1960s which indicated that a lower-middle-income family spent one-third of its income on food. The current poverty level is determined from the 1963 base year with annual adjustments made reflecting changes in the Consumer Price Index. In addition, it is assumed in calculating the poverty index that farm families require 85 percent of the corresponding nonfarm level of income for the same standard of living.

A more subjective assessment of poverty status as opposed to Orshansky's market-basket approach is that of relative poverty describing a position on a scale relative to others. According to this measure, at whatever point the poverty threshold is drawn—for example, the lower fifth or third of the population—the numbers of people in poverty will remain fairly constant.[1]

The poverty index developed by the SSA in 1964 is based entirely on money income. It contains no adjustment for such in-kind supplements as food stamps, subsidized housing, or health care under Medicare or Medicaid. Poverty index data for selected years are presented in Table 3.1.

For 1980 the poverty threshold was calculated at $8,414 for a nonfarm family of four and $7,151 for a farm family of four. Based on the 1980 threshold, 13 percent of the total U.S. population or 29.3 million persons were at or below the poverty line. This represented an increase of 3.2 million persons below the poverty line between 1979 and 1980, and one of the largest annual increases since 1959, the earliest year for which poverty statistics are available. For the year 1979–1980, urban poverty increased from 10.7 to 11.9 percent or by 1.9 million people while comparable data for rural populations (including rural farm) were 13.3 to 17.5 percent or 1.3 million people (U.S. Bureau of the Census, 1981). In addition, it was recently reported that one-third of the households with very low incomes (defined to be at most 50 percent of the median income of a family of four in a particular area), were in rural areas (Economic Research Service, 1981).

[1]For a detailed discussion of the issues surrounding the relative and absolute definitions of poverty the reader is directed to the work by Patrick J. Madden, *Poverty Statistics: A Guide to Interpretation*. Department of Agricultural Economics and Rural Sociology, Pennsylvania State University, revised October 16, 1972; and to Morton Paglin, "Poverty in the United States: A Reevaluation," *Policy Review*, Spring, 1979, 7–24.

Table 3.1.   Persons below the Poverty Level: 1960–1979*

Year	Persons below Poverty Level		Average Income Cutoffs for Non-Farm Family of 4	Median Family Income of All Families
	Number (millions)	Percent	At Poverty Level	Total
1960	39.9	22.2	$3,022	$ 5,620
1965	33.2	17.3	3,223	6,957
1970	25.4	12.6	3,968	9,867
1975	25.9	12.3	5,500	13,719
1979	25.3	11.6	7,412	19,661

*U.S. Bureau of the Census. *Current Population Reports*, Series P–60, No. 130, 1969, Series P–23, No. 28, 1981; and earlier issues.

For families in rural areas, 12.1 percent live below the poverty level as compared with 9.4 in urban areas. This translates into 11 million, 251 thousand people or 38.4 percent of the total (rural and urban) poverty population. Put another way, the rural population in 1980 composed 26.7 percent of the total U.S. population but represented 38.4 percent of the total U.S. population below the poverty line (U.S. Bureau of the Census, 1981). Furthermore, rural poverty is found disproportionately in the South where 13 percent of the total population is below the poverty level. This compares with 9 percent in the Northeast, 8.8 percent in the North Central region, and 9 percent in the West. Likewise, minorities experience proportionately greater poverty in rural areas than do whites. For the rural black population 40.6 percent were reported as below the poverty level in 1980 (compared with 30.1 percent of urban, central city blacks), and 26.3 percent of rural minorities of Spanish origin were below the poverty level compared to 25.5 percent for their urban counterparts. A comparable figure for rural whites in 1980 was 12.9 percent rural and 8.8 percent urban below the poverty level (U.S. Bureau of the Census, 1981).

Especially important from a policy perspective is the finding that rural people, although poor by the standard definition, are more often than their urban counterparts, employed. Twenty-five percent of rural, poor families have a full-time worker who heads the household, and nearly one-third have two or more employed workers in the household. Taking into account this finding, rural poverty reflects a situation of underemployment with relatively low wages and/or part-time work. Such employment characteristics are reflective of the types of jobs available in rural areas as well as a population characterized by inadequate skills, training, and education (Deavers & Brown, 1979).

Federal Expenditures in Rural Areas

Although the income levels of rural people remain low, Bluestone (1980) suggests that progress was made between 1968 and 1975 in reducing the disparity between rural and urban incomes, with personal income growing 25 percent faster in nonmetropolitan counties than in metropolitan counties. Much of the growth in personal income is the result of government transfer payments to individuals which increased from 8.4 to 13.1 percent of personal income for rural people in the period 1968 to 1975. This growth is attributed to policy changes in income maintenance programs and a larger number of rural people receiving benefits through these programs.

A further word is in order about government outlays to rural areas. While Osgood (1977) states that federal expenditures for income and other welfare programs were only 25 percent of the amount expended in urban areas, more specific data will enhance the critical examination of strategies of income security. Deavers and Brown (1979), in a grouping of federal, nondefense expenditures into four categories of targeted economic development, public and private infrastructure, human capital, and transfer payments, closely examined the extent of federal expenditures in rural areas. Expenditures in each area are summarized in Table 3.2, using as a source the Community Services Administration as reported by Deavers and Brown (1979, p. 33).

Transfer payments to individuals and households in fiscal

Table 3.2.   Percent of Rural–Urban Distribution of Nondefense Federal Spending, 1976*

| | Federal Program Category | | | |
	Targeted Economic Development	Public and Private Infra- structure and Housing	Transfer Pay- ments to Individuals	Human Capital Programs
Rural	34	25	27	20
Urban	66	75	73	80

*Deavers, K.L. and Brown, D.L. Community Services Administration, 1979.

year 1976 were $136 billion of total federal expenditures. Twenty-seven percent of these dollars ($36.7 billion) went to individuals living in rural areas as follows: Social Security retirement and disability, 65 percent or $24 billion; public assistance, 13 percent or $4.6 billion; veterans' benefits, 6 percent or $2.3 billion; and Medicare, 5 percent or $1.8 billion; and other, 11 percent or $4 billion.

Targeted economic development in rural areas accounted for about one-third ($3.3 billion) of government expenditures in this area. Among the programs included are those for American Indians, the Farmers Home Administration (FmHA), Small Business Administration (SBA), Tennessee Valley Authority (TVA), Community Development Block Grants under the Department of Housing and Urban Development (HUD), the Appalachian Regional Commission (ARC), and the Economic Development Administration (EDA). The type of assistance—grants, loans, and loan guarantees—varies by program. There is a good deal of government discretion in the allocation of these funds, yet they are generally targeted to economically depressed areas.

Federal outlays of $9.3 billion, or 25 percent of the total directed toward public and private infrastructure, was expended in rural counties in fiscal year 1976. Expenditures under this category are targeted to communities for housing, transportation, communication, environmental protection, parks and recreation, and become more or less permanent contributions to the community.

Programs within the human capital category include education, health, manpower, and training. For the most part these programs provide services through loans to individuals and through program grants. According to Deavers and Brown (1979), it is in this category that expenditures in nonmetropolitan areas were disproportionately small, representing 20 percent ($5 billion) of the total expenditure. With the documented problems of underemployment, poor education, and lower health status in rural areas, human capital expenditures warrant careful analysis by policy decision makers. However, our further examination of income security will focus on transfer payments to individuals.

Programs Directed toward Income Security

Historically, social policy focused on income security in industrialized nations has been a response to the exigencies of economic systems that place individuals in particularly vulnerable situations vis-a-vis the productive market economy. As a result, income policy has been directed at two primary issues: (1) the assurance of a minimal level of support to persons who are unable, for a variety of reasons, to participate in the labor force, that is, to provide for some adequacy in meeting basic needs; and (2) the redistribution of income from one group in society to another group with less financial resources, that is, to provide for an equitable distribution of the resources of society. Underlying the policy decisions relative to adequacy and equity are values inherent in the Judeo-Christian ethic of helping others and the value and integrity of the human being. Juxtaposed against this ethic in American society is the Protestant work ethic and the capitalist focus on competition and profit. The tensions that have developed in applying these values to policy decisions of an industrial society have resulted in a dual system of income security, with one component (the social insurance mechanism) based on the concept of shared risk and the other (public assistance) based on the residual concept of the social welfare institution. Permeating the broader discussion, particularly in recent months, is the issue of the extent of government responsibility for insuring either adequacy or equity in addressing human need. As noted in a lead article in a recent issue of *The National Journal,* Havemann (1982), states "But there can be no doubt about one of the consequences of Reagan administration policies: income will be distributed more unevenly than before between the rich and the poor" (p. 1788). In an advanced industrial society the debate and search for alternatives intensifies. However, one must be aware of the complexities of the present system in order to think perceptively about the future.

Social insurance programs, according to Burns (1956), are based on a principle derived from private insurance, that is, benefits are closely related to contributions made by an individual, the beneficiary, during a defined period of time, usually the working years. This basis, as will be seen shortly, has implications that go beyond actuarial soundness. The concept of insurance conveys a right to a benefit based on a contribution, thus reducing the stigma associated with publicly enacted programs of which public assistance based on poor law tradition was the major precursor. The provision of social insurance basically adheres to the principle of universality in the allocation of benefits.

Public assistance, in contrast to social insurance, is based on need rather than on contribution. A selected group of recipients is targeted and eligibility is based on a means-test of income need. Applying the value premise of the Protestant work ethic and the assumptions of a capitalist industrial society gives public assistance an overtone of stigma for the recipient and raises continual public outcry about public expenditures for people thought able to work.

Social Insurance

For purposes relative to policy implications for rural settings, the major points and issues relative to four American social insurance programs, OASDHI, Unemployment Compensation, Workers' Compensation, and Medicare, are summarized. Although Medicare is viewed as part of OASDHI, it is included as a separate discussion from the retirement and disability benefits because of its overall importance in social and economic terms. The implications for rural populations are pointed out with the discussion of each program.

Old Age, Survivors, Disability, and Health Insurance (OASDHI)

The provision of a minimum level of coverage for American workers upon retirement at age 65 was the cornerstone (Title II) of the social insurance provisions of the Social Security Act of 1935. Later additions to the initial old age coverage were coverage for survivors (1939), for disability (1956), and for health (Title XVIII, 1964), Medicare. Although the initial OASDHI covered only workers in industry and commerce, the beneficiary group has now been expanded to cover approximately nine-tenths of all gainfully employed persons. Those not covered are primarily government (federal and state) employees and some additional persons whose income has not been reported. With each additional beneficiary group added to the program and the subsequent reduction in the number of quarters workers were required to be in covered employment to attain beneficiary status, the OASDHI program became less of an insurance program according to the criteria of private insurance on which it was initially based. The beneficiary does not in the strictest sense receive payments according to the level of contribution and subsequent interest on that contribution.[2] Therefore, with a high percent of benefit in the form of a subsidy, OASDHI resembles more a transfer program from one group to another group, rather than an insurance program in which benefits are closely related to contribution.

The rationale behind this transfer arrangement can be seen in the following hypothetical example: If one had to contribute 20 years before a benefit could be drawn, the system would do nothing to solve the financial dilemmas of those persons already approaching or at retirement age at the inception of the program. Therefore, the policy decision in the case of social security was to be more inclusive of beneficiary groups and fund the benefits from the contributions of those workers currently employed in the labor force as an intergenerational transfer. During periods of high employment and an expanding workforce and economy, this rationale raises little concern, even from the critics of such social responsibility. However, the current fiscal dilemma of the social security system is directly, but not entirely, related to a shrinking workforce, an economic downturn with high unemployment, a rapidly expanding group of people age 65 and over, the indexing of benefits to inflation, and the reluctance of the Congress to transfer revenues from the general fund to support the social security trust fund. This reluctance reinforces the philosophic importance of the insurance principle even though social security (OASDHI) is far removed from adhering to the conditions incumbent on a private insurance fund. With subsidies now constituting a large percent of benefits and payroll taxes that are regressive, Ozawa (1982) points to the appropriateness of using general revenues to solve the fiscal problems of the system.[3]

[2]In a recent article by Martha N. Ozawa, "Who Receives Subsidies Through Social Security, and How Much?," *Social Work*, 1982, 17(2):129–138, the difference received by a beneficiary is referred to as a subsidy which carries out the welfare or adequacy function of social security. Ozawa shows that, if viewed in absolute terms, subsidies favor highly paid workers rather than those who are low paid. Thus, greater amounts of income in the form of subsidies have been redistributed (the welfare function of adequacy) to those who have been highly paid workers before retirement. This poses major social policy questions about the adequacy or welfare function of the social security retirement program.

[3]At the time of this book's publication, that transfer may have occurred as it is being viewed by increasing numbers of politicians as a viable economic option to guarantee the solvency of the social security system. In addition, a National Commission on Social Security Reform was recently established by President Reagan with the charge to develop proposals to guarantee the fiscal soundness of the system.

The benefit rate and eligibility criteria for OASDHI are determined by legislative action as a social policy decision. Also determined is the dual contribution rate of the employee and the employer and the lower rate for self-employed persons. At the present time the contribution rate is 6.7 percent from both employer and employee on earnings up to $32,400. For self-employed persons, for example, farmers and sole proprietors of businesses, the contribution rate is 9.35 percent. The legislative determination of eligibility and contribution rate with the distinct possibility of change or modification of the program at any point in time through the legislative process is another violation of the insurance principle which involves a legal and binding contract between the company and the beneficiary. This has caused great alarm in recent months as Social Security beneficiaries see the modifications proposed in the form of cutbacks as detrimental to their relative economic position and well-being.

The reader is reminded that transfer payments under OASDHI to individuals in rural areas totaled $24 billion or 65 percent of all transfer payments to rural people in fiscal year 1976. These global figures, however, tend to mask some of the more complex issues for rural policy. First, OASDHI benefits are based on earnings with a minimum benefit in 1981, now abolished for new applicants, of $170.30 for a single retired individual and $255.45 for a couple with both age 65 or over. Whereas a significant number of rural people have been employed in low-wage jobs or in seasonal employment, it is expected that many qualify to receive only the minimum benefit (now a low work-related benefit) or, at best, lower payments than their urban counterparts (Hoppe & Martin, 1982). It is also thought, although difficult to document, that many of these same people have not had their incomes reported by the employer, making it extremely difficult to establish an adequate work history when applying for Social Security. In addition, self-employed persons may not have reported a net business profit and may not have, therefore, paid sufficient Social Security taxes to qualify for a benefit at age 65. Furthermore, the type of employment (self-employment, sporadic, and seasonal), is seldom supplemented by additional retirement benefits, characteristic of fringe benefit packages in large, unionized occupations. With some extractive and manufacturing industries as exceptions, rural workers are also less likely to be unionized than are their urban counterparts, another factor contributing to lower wages. Nevertheless, it is appropriate to say that at present, with benefits related primarily to income during the working years and greater subsidies to highly paid workers, the policy of benefit payments (allocation) is clearly discriminatory against low-income rural populations. These are people who, for the most part, have not been unionized and consequently have not benefited from the collective bargaining process to secure higher wages and adequate benefit packages. Yet, with low incomes the benefit payment, although inadequate, remains a significant source of steady income to many rural people.

Under the Omnibus Budget Reconciliation Act of 1981 (P.L. 97–35) enacted on August 13, 1981, several important changes were instituted in OASDHI, and one important recision was made in an amendment to the law, signed by President Reagan on December 29, 1981. These changes are noted here as they represent trends or decisions that bring into question the issues of adequacy and equity and how they are viewed in current social policy decisions.

The initial law (August 1981) eliminated the minimum benefit for all persons who would become eligible for OASDHI after October 1, 1981. For all currently enrolled beneficiaries the abolition of a minimum payment would have taken place after February 1982. Henceforth, payments would be wage-related. The impact of such a change on low-wage rural populations is obvious. The lowered benefit would, if other eligibility requirements were met, also render the beneficiary eligible for a Supplemental Security Income (SSI) payment. This action, based on economic concerns of the solvency of the Social Security system, as well as the intent of the federal government to cut expenditures, may be viewed as a way of decreasing the Social Security subsidy and turning to a welfare benefit (SSI) as a substitute with the potential for increased stigmatization of the beneficiary.

Through an amendment to the law, the minimum benefit provision was restored for all beneficiaries who became eligible in 1981 or earlier. This amendment followed considerable constituency reaction voiced against the elimination of the minimum benefit. However, for people who become eligible after 1981 (62 years, disabled, or survivors), the minimum benefit provision is still eliminated (Svahn, 1982).

Disability insurance (DI) under OASDHI provides, through the payroll tax, coverage for disabled workers and their dependents. A significant expansion in this program over the 1970s has occurred, with those insured for disability increasing by 34 percent since 1970. Although the number of persons receiving disability benefits was 4.9 million in 1978, this number has decreased by more than 400,000 during the past three years. The dollar amount paid out in benefits was $17.2 billion in 1981. This translated into an average monthly payment to disabled beneficiaries of $413.15. In an analysis of these data, Lando, Farley, & Brown (1982) show that disability denial rates are higher than they were previously, both at the time of initial application and at several points of reconsideration. The DI program and workers' compensation are coordinated with one another and as a further attempt to reduce federal expenditures, stringent, and in the view expressed by Cater (1982), arbitrary review processes have been implemented. According to Cater, 139,000 workers and their dependents had been dropped from the DI roles in the past 18 months, and 35 percent had shown little or no improvement in the condition that initially led to their beneficiary status.

A second provision of P.L. 97–35 with implications for our analysis is the implementation of a "Megacap" on disability earnings. Under this provision, Social Security disability benefits "will be reduced (if necessary) so that the sum of all benefits payable under certain Federal, State, and local public programs on the basis of disability will not exceed 80 percent of the person's 'average current earnings' " (Svahn, 1981, p. 16).

To illustrate the nature of rural poverty and the impact of income from a social insurance transfer program, one need not look far as exemplified in the following case example.

Mr. L., age 65, and his wife, age 62, are long-time residents of an isolated, rural community of 458 people in the Northeastern U.S. They own their small, modest home which was only recently modernized to include indoor toilet facilities. Mr. L. worked for most of his life as a farm laborer, engaged primarily in seasonal employment, moving among the large-farm operations within a 70 to 90 mile radius of his home. His wife worked in the home raising their three children, one of whom was severely impaired in a tractor accident, required constant nursing care, and died several years ago at the age of 30. The other two children migrated to the nearest city some years ago where each is employed in manufacturing shoes. Mr. and Mrs. L. were taken by an outreach worker from a regionally based Area Agency on Aging (AAA) to the Social Security office 60 miles away to apply for Social

Security benefits. They had come in contact with the outreach worker at a meal site for the elderly.

As a result of Mr. L.'s work and family status, the following outlines his participation in the Social Security system of income benefits.

The Social Security benefit amount depends on the level of wages over a long period of time that is credited to his record; this is difficult to document because of the inaccuracy of the records due to his rather sporadic, low-income work history, and to inaccurate reporting by his many employers. Nevertheless, once documented, his Social Security benefit is determined to be $178 per month. Mrs. L. qualifies to receive 75 percent of one-half of Mr. L.'s benefit, or $66.75. With this low benefit level, Mr. L. finds that he also qualifies for a Supplemental Security Income (SSI) benefit of $136.60, which includes a $10 state supplement. (See p. 81 for a more detailed discussion of SSI.) He also qualifies for Medicare coverage and is Medicaid eligible. Medicaid pays the Medicare Part B premium and other health care costs incurred that are not covered under Medicare. Mrs. L., not yet 65, qualifies for health care under the medically needy program in the state in which she and Mr. L. reside. The L.'s also find, much to their surprise, that they qualify for a food stamp allotment of $125.

The interlocking nature of social insurance and public assistance is immediately apparent in the case Mr. and Mrs. L. Although Mr. and Mrs. L. receive benefits from a total of six different programs including cash, in-kind, federal, state, social insurance, and public assistance, their income level is still below the poverty level. Social policy decisions of income security have created a system that is bewildering to the beneficiary, administratively complex, and ineffective in providing a benefit level adequate to meet the needs of Mr. and Mrs. L. in a comprehensive and coordinated manner and lift them above the poverty level.

Unemployment Compensation

In response to the economic crisis of the Great Depression with approximately 25 percent of the labor force unemployed, Title III of the Social Security Act of 1935 represented the introduction of a nationwide system for compensating individuals during times of unemployment. Viewed as an insurance program like OASDHI, its intention was to provide a minimal level of financial support during periods of temporary unemployment and thus maintain an income base to unemployed workers and their families.

Unlike OASDHI with federal administration and legislatively mandated benefits and contributions, unemployment compensation represents a system of federal–state cooperation. Administered by the states under the supervision of the U.S. Department of Labor, benefit schedules as well as employer payroll tax contributions vary from one state to another. The amount of tax levied on an employer's payroll is based on an "experience rating." That is, employers with better employment histories pay a lower tax than those with records of pronounced fluctuation of employment stability. In principle, the lower tax rate acts as an incentive to the employer for maintaining conditions of employment stability.

The benefit level for unemployment compensation is usually computed as a fixed percent of the worker's previous weekly salary before tax wages, generally not to exceed 50 percent. Minimum and maximum amounts apply. During such recent recessionary periods as 1974 and 1975, the federal government, using general tax funds, extended the benefit time of eligibility beyond that to which the various states were committed. Eligibility is determined by the worker having been employed a specified number of weeks in covered employment.

The questions of importance for rural areas revolve primarily around the indexing of benefit level to previous weekly earnings and the ways in which unemployment levels are measured. With already low wages, indexing benefits means unemployment with even greater marginality of income. A benefit level related to need, for example to family size, family income, and expenses, would seem to be more appropriate.

A major difficulty in determining unemployment levels in rural areas lies in the type of statistics used (National Research Council, 1981). This has important implications with government allocations to geographic or political subdivisions tied to statistical formulae. The problems of statistical representation of unemployment in rural areas is exacerbated by those who are discouraged from job seeking when opportunities are not available over long periods of time and when the costs of job searching with few available employers exceeds the perceived gains (National Research Council, 1981, pp. 141–142). Such individuals are not counted in the unemployment statistics and make reported rates of unemployment lower than they are in actuality.

Unemployment compensation as a policy response is clearly tied to one's previous work status in a covered occupation. Since variations exist from one state to another, lower tax rates on employer payrolls in some states may serve as incentives to businesses to locate in low-tax states. When one examines the need for the development of well-paid, steady employment in rural areas this becomes a critical component in the overall economic health of an area. Another important policy issue is the relative importance attributed to a standard benefit based on need or, by contrast, the continuation of a state-by-state system that is particularly vulnerable to more localized economic and political fluctuations.

A further issue, having to do with the source of funds, primarily the tax levied against an employer's payroll, is the extent to which this best serves broader social policy goals. For example, funding from federal general revenues, with standardization between the various states may, as with SSI, serve to increase the adequacy and the equity of the program. Such a response is necessary when the economic vulnerability of workers is recognized as inextricably influenced by federal economic policies.

One need only survey the recent data on unemployment to see this influence. For example, since April 1981, total unemployment for all civilian workers increased from 7.3 to 9.8 percent (July 1982), and was expected to move higher in future months. Workers who are historically more vulnerable to fluctuations in the economy are currently experiencing higher than average levels of unemployment. The data for July 1982 show unemployment among women who maintain families to be 12.0 percent, blacks 17.3 percent, and youth age 16 to 19, 24.1 percent (*Economic Indicators*, August, 1982).

Workers' Compensation

The recognition of government responsibility to the workforce was manifest in the establishment of workers' compensation (disability insurance) under the Social Security Act. One of the earliest programs to be enacted (1908) protected federal employees from loss of income due to disability. Today, workers' compensation programs are based on state law and financed almost exclusively by employers who purchase coverage from private insurance companies. The amount of coverage required is dependent on the risks of the industry, as determined by an experience rating in a way similar to that used in determining unemployment compensation. It is assumed that through the experience rating, workers' compensation programs encourage industrial safety to reduce premium costs to the employer. Approximately 89 percent of all wage and salary workers are protected under the workers' compensation laws. In 1979, $11.9 billion were paid out to beneficiaries at a cost of $20.0 billion to employers.

Underlying workers' compensation is the belief that the social risks of an industrial society, for example, work-related disability and death, necessitate provision of some level of income security for disabled workers and their families, or in the case of death, the workers' survivors. Benefits are generally for a percent of employment income and medical care persuant to the work-related accident or injury. Rehabilitative services may also be included. The determination of criteria for work-related accident and injury is not always clear and has resulted in numerous court cases to obtain a judicial opinion and establish legal precedents.

From the health care field it is known that rural workers often face great safety risks in their jobs related to agriculture, extractive industries, and heavy manufacturing. This raises questions about the adequacy of a state-by-state approach to workers' compensation in which benefits may vary widely. An additional concern is that sole proprietors (self-employed) workers in very small firms, and those in "casual employment" (that is, irregular, occasional employment) are frequently exempt from workers' compensation under state laws. These types of employment, according to the National Research Council (1981), involve a substantial number of rural people.

Medicare

The final social insurance program to be discussed is Medicare. It constitutes one piece of the OASDHI benefit package of the Social Security Act and was established under Title XVIII in 1964, implemented in 1965. As a social insurance program, Medicare provides hospital and physician reimbursement for costs incurred primarily by those people 65 years and over in our society. Approximately 90 percent of those enrolled in Medicare are 65 years or older. Exceptions are the inclusion of people with long-term, chronic health care problems, such as end-stage renal disease, and certain disabled persons. With the high usage of the health care system by the elderly, Medicare qualifies as part of the American response to income need. As an insurance program, Medicare pools the risks of a population that is primarily elderly. This is unlike the majority of commercial or nonprofit plans like Blue Cross/Blue Shield in which health risk is spread across the life span to include health-vulnerable as well as predominately healthy individuals.

Medicare is generally viewed as an in-kind benefit since the cash reimbursement goes directly to the reimbursable provider according to "usual and customary" fees in the case of physicians and according to "reasonable" costs for hospital care. Beneficiaries are expected to pay a deductible amount before drawing on the insurance, and a co-payment is levied at certain points. For example, under 1982 policy the beneficiary is required to pay the first $260.00 of expense (deductible) incurred in a benefit period. A co-payment of $65.00 per day is charged to the beneficiary for hospitalization between 61 and 90 days unless the beneficiary wishes to draw on what are called "reserve" days. The deductible and co-payment as well as the types of services covered are at the discretion of Congressional action and the subsequent regulatory process. Part A of Medicare covers hospitalization and is funded by an earmarked percent of the paycheck contribution to the Social Security trust fund. In 1981 this rate was 2.6 percent of the combined employer/employee tax. Part B, to cover physician services, is voluntarily subscribed to by the individual with funding from a beneficiary-paid monthly premium that is matched by a federal contribution from general tax revenues. For July 1, 1982, this premium was fixed at $12.20.

Medicare and the companion piece of legislation, Medicaid, operate within the private fee-for-service structure of the health care system. The spiraling costs of health care have frequently been attributed to the reimbursement mechanism for Medicare in which hospital care is reimbursed on the basis of incurred costs. In the words of Ginsburg (1982), "Hospitals report their costs to Medicare, and the program, through its intermediaries (private insurance companies, Blue Cross plans and claims processing companies), determines what portion should be attributed to Medicare patients" (p. 934). Critics of this process point out that there are no built-in incentives to keep costs at a reasonable level (Friedman & Wendorf, 1977; Somers & Somers, 1977). Current proposals to deal with this situation include prospective reimbursement wherein the hospital calculates costs ahead and is penalized by excess expenditures or rewarded financially by an expenditure level that is under projected costs. Reimbursement at a flat rate according to the diagnosis is being implemented in an attempt to contain costs.

A major question raised about prospective reimbursement pertains to maintenance of quality care. That is, will hospitals jeopardize quality care in an effort to cut costs and hence participate in the incentive system?

From the perspective of a rural setting there are two major disadvantages of Medicare. Although providing significant health care reimbursement for a large number of low-income people, Medicare does little in the way of guaranteeing access to health care. Rural elderly people pay the same monthly premium as do their urban counterparts (as a percent of payroll tax and the monthly premium for Part B), yet health care services are concentrated and more readily available in urban areas. It has been suggested by Roemer (1980) that the Health Maintenance Organization (HMO), a prepayment mechanism which guarantees availability and contains a strong preventive thrust, is a rural health care delivery mechanism for integrating reimbursement and accessibility that deserves attention in discussion of alternatives. In spite of the attractiveness of the HMO concept, its implementation in areas with a widely dispersed population has been difficult.

The reimbursement process associated with "usual and customary" and "reasonable costs," translates into lower reimbursement rates of rural health care providers than that received by their urban counterparts. This policy has worked to increase the maldistribution and the specialization of providers, with rural areas and primary practice less attractive monetarily than with urban settings and medical specialties (Somers & Somers, 1977).

The Rural Health Clinics Bill of 1977, which allows Medicare reimbursement of services provided by a nurse practitioner or physician assistant without a physician on the premises in federally certified rural clinics was designed to deal with some access issues. However, the suggested use of new health practitioners as a way of bringing health services to underserved areas and disadvantaged populations is interpreted by Roemer (1977) ". . . as an abdication of social responsibility by doctors . . ." and is ". . . attributed to an unwillingness to impose social obligations on the physician (e.g., location in areas of need) and to train adequate numbers of primary care doctors" (p. 553). It has been noted also, that the certification of rural clinics has been extremely slow and hence blocks the real intent of the legislation (Douglas, 1980).

For the rural population, payments through Medicare were 5 percent of the total federal transfer payments in fiscal year 1976. This amounted to $1.8 billion, or 8.6 percent of total Medicare expenditures of nearly $21 billion to rural and urban populations in fiscal 1976. It should be noted that the rural elderly are 44.7 percent of the total U.S. elderly population. This demonstrates, in a rough sense, that Medicare expenditures in rural areas were not in proportion to the eligible population. Under the Omnibus Budget Reconciliation Act of 1981 (P.L. 97–35), changes increasing deductible and co-payments were implemented and the continuous open enrollment period was curtailed (Svahn, 1981). Additional proposals to reduce expenditures include reducing hospital reimbursement rates, requiring federal employees to contribute to the fund, and stimulating competition in the health care sector (Clark, 1982).

Public Assistance

In contrast to social insurance is public assistance as a strategy for income provisions wherein participation is based on a test of income need, that is, a means-test. Public assistance programs are funded not through special earmarked beneficiary contributions but rather from the general revenues of federal, state, and local governments. The public assistance programs to be discussed are Aid to Families with Dependent Children (AFDC), Supplemental Security Income (SSI), Medicaid, and the Food Stamp Program. All but the last of these have their legislative base in the Social Security Act. A fifth program which will be mentioned only briefly is General Assistance (GA).

As a result of the enactment of the Social Security Act, several principles were established which, over the years, provided a common base to programs. The more general principles established and embodied in the public assistance programs were: (1) the establishment that grants to individuals were to be in cash; (2) individuals were entitled to a fair hearing if their application for assistance was denied; (3) in submitting plans for participation in the assistance programs, states were required to show that the program was available to people in all political subdivisions (counties) of the state; and (4) a state level office was to be established to implement and monitor the program for efficiency and effectiveness (Axinn & Levin, 1982). Equally important was the fact that inclusion of insurance and assistance programs within one basic piece of legislation, the Social Security Act, in the words of Axinn and Levin ". . . gave some support to the concept of the 'right to assistance' for eligible recipients" (p. 200). However, the nature of the legislation, representing compromise between the interests of the federal government and the states as well as basic philosophic differences on the issue of governmental responsibility for income security, allowed for program details which differed from one state to another. That is, states were allowed some discretion in the implementation of programs. These differences are now seen, for example, in the AFDC and Medicaid programs. In enacting the public assistance provisions of the Social Security Act it was believed by some policymakers that the gradual expansion of the insurance provisions would eventually make government participation in public assistance unnecessary (Axinn & Levin, 1982).

Each of the four public assistance programs will be reviewed briefly and the issues generated for rural populations examined collectively since there is overlap among them on a program-by-program basis.

Aid to Families with Dependent Children (AFDC)

The current AFDC program has as its historical base the establishment of the Aid to Dependent Children (ADC) under Title IV of the Social Security Act. The purpose of this program was to provide financial assistance for dependent children, that is, children under the age of 16, deprived of parental support and care, and living with a relative. This usually meant a widowed woman raising young children. The program required, as it does today, state financial participation.

The current AFDC program was the result of the Public Welfare Amendments of 1962 (P.L. 87–543). The previous program (ADC) was strengthened under the 1962 amendments by enabling states to provide assistance which would include rehabilitation, services, and income for the parent or relative caring for the child with the purpose of strengthening family life. For purposes of definition, the AFDC program targets "dependent children" as the primary beneficiary. This child is one ". . . who has been deprived of parental support or care by reason of death, continued absence from the home, physical or mental incapacity of a parent which must be expected to last at least 30 days, or unemployment of a parent and who is living with (stated relative) . . ." (U.S. Department of Health and Human Services [HHS], 1981, p. 21). Under the 1962 Amendments, funds were also provided for the training of personnel to enhance the effectiveness of the law. Furthermore, the federal share of funding was increased to 75 percent. States, and in some instances, local governments (eleven) provided the matching funds. However, as a compromise in the policy process, states were to retain autonomy in establishing assistance levels, thus specifying the target population.

Under current federal requirements individual states were allowed to determine a standard of need and the amount of assistance to be paid toward meeting that need. This means, for example, that in 1980 Alabama determined $240 for a family of four persons (1 adult and 3 children) to be the standard of basic need. Basic need, usually, but not in all states, refers to food, clothing, shelter, and utilities. In the same state (Alabama) the amount of the assistance payment to the family with no income was $148 or approximately 62 percent of basic need. Again, from 1980 figures, 27 states paid the full amount of their standard of need (U.S. Department of Health and Human Services, 1981). The variability among the states in amount of state need standard for one adult and three children in 1980 is seen when one looks at Texas with a need standard of $187 and Utah with $572. As a general rule, states with large rural populations, particularly those in the South, have low assistance payments. For example, the HHS figures (1981) show that Mississippi monthly benefits ($120) for AFDC were only 25 percent of the monthly benefits paid in New York ($476). Further variation exists among the states in definition of "continued absence," appropriate relatives, and incapacity. Provisions for assistance in the case of an unemployed parent is made in 27 states (AFDC–UP) (U.S. Department of Health and Human Services, 1981).

As an example of state computation of AFDC benefit level, the following case serves as an example. This example is offered without burdening the reader with the many exceptions that exist since to do so would detract from the fundamental purpose of this volume.

Mrs. A., age 34 years, was recently deserted by her husband of eleven years. His whereabouts is unknown. She has three children, ages 10, 6, and 2, a sporadic work history, little education, and few marketable skills during a period of high unemployment (national average of 10.1 percent). In addition, the small community of 765 residents in which she rents a one-bedroom apartment for $200 has an unemployment rate of 19.4 percent. This is due primarily to the closing of a leather-tanning factory several months ago. Residents blame the closing on the general economy and the competition in the shoe industry from foreign imports and increased reliance on synthetic materials in shoe manufacturing.

The state in which Mrs. A. resides has determined the basic standard of need for a family with one adult and three children and no source of income to be $564. This would clearly place Mrs. A. below the 1980 poverty level of $8,414 for a nonfarm family or $7,151 for a farm family. This same state, however, computes standard of need based on the 1972 poverty level, and has determined, furthermore, as a policy decision that it will pay all AFDC recipients only 72.5 percent of the standard need. This means that Mrs. A.'s total AFDC benefit will be $408 per month.

Mrs. A. also, because of her low income, is eligible to receive a food stamp bonus of $191 per month. Because she is eligible for AFDC she also qualifies for Medicaid.

If Mrs. A. were to find a job her earned income would reduce her AFDC benefit a certain amount as can be seen in the computation below:

Earned Income	$341.70	
Less standard deduction for work related expenses	− 75.00	
	$266.70	
Less $30 and	− 30.00	
1/3 of the remainder	$236.70	
or	− 78.90	
	$157.80	as countable income in computing her AFDC benefit

$564.00   Full need (used by this
          state for computing
          benefit level)

−157.80
─────────
$406.20   AFDC Benefit

The benefit reduction is less than $2.00 and Mrs. A.
then has a total income (AFDC + Earnings) of $747.70. This
is referred to as a positive work incentive and is discussed
further under the discussion of Public Assistance and Rural
Poverty. As Mrs. A.'s earnings increase and after a four-
month period of time, under current federal policies her benefit amount will be dramatically reduced because of the manner in which the deductibles are computed.

As a social policy response, the AFDC benefit level does not
raise Mrs. A. and her family above the current poverty level, and
thus it fails to fulfill the basic adequacy function of the income
maintenance system. It also fails, within the boundaries of our
current knowledge, to provide an equitable redistribution of income. Instead, the basic function of stringent eligibility criteria,
while purportedly to reduce costs, is, at the risk of escalating
social devisiveness, increasing the income disparities between the
wealthy and the poor (Cater, 1982).

Furthermore, the small community of which Mrs. A. and her
children are members suffers disproportionately in terms of high
unemployment and its attendant problems of despair, frustration,
and social breakdown. We will look further at communities and
the policy process in later chapters.

Under the Omnibus Budget Reconciliation Act of 1981 (P.L.
97–35), changes in the AFDC program will, of course, affect all
states and individuals differently. However, the basic intent of
the Act was to cut public expenditures by redefining what constitutes income, for example, income of stepparents, the extent of
allowable deductions, and greater limitations on property assets.
For the year 1983 it is estimated that the above restrictions plus
others designed to increase program efficiency and encourage recipients to work would result in savings of $1.2 billion or a pro-
posed spending level of $5.5 billion (Clark, 1982). Within AFDC
alone, total national cuts will equal approximately 17 percent over
the years 1981 and 1982. This exceeds cuts in any other federal

income transfer program and will affect most harshly those persons with some source of income, or those at the top of the eligibility range (Cater, 1982).

Supplemental Security Income (SSI)

A second major public assistance program, SSI, was implemented in January 1974, by combining and federalizing (placing under the control of the federal government) three previously categorical programs that had been funded by a federal–state match in a way similar to AFDC. The categorical programs were originally components of the Social Security Act of 1935 and included Old Age Assistance (OAA), Aid to the Blind (AB), and Aid to the Permanently and Totally Disabled (APTD) added in 1956.

The primary target population for SSI is low income adults over the age of 65, or those blind or disabled. In addition, blind or disabled children as well as adults under the age of 65 may be eligible for SSI benefits. This includes mental and physical disability that is expected to last no less than 12 months or to result in death. Furthermore, persons who are mentally retarded, according to specific policy guidelines, may be eligible for an SSI payment. This includes children living at home and persons living in small community group residences.

The SSI program, as a federally funded income transfer program, drawing funds from the general revenues of the federal government, is administered by the Social Security Administration and provides a minimum standard cash benefit to individuals who meet the qualifications of income need. In 1980 there were slightly over 4 million participants in the SSI program, with federal expenditures at nearly $6 billion. The minimum floor benefit established in 1974 was $130 per month for a single individual or $195 for a married couple. Over the years, the minimum benefit has been raised to a current (July 1, 1982) level of $284.30 for an eligible individual and $426.40 per month for an eligible couple. In addition to being indexed to inflation should it exceed an annual rate of 3 percent, states are allowed to supplement the basic benefit amount. In 1980, 16 states provided such a supplement. When the program was first implemented, states were required to provide a supplement if the previous categorical grant to an individual under OAA, AB, or APTD had been higher than the new SSI floor benefit level. Projected SSI expenditures for 1982 are in excess of $7 billion.

A guiding principle in public assistance programs has been to reduce the benefit level by some proportion (a policy decision) as the individual has earned income. This was seen previously in the case example of Mrs. A. However, a major concern with SSI and its response to disabled persons has been the cutoff of benefits when one becomes employed, yet earnings are not enough to cover the special needs of the disabled person. In 1981, under an experimental program, disabled or blind persons could continue to receive SSI, Medicaid, and social services even though their earnings exceeded the level of what is considered substantial gainful activity.

> In the case of C.M., a 23-year-old male paraplegic with limited movement of his arms, confined to a wheelchair and in need of a personal attendant to help with hygiene, dressing, and other activities of daily living, the experimental program provided new hope for a life of independent living. C.M. had been attending college, preparing for a career in a helping profession. However, he was constantly discouraged by the prospect of not earning enough money after graduation to continue living as he had for the past three years in an independent living center. Under the new program, C.M. has now completed his education, is employed full-time, lives independently, and retains his eligibility for SSI (to be gradually phased out as earnings increase), Medicaid, and social services.

Under the present administration it is being proposed that savings in the range of $1 billion over the 1982 to 1987 period might be realized by tightening up on the computation of SSI benefits. This would be accomplished by computing benefits from the first day of eligibility rather than the first day of the first month of eligibility and defining disability according to more stringent guidelines, for example, a required prognosis of 24 months inability to work rather than the present 12 months.

Food Stamp Program

The precursor of the current food stamp program was initiated under The Potatoe Control Act of 1935 (P.L. 72–320, Sec. 32) and has expanded into a major part of the American income security system. It is the outgrowth of negotiation and compromise from its beginnings as a means of disposing of farm (agricultural) surplus and providing additional relief during the Depression, to a program with an expanded goal of providing low-income households with a nutritionally adequate diet, as seen in the Food Stamp Act of 1964 (P.L. 88–525).

The program provides in most instances food coupons to households, which upon presentation through the "natural channels of trade and commerce," may purchase food at the market value. Eligible households are determined by income level and family size. Administered by the Federal Government through the Department of Agriculture, the cost of food stamp coupons is entirely federally financed. Administration is at the local level by a designated state agency with the cost of administration financed 50 percent by the federal government.

The Potatoe Control Act, as the basic piece of legislation, encouraged the consumption and distribution of agricultural commodities in other than the normal market channels. This was accomplished by the distribution of actual food commodities to families and school lunch programs, under the administration of the Federal Surplus Commodities Corporation (FSCC). It is important to remember that this program served an economic function of upholding market prices for agricultural products by keeping surpluses from glutting the market and depressing prices (MacDonald, 1977). The general concern about problems of malnutrition and poverty were to be expressed in later legislation.

In response to widespread dissatisfaction among recipients as well as distributors about the monthly distribution of commodities, which included perishable items and made budgeting food consumption difficult at the household level, the first food stamp program was operationalized from 1939 to 1943. This initial stamp program also responded to pressures from the food industry which lobbied for a program that operated within the normal market channels of both production and retail sales. However, with the advent of World War II the stamp program was suspended because of decreasing surpluses and decreasing numbers of public assistance cases, to be reinstituted as a food commodity program during the 1950s.

The most recent history of the Food Stamp Program is embodied in the Food Stamp Act of 1964. Stimulated by the "rediscovery" of poverty and malnutrition, the stamp program provided an income supplement to families. The transaction involved a family purchasing food stamps and receiving, without charge, bonus stamps—the amount inversely related to family income. Under this basic system the program expanded from a pilot program in 22 states with 360,000 participants to mandated food stamp participation by 50 states in 1974 with 13.5 million participants and a federal bonus stamp cost of $2 billion, 714,000.

The purchase requirement was found to hinder the participation of many low-income families and became a target for change throughout much of the late 1970s. Concerns were also expressed about abuse of the program by vendors, those distributing the stamps, and resulted in the passage of a Vendor Accountability Act in June 1976. This Act required vendors to make routine deposits of food stamp monies and thus curtail the practice of accumulating interest on the funds deposited in high interest accounts.

In 1978 Congress eliminated the purchase requirement for food stamp participation. By this action, a household eligible to purchase $150 in food stamps for $100 now receives $50 in food stamps. In some pilot projects several states are "cashing out" this amount by providing the household, for example, with $50 in cash rather than food stamps.

Projected federal outlays for food stamps in 1982 are just over $10 billion. The administration is attempting to cut this expenditure by more than $2.5 billion by 1987 through various measures including a work requirement, counting energy assistance benefits as income, and cutting benefits 35 cents (rather than 30 cents) for each dollar of income (Clark, 1982). Other proposals for cutting costs include further restrictions on deductions, gross income limits, and liquid assets.

The development of the food stamp program provides an excellent example of social policy that, when implemented in the form of food commodities, controls behavior at the point of consumption, stigmatizes the recipient, and supports the agricultural economy. In moving first to stamps and then to a "cash out" benefit, we see social policy that on the one hand exerts less control of the recipient and on the other hand supports the market mechanism in the distribution of food through community retail outlets. One must remember, however, that little choice is actually exercised when the dollar amount of the benefit is very low. In the above case of Mrs. A., for example, the food stamp benefit was determined to be $191 per month for herself and three children.

Medicaid

The inclusion of Medicaid in the discussion of public assistance is twofold: First, the benefits, if figured as cash, would substantially influence the income level of vulnerable populations—those who are heavy users of health care; and second, Medicaid is generally available to all participants in the AFDC and SSI programs as well as other groups at state option. For example, it is reported by Rein (1982) that Medicaid provides the equivalent of $168 per month to a four-person family in Massachusetts.

Medicaid was passed in 1965 as Title IXX of the Social Security Act to fund health care services for people unable to obtain care in the private, fee-for-service market. The history of Medicaid has been controversial. From its beginnings, it was viewed as a temporary step toward the enactment of a national health proposal which its framers anticipated would be enacted in the late 1960s or early 1970s. Many provisions, primarily around reimbursement, have proven substantially problematic in interpretation, and in the view of many critics, they have served as an open faucet of funding for the health care provider and a second rate system of care for poor people. Other critics (Friedman, 1977; Somers & Somers, 1977) suggest that Medicaid does nothing to promote incentives to health promotion and in fact results in overuse by participants. This criticism is also, although not as frequently, raised about other health care insurance programs.

Medicaid is a federal–state program with a federal input of dollars ranging from 50 to 83 percent depending on the per capita income of the state. In 1981 Mississippi had the highest federal match at 77.36 percent followed by Arkansas, Alabama, and South Carolina (USDHHS, 1981, p. 237). Under the provisions of Medicaid, certain services are mandated while others are at state option. The participant population may be expanded at state discretion to include persons other than AFDC and SSI recipients. The same reimbursement concerns as those seen with Medicare are evidenced with Medicaid. In addition, health care providers in accepting the assignment of a Medicare or Medicaid case, agree to reimbursement of covered services according to the established guidelines with no further billing to the consumer even though the reimbursement may be a smaller amount than that received through private fee-for-service or other third-party insurers.

Unlike Medicare, there are no deductible or co-payment mechanisms in Medicaid. However, changes are anticipated in the near future with administration proposals to charge beneficiaries $1 for hospital visits and $2 per day for hospitalization (Clark 1982). In addition, to decrease Medicaid expenditures by almost $5 billion by 1987, the Federal Government is proposing to decrease the federal match for optional state programs and allow that states may collect the costs of long-term care (usually defined as nursing home care) from estates. With fewer people eligible for AFDC and SSI and the growing reluctance of states to provide benefits or include populations beyond those specifically mandated, a decrease in Medicaid participation, particularly of persons more categorically borderline in their income levels, is to be anticipated.

General Assistance

As the most residual of all income transfer programs, general assistance serves as very temporary assistance available to individuals who fail to meet the eligibility of other programs. The administration of general assistance varies from state to local, and includes some well-designed, highly professional programs as well as many that operate on an "as needed" basis with the local town officeholders making eligibility and benefit determination. Financing of General Assistance also varies, ranging from complete local or state funding to combinations of funding sources.

Public Assistance and Rural Poverty

With the complexity of federal, state–federal, and local programs designed to provide some level of income security, and with the rapid increase in income transfer benefits in the past decade, what major issues are raised for rural people? Relative to the previous discussion of public assistance the issues will be highlighted. They are, however, not entirely unlike those relative to social insurance; thus, some overlap may be apparent, yet reinforcing of the basic dilemmas.[4]

A basic dilemma of the federal–state public assistance programs of AFDC and Medicaid has been alluded to earlier, that is,

[4]For a detailed presentation of public assistance in rural areas see, National Rural Center, *The Rural Stake in Public Assistance*, Washington, D.C.: Publication Series, Vol. 10, 1978.

the great variation among programs from state to state and the particularly low benefit levels in states with a high proportion of rural people—for example, Mississippi, North Carolina, and Kentucky. The most impoverished rural populations remain in poverty under these programs and have fewer services available to them.

When one looks at the beneficiary group for public assistance it is abundantly clear that it is composed primarily of children and single parent families (AFDC), the elderly, blind and disabled (SSI), and families qualifying for food stamps, Medicaid, and in a minority of states, AFDC-UP. This, in summary, excludes low-income people living as single persons under the age of 65, and couples under age 65 without children. According to statistics on household characteristics of rural families, the inequities of the present system for rural people are well documented.

A third dilemma, and one that permeates the history of welfare and discussions of welfare reform, is that of the work incentive. The dilemma involves the tension between providing an income benefit and maintaining an individual's incentive to work. Critics of generous public assistance income benefits maintain that receiving the benefit decreases the desire to work or to search for work in the marketplace. To such critics, almost all benefit levels are viewed as generous and provision of an adequate benefit level will only encourage people to apply for public assistance. The proponents of more generous benefit levels point out that poor people indeed want to work and that the vast majority of public assistance recipients are unable to work by reason of age and/or disability. Few recipients fall into the category of the "able-bodied" poor and those who do are most often the victims of racism, sexism, and ageism with a resulting lack of job skills and access to opportunities to develop such skills, not to mention a current (July) rate of unemployment that surpasses 9.8 percent as a national average. Figures are much higher for minorities (17.3) and for women who maintain families (12.0) (*Economic Indicators*, August, 1982).

The issue of the work incentive has been dealt with in a number of ways in our present public assistance system. Within AFDC (as seen in the example of Mrs. A.), SSI, and food stamps, certain deductibles are subtracted from the earned income before the benefit level is determined. These deductibles are often such work-related expenses as transportation, uniforms, and child care expenses. Income derived from work has an implicit tax rate so that benefit payments are reduced as income rises. Through this benefit reduction rate, the recipient may have a total income that is greater than the assistance payment. In other words, the less of benefit dollar lost per earned dollar to a predetermined cutoff point, the stronger is the incentive to work and the more likely it is that the recipients will have an income above the poverty level. This is demonstrated by the case of Ms. S. who has income from three sources, Social Security Retirement, SSI, and earnings from a job.

Ms. S., age 65, lives by herself in a small home she owns. Her only income is a Social Security Retirement benefit of $182.00 per month. She subscribes to Medicare Part B (physician coverage) so the $12.20 premium is deducted from her check leaving an income of $169.80. Ms. S. takes a babysitting job from which she earns $75.00 per month. Her total benefits when she applies for SSI are calculated in the following manner:

Monthly Social Security Benefit	$182.00	
Less $20.00 (Standard exclusion in determining as SSI benefit)	− 20.00	
Remaining countable income not from earnings	$162.00	$162.00
Earnings for the month	$ 75.00	
Less $65.00 (Standard exclusion on earned income in determining an SSI benefit)	− 65.00	
Divided by 2	$ 10.00	
Countable income from earnings	$ 5.00	5.00
Total Countable Income		$167.00
Basic SSI Benefit	$284.00	
Less total countable income	−167.00	
Monthly SSI Benefit	$117.00	$117.00
Monthly SS Benefit		$182.00
Monthly earnings		$ 75.00
Total Monthly Income		$374.00

Ms. S.'s eligibility for SSI makes her in most instances eligible for Medicaid. This would be used to pay her Medicare Part B premium and any additional services not covered by Medicare.

Not only are recipients encouraged to work by systems of deductibles and low benefit reduction rates, but other means are used with much more coercive characteristics. The Work Incentive Program (WIN) enacted in 1967, requires adults (mothers with children under 6 were excluded) and older, out-of-school children, to accept employment or to participate in job training programs or lose their benefits. Although the work requirements and incentives have had questionable impact (Rein, 1982), present trends indicate a strengthening of work requirements as seen in the increase of "workfare" plans at the local level. Work requirements in rural areas with fewer job opportunities in the private sector and a smaller number of public service jobs that would provide job skills marketable in the private sector pose especially difficult issues.[5]

Even though incentives to work exist in benefit determination, it should be remembered that, with the concentration of rural people in low-benefit level states (AFDC), there is less likelihood that such recipients will continue to receive a benefit once their total income from assistance and earnings moves above the poverty level. Public assistance will fail more often to lift rural people out of poverty than it will those living in urban areas.

With the problems of underemployment more prevalent in rural areas, the work incentive serves a less positive function. Rural people have a high degree of attachment to the workforce. Carlin and Pryor (1980) suggest that a diminished work incentive exists in that approximately one-half of the states have benefit levels higher than employment earnings at minimum wage.

According to Carlin and Pryor (1980), the way in which assets are treated in the determination of benefit eligibility for AFDC, SSI, and Food Stamps is particularly important to rural people. For a large proportion of rural people who are self-employed having low incomes yet considerable business assets—for example, farmers—benefit status may not be possible until assets

---

[5]The reader is referred to the work of Mildred Rein, "Work in Welfare: Past Failures and Future Strategies," *Social Service Review*, 56(2):211–229, 1982, for an excellent presentation of the effects of work requirements and incentives on the reduction of dependency on public assistance income.

have been sold. In essence, the public assistance system forces the self-employed to forego their source of income, albeit low and perhaps sporadic, in order to receive a more predictable, assistance level of income.

Related to the often sporadic nature of rural employment is the income period considered in determining eligibility. It has been determined (Carlin & Pryor, 1980) that long accounting periods decrease the size of the poverty population. Furthermore, ". . . the longer the accounting period, the less likely that small farmers, for example, would be eligible to participate in a given welfare program. For considerable periods of time, however, their income might be extremely low" (p. 14).

It is generally accepted among proponents of progressive welfare reform that federalization of AFDC and Medicaid would be to the benefit of potential and present beneficiaries by standardizing eligibility and benefit levels as with SSI. However, it is recognized that variations in the cost of living do exist from one region of the country to another, and that it costs less to live in rural areas. Even though many rural residents would benefit from a standardized benefit level enacted in low benefit states, there is little agreement as to how or if regional variations should be calculated. For example, housing is usually less costly, but transportation costs, in the absence of public transportation, are more expensive. Taxes may be lower, but the quality of public services—water, fire protection, utilities, and so on—may also be less than adequate resulting in self-provision, increased insurance rates, or simply doing without the necessities taken for granted in urban areas of the country.

According to the National Research Council (1981), measuring cost-of-living differences between rural and urban areas and among rural regions is problematic since good measures of the differences do not exist. An imperative to sound policy formulation is the development of more sophisticated information systems that include rural data.

Reform of the Public Assistance System

The ongoing concern about income security in an advanced industrial society has led to periods of stormy debate and designs for reform. The social insurance programs have emerged relatively unscathed from the discussion because of their close tie to work, the universality of their target population, and their coverage of populations seen as deserving in the view of most policymakers and the general public. Furthermore, the political power of the constituency groups, for example, the elderly (OASDHI), has proven to be a formidable force against decrease in benefit levels in even the most difficult economic times; witness the restoration of certain minimum benefits in OASDHI several months after being legislatively removed by the Congress under the Omnibus Budget Reconciliation Act of 1981 (Svahn, 1982).

The reform of public assistance has been continually and vociferously debated. General concern is expressed because the recipients are frequently thought able to work and the expenditure of funds for public assistance has increased substantially in the past two decades (See Table 2.1). These arguments fail to recognize the fact that most participants in AFDC and SSI are children and older, disabled adults. Reform proposals are viewed as either incremental, that is, building on the currently available system, or comprehensive in that an essentially new system is proposed. The past decade has witnessed some incremental changes in the system, for example, the establishment of SSI, experimental cash-out provisions for food stamps, and unemployed parent benefits under AFDC. These changes have not, in a comprehensive sense, addressed the real issues of income support in a highly technical, complex, and fluid advanced industrial society.

From an incremental perspective, reform in the public assistance system that would most increase benefits to rural areas would include:

1. eradication of the benefit differences from one state to another, except those differences that can be documented as realistically based on regional differences needed to maintain a standard of living;
2. liberalization of the work incentives since it has been shown that they do not diminish attachment to the workforce on the part of rural people and that the present benefit reduction rates place an unequitable tax on income, perpetuating the already existing inequities of the system.[6]

[6]The reader is referred to the following for discussions of welfare reform: Martha Ozawa, "Issues in Welfare Reform," Social Service Review, 52(1):37–55, 1978; Irwin Garfinkel, "What's Wrong with Welfare?" Social Work, 23(3):185–191, 1978. In addition, rural issues related to the work incentive are found in, U.S.

3. extension of coverage to those persons currently ineligible which, in rural areas, would include substantial numbers of underemployed two-parent households and households consisting of non-elderly adults.

These proposals are thought best accomplished by increased federal support of the public assistance system and the standardization of eligibility criteria and accounting periods for determining eligibility across programs. Reform proposals which incorporate the points outlined above would increase the adequacy and the equity of the income security system. They are also thought to increase the monetary costs by expanding the target population and raising benefit levels in many states.

In a depressed economy with an administration focusing its efforts on decreasing inflationary pressures by a reduction in government expenditures for programs, progressive, comprehensive welfare reform will not be given a priority. Rather, reform as currently defined refers to initiating cutbacks in assistance benefits, restricting the recipient population through more restrictive eligibility criteria, and placing greater responsibility (funding and management) at the state and local level.[7]

Summary

The focus of this chapter has been on programs designed to maintain a level of income security in American society and the ways in which rural populations participate in these programs.

The extent of poverty is greater in rural than in urban areas. However, many rural people work full time in underpaid occupations or work part time in seasonal employment. The income disparities between rural and urban populations are only perpetuated with social insurance income transfer payments so closely related

Department of Health Education and Welfare, *The Rural Income Maintenance Experiment, Summary Report*, SR10, Nov., 1976.

[7]In his attempts to further the New Federalism and ultimately reduce government expenditures, President Reagan has proposed a federal takeover of Medicaid with complete state responsibility for AFDC. In June 1982 this proposal translated into the federal government assuming $18.3 billion in state Medicaid costs, placing $20.4 billion into a trust fund for AFDC and other federal aid programs that states would take responsibility for over a period of eight years. This would involve $8.1 billion in federal AFDC costs and $30.6 in other program costs to be assumed by the states (Clark, 1982, p. 278).

to work history. Furthermore, public assistance benefits which are woefully inadequate in all states are even more deficient in very rural states—seldom meeting poverty level guidelines.

The close attachment of rural people to the workforce—often at substandard wages—the greater numbers of self-employed rural people, and the lack of job opportunities in many rural areas, indicate a differential participation of the rural population in the economic structures of society. This in turn suggests that the conventional solutions based on urban models, that is, job training, benefit reductions for earned income, and wage-related benefits, are not necessarily appropriate to rural populations. Policy alternatives to the present income security system of social insurance and public assistance must consider the rural/urban differences and seek a more equitable distribution of society's resources.

References

Axinn, June and Levin, Herman. *Social Welfare: A History of the American Response to Need*, 2nd ed. New York: Harper and Row, 1982.

Bluestone, Herman. "Rural Income Growing and Changing" in Brown, David L., Steward, Donald D., and Ingalsbe, Gene (Eds.), *Rural Development Perspectives: Focus on Rural Poverty*. Washington, D.C.: Economic Development Division, ERSC, USDA, 1980, 27–28.

Burns, Eveline M. *Social Security and Public Policy*. New York: McGraw Hill Book Co., 1956.

Carlin, Thomas and Pryor, Shirley. "A Rural Perspective of Welfare Reform: Part I—Issues" in Brown, David L., Steward, Donald D., and Ingalsbe, Gene (Eds.), *Rural Development Perspectives*, Washington, D.C.: Economic Development Division, ERSC, USDA, 1980, 12–15.

Cater, Morrow. "Trimming the Disability Rolls—Changing the Rules During the Game?." *National Journal*, 1982, 14(36):1512–1514.

Clark, Timothy. "Reagan's Budget: Economic, Political Gambles," *National Journal*, 1982, 14(7):268–285.

Deavers, Kenneth L. and Brown, David L. *Social and Economic Trends in Rural America*. The White House Rural Development Background Paper, Economics, Statistics, and Cooperative Services, USDA, 1979.

Douglas, Virginia T. "Rural Health Clinics Serve 'Invisible Poor,' " *Forum*, 1980, 4(3):22–28.

Economic Indicators. Department of Labor, Bureau of Labor Statistics,

Washington, D.C.: U.S. Government Printing Office, August, 1982.

Economic Research Service. "Housing Rural America." Prepared by the Housing Program Area, Economic Development Division, Washington, D.C.: U.S. Department of Agriculture, 1981.

Friedman, Emily. "Medicaid: The Primose Path," *Hospitals*, 1977, 51 (Aug. 16), 51–56.

Friedman, Emily and Wendorf, Carl. "Medicaid: A Garden Sown with Dragon's Teeth," *Hospitals*, 1977, 51 (Sept. 1), 59–63.

Garfinkel, Irwin. "What's Wrong with Welfare?" *Social Work*, 1978, 23(3):934–937.

Ginsburg, Paul B. "Issues in Medicare Hospital Reimbursement," *National Journal*, 1982, 14(21):934–937.

Havemann, Joel. "Sharing the Wealth: The Gap Between Rich and Poor Grows Wider," *National Journal*, 1982, 14(43):1788–1795.

Hoppe, Robert A. and Martin, Glenda V. "Transfer Payments: An Important Source of Nonmetropolitan Income" in Morris, Lynne Clemmons (Ed.), *Dignity, Diversity, and Opportunity in Changing Rural Areas*. Paper presented at the Sixth National Institute on Social Work in Rural Areas, University of South Carolina, 1982, 140–152.

Lando, Mordechai E., Farley, Alice V. and Brown, Mary A. "Recent Trends in the Social Security Disability Insurance Program," *Social Security Bulletin*, 1982, 45(8):3–14.

MacDonald, Maurice, "Food Stamps: An Analytical History," *Social Service Review*, 1977, 51(4):642–658.

Madden, P.J. *Poverty Statistics: A Guide to Interpretation*. Department of Agricultural Economics and Rural Sociology, Pennsylvania State University, revised October 16, 1982.

National Research Council. *Rural America in Passage: Statistics for Policy*. Washington, D.C.: National Academy Press, 1981.

Orshansky, Mollie. "Counting the Poor: Another Look at the Poverty Profile," *Social Security Bulletin*, 1965, 28(1):3–29.

Osgood, Mary H. "Rural and Urban Attitudes Toward Welfare," *Social Work*, 1977, 22(1):41–47.

Ozawa, Martha N. "Who Receives Subsidies Through Social Security, and How Much?," *Social Work*, 1982, 17(2):129–138.

Paglin, Morton. "Poverty in the United States: A Reevaluation," *Policy Review*, 1979, 8(Spring):7–24.

Rein, Mildred. "Work in Welfare: Past Failures and Future Strategies," *Social Service Review*, 1982, 56(2):211–229.

Roemer, Milton I. "Primary Care and Physician Extenders in Affluent Countries," *International Journal of Health Services*," 1977, 7(4):545–555.

Roemer, Milton I. "Health Maintenance Organizations—New Develop-

ments of Significance for the Elderly in Rural Areas." Unpublished
    paper, 1980.

Somers, Anne R. and Somers, Herman M. "A Proposed Framework for
    Health and Health Care Policies," *Inquiry*, 1977, 14:115–170.

Svahn, John A. "Restoration of Certain Minimum Benefits and Other
    OASDHI and Medicare Provisions," *Social Security Bulletin*, 1981,
    44(10):3–24.

Svahn, John A. "Restoration of Certain Minimum Benefits and Other
    OASDHI Program Changes: Legislative History and Summary of
    Provisions," *Social Security Bulletin*, 1982, 45(3):3–12.

U.S. Bureau of the Census. *Current Population Reports: Special
    Studies*, Series P-23, No. 28. Washington, D.C.: U.S. Government
    Printing Office, 1969.

U.S. Bureau of the Census. "Money Income and Poverty Status of Families
    and Persons in the United States: 1980." *Current Population Reports*,
    Series P-60, No. 127, U.S. Dept. of Commerce, 1981.

United States Department of Health and Human Services. *Characteris-
    tics of State Plans for Aid to Families with Dependent Children*.
    Washington, D.C.: SSA Pub. No. 80-08005, 1981.

4

Contemporary Policy Themes: Organization and Delivery of Services

Introduction

The purpose of this chapter is to examine the primary social policy themes that have developed during the past decade and have had a decided impact on service organization and the delivery system. While these themes—continuum of care, formal/informal networks, deinstitutionalization, and services co-ordination strategies—are in part a response to the conditions of an advanced industrial society, they are not to be construed as absolutes or as discrete concepts. Rather, each is a contemporary and in some ways pragmatic response based on an historical and philosophical antecedent and reflective of the multidimensional nature of the delivery system. For purposes of clarity in presentation, this examination will view the themes as discrete concepts and alert the reader to their fundamental interdependence. The themes examined in this chapter represent responses to the questions posed by Burns (1956) and Gilbert and Specht (1974) relative to the delivery of income or service provisions.

Each theme becomes manifest in a variety of policy products and hence action, cutting across such service sectors as health, aging, income security, and housing. As in Chapter 3, the analytic presentation of the theme includes a brief review of the historical context to provide the reader with a broad view of the theme and to suggest the dynamic context of the policy process. Examples from contemporary legislation are used to clarify each theme and its possible impact on the rural environment. Throughout, the reader will be alerted to the theoretical perspective and value base underpinning the theme as well as the applicable generic policy choices presented in Chapter 2.

Delivery System Goals

The baseline goal of a delivery system for the distribution of income or service provisions is to provide for the general welfare by redistributing, according to the principles of equity and justice, income to sustain a defined adequacy or quality of life and/or to provide services which enhance the interactions between people and their environments. Interfering with the full realization of this goal at the delivery level are commonly recognized dysfunctions: a lack of system as well as program and agency accountability; poor or limited access to the system by potential participants; difficulties in moving through the system to receive the appropriate benefit; and gaps in needed services (Gilbert & Specht, 1974; Rein, 1970). The social policy themes examined in this chapter are intended to address such dysfunctions. At the same time, as will be pointed out, the potential exists for each to generate unintended consequences of a sizable magnitude for rural as well as urban populations. The various themes, as the embodiment of policy choices, represent the means by which the larger system goal is addressed.

Continuum of Care

The continuum of care concept has recently gained prominence both as a tool of policy analysis and as an organizing concept for service delivery. Its recent history dates to the report of the *President's Panel to Combat Mental Retardation* (1962), established by President John F. Kennedy. According to that report, the concept of continuum of care embodied several important principles. It suggested that there were transitions and linkages both among various providers and professionals and within service agencies which needed attention and focus as the individual moved from one service to another, meeting uniquely individual needs throughout the life span. According to the report, assuring a continuum of care was to be the focus of service planning and coordination. The passage of P. L. 88–164, Mental Retardation Facilities and Community Mental Health Centers Construction Act of 1963, signed into law by President Kennedy in 1963, had widespread implications for government responsibility in addressing the needs of the mentally retarded and several other groups defined as developmentally disabled, whose service needs were thought to persist at one level or another throughout the life span. Its intended consequence was to promote a fully developed service system that was accessible, continuous, and unfragmented in its response to the needs of the developmentally disabled.

Passed during a period of social optimism, P.L. 88–164 was underpinned by a belief that delivery systems could be comprehensive, responsive, and expansionary. Furthermore, the recognized responsibility of a government to those people more vulnerable was to intervene through a service system and foster the full development of the individual. The continuum of care theme has continued and recently was incorporated as a primary component of The Older Americans Act as amended, 1978. However, it still is not entirely clear what is meant by continuum of care.

Under the direction of Arabella Martinez, then Assistant Secretary for Human Development Services, The Office of Human Development Services (OHDS–HEW) commissioned a paper by Ecosometrics (1978) on the continuum of care as related to the OHDS mission. In keeping with the OHDS mission it addressed need in a universal sense, not targeting a specific categorical population such as the developmentally disabled. The continuum of care, according to Martinez (1980), involves an appropriate range of responses to a predictable range of needs as a person progresses through the life cycle. Furthermore, responses in a continuum of care are oriented toward maximizing independence, self-sufficiency, and growth. The primary assumption of the concept of continuum is that need can be predicted and a rational network of services designed in the anticipation of need.

The concepts of the developmental continuum and continuum of need are, in Martinez' view, used interchangeably with continuum of care. However, it appears that developmental continuum is more accurately derived from developmental theory underlying continuum of care when it is viewed as a service delivery concept. The continuum of need describes the situations which call for a response on the part of organized formal and/or informal service networks. Continuum of care as defined by Ecosometrics and reported by Martinez actually consists of five continua across which people would be expected to move from dependence to independence as the result of service and/or economic intervention.

The five continua are:

1. The growth/loss continuum which refers to the changes in the human/biological organism over time in its capacity and need for independence or dependence. It is identified as the developmental continuum;
2. The continuum of residence which refers to the range of living environments from independent living in one's own home to residence in a large institution;
3. The continuum of employment which refers to employment that is gainful and meaningful (supposedly long-term and full-time) to the unemployability of the individual at the opposite end of the continuum;
4. The impairment continuum which refers to the dichotomous positions of positive health versus permanent and total disability; and
5. The economic status/income continuum which refers to the range between economic dependence on the public system of maintenance to improved economic status.

The input (intervention) side of continuum of care is conceptualized as levels of care designed to impact the continua of need either separately or in combination with one another.

The levels of care are as follows:

1. Professional care which involves professionally trained persons in a variety of helping professions and settings;
2. Paraprofessional care which involves persons with technical training in specialized areas;
3. Caring network which includes those activities performed by friends, churches, families, and often referenced in the literature as the informal network;
4. Self-care which is provided by the person her/himself and exemplified by the self-care and self-help movements; and
5. Nonservice which refers to those activities thought to generate widespread benefits, for example, tax credits, stimulation of industrial growth in the private sector, zoning regulations, and so on, affecting in a variety of ways employment, day care, and so on.

The need for a conceptual framework for policy development and service delivery was cited by Benedict (1977;1978). Building on the earlier work of Benedict and Hoke (1976), the continuum of care was advocated to serve this purpose. From Benedict's (1977) perspective, the continuum of care is defined as an array of services which correspond to the needs and preferences of the individual. Forming a range of services to include those least restrictive to those most restrictive a system of long-term care is formed—for example, community care, in-home care, personal care, and institutional care.

According to Benedict (1977), writing from the context of the elderly as the target population, the purposes of continuum are: (1) a way of channeling scarce resources to the frail or most vulnerable of the elderly; (2) a concept that provides unity to the service network; and (3) a mechanism that provides more appropriate and efficient utilization of the delivery system.

As a unifying concept, continuum of care brings together long-term institutional care and community social services into one service network for a homogeneous target population such as the mentally retarded or the elderly. From a policy perspective Benedict (1977) makes the important observation that individuals in the two systems of care (institutional or community social services), differ only in that the illness or disability of the institutional group exceeds "the capacity of the community service network to maintain him or her outside an institution at the present time" (p. 8). This view has strongly influenced recent policy decisions related to institutional/community-based services and will be discussed more extensively when deinstitutionalization is examined in a subsequent section.

As a concept for providing unity to the service network, continuum of care unites two dichotomous positions on the continuum, institutional and community-based services. As applicable to services for the elderly which was Benedict's (1977) chief concern as Commissioner of the Administration on Aging (AOA), are the following observations:

Within these unified parameters, which can, for the time being, be called Long-Term Services, the chronically ill elderly should be able to choose the medical and social services they need, in whatever setting is most appropriate, with reimbursement related to the per capita cost of meeting the individual's needs—not according to the location or provider of services. (p. 9)

The intermingling of concepts and value underpinning is clearly seen in the following statement found in the AOA position paper, "AOA's Approach to Long Term Care."

> Long-term care, in our view should be defined as health care, social services, or personal care, including supervision, treatment or any sort of simple help with everyday tasks, provided formally or informally, on a recurring or continuous basis as needed, to functionally impaired individuals, in living environments ranging from institutions to their own homes, whose chronic illness or incapacity requires that they receive assistance with one or more essential physiological functions or activities of daily living.
>
> Ideally, the care and services are the most appropriate for, and are provided in the least restrictive setting consistent with, the person's needs and optimum functioning (Benedict, 1980, p. 3).

Benedict (1977) and Benedict and Hoke (1976) proposed that a continuum of care be established under the control and sponsorship of local government, perhaps as a local human service authority. In their view, local government would increase the legitimacy of the structure by targeting the locality as the focus for services planning and management. On the one hand, for communities with many service providers, a rich service mix may result. For those communities without an adequate service base, as is frequently the case in rural areas, local structures may lend more legitimacy to their establishment. On the other hand, the researchers do not acknowledge the possible constraints that traditionally conservative local belief systems might impose on the local human service authority, constraints analogous to those found in general assistance (GA) programs.

The value perspective reflected in the continuum of care concept is the worth and dignity of the unique individual. The concept addresses with fluidity the changing needs of the individual over the life span. It reflects an institutional view of social welfare, recognizing that some exigencies of life demand resources not routinely provided by other institutions, namely the family and church, and that the service needs for several target populations are long-term.

The intent of a continuum of services is to provide a better level of health and well-being for those target populations living in the community and to prevent the future institutionalization of an undetermined number of individuals, be they elderly, mentally retarded, mentally ill, or juvenile offenders (E. Brody, 1979).

Achieving these goals will require close collaboration between formal and informal caring networks, a topic to be examined in a subsequent section in this chapter.

The impact of developmental theory on the continuum of care concept is readily apparent. With an emphasis on individual psychological and personality aspects of the developmental process, a note of caution is raised. Estes (1979) suggests that developmental theory, in the context of the elderly as a target population, reinforces the stigma of declining independence, promotes intergenerational conflict in the struggle to acquire scarce resources, and focuses services on deficiencies rather than on prevention.

To address these issues Estes proposes the use of symbolic interactionist theory as an underpinning to social policy development. By addressing the interface of self and environment, social policy is guided toward addressing the parameters of social class, gender, ethnic identification, and geographic context. Such a perspective is clearly congruent with the mission of social work practice and helpful within the rural context. The interactionist approach, although not sufficiently tested, does concern itself with the meanings that are attached by the actors to what they do and experience. "Such differential meanings provide a basis for assessing whether young and old can find common ground for approaching the problems generated in old age and the potential for political mobilization on old age policy issues" (Estes, 1979, p. 11).

As a delivery concept that includes a comprehensive core of services, the continuum of care is generally recognized to include, at the direct service level, those services which facilitate entry and movement within the system, planning to assess client goals, follow-up, and basic services. The latter is represented by an array of services from in-home, community-based, and institutional arrangements. Important from a policy perspective is the general agreement that local communities should exercise discretion in the range of services provided and the way in which they are organized and coordinated.[1]

[1] Material for this section on continuum of care was developed in part under Grant #90-AR-2073/01, from the Administration on Aging. For further discussion of the concept the reader is referred to the work of Watkins, Dennis A., and Watkins, Julia M. *Toward a Continuum of Care Policy Framework for Decision Making by State Units on Aging and Area Agencies on Aging: Issues and Opportunities in Rural Service Provision*. Final Report submitted to the Administration on Aging, Grant #90-AR-2073/01, July, 1981.

The case of Mr. E. serves as an example of the policy impact of continuum of care on an individual client.

> Mr. E., age 76, was identified by an outreach worker from the local area agency on aging (AAA). He was living alone, caring for himself in his small home near the center of a small Southwestern community. Little was known of his history or background. In discussion with Mr. E. the outreach worker determined that he subsisted on a very meager SSI benefit. Although Medicaid eligible, he had not seen a physician in more than 15 years—in spite of the observation that he moved around his house with difficulty and seldom got out to do any shopping or to socialize with a few remaining friends.
>
> The outreach worker made a referral to the coordinated care program under the auspice of the AAA. As a result, Mr. E. was linked, through a collaborative case-planning process, to the following community-based services: transportation, a congregate meal site operating three days a week in a neighboring community, a social club meeting in conjunction with the meal program, and a health screening program located in the local church where the meals were served.
>
> The health screening program nurse detected high blood pressure and chronic arthritis. As a result, follow-up with a local physician was initiated to prevent as much as possible further deterioriation of Mr. E.'s condition and to serve as a referral point should Mr. E. need hospitalization in the future.
>
> In-home services of homemaker and chore services were initiated. In addition, a visiting nurse was introduced to Mr. E. to follow up with some home health care, should Mr. E. be unable to get to the meal site for appropriate monitoring of medication and diet.

The activation of home and community-based services for Mr. E. clearly adheres to the principles of service delivery embodied in the continuum of care concept. The strategy for assuring access and usability of services on the part of Mr. E. is that known as case management through which the appropriate services are managed in a purposeful and planned effort to maintain Mr. E. in an environment least restrictive of his daily living.

As a policy theme it is clear that continuum of care has

relevance at several critical points in the provision of services and income to rural populations. Rural isolation, poverty, and its attendant problems of a higher-than-average population at risk, would suggest that a service system, conceptualized as a continuum, or several continua, would be helpful in assessing which continua are deficient and what levels of care might be strengthened or alternatives developed in any given community.

A marked disadvantage of the concept is the tendency to define needs of a population by the services that do exist. This approach, as discussed by Golant and McCaslin (1979), has as its risk that services define need. Particularly in rural areas where services are notably sparse, the service planner may be tempted to overutilize unneeded yet available services and thus not expend effort toward more comprehensive service development.

Another equally problematic aspect to this policy theme is, on the one hand, that when mandated under a piece of legislation with the service dollars dependent on its implementation, rural areas are at a decided disadvantage with fewer services to pull into a continuum of care. On the other hand, a legislative mandate may provide the leverage needed with local politicians for the social worker or service planner to enter into contractual agreements for service with more distantly located providers. Likewise, these providers may see an extension of their services to a new community as a way of generating income in a time of general resource scarcity. Mandates can also sensitize such area-wide planning agencies as Area Agencies on Aging (AAAs) and state, regionally based offices to act in more responsible ways to provide for rural constituencies.

Formal/Informal Support Systems

Recently, a series of policy statements and reports has generated an increased visibility for the interaction between formal and informal support systems as a way of assuring a comprehensive service system available to the general population (*President's Commission on Mental Health,* 1978; National Commission on Neighborhoods, 1979; Wingspread Report, *Strengthening Families through Informal Support Systems,* 1978). More dramatic have been recent pronouncements that the nation must return to a service system of local control and voluntarism congruent with the American values of independence and family stability.

The purpose of this section is to examine the concepts of formal and informal service networks and their mutual interaction as an emerging theme in policy decisions. The examination will elucidate the meaning of formal and informal, capture the relative importance of both for rural settings, and show how the theme is translated from legislation into such mechanisms as the self-help and voluntarism movements. Issues will also be addressed relative to the interaction between the formal and informal service networks as the relative advantages and disadvantages for rural areas are explored.

The formal support system is that part of the service network with which social workers frequently interact and are most familiar. Included are agencies and organizations with an identifiable structure and recognized collective concern of society through legislative mandate or incorporation under prevailing state laws as an entity to provide for the well-being of the society. They embody to one degree or another the characteristics of formal organizations: goals, tasks, roles, and status heirarchies to name a few. They are also staffed primarily by professionally trained people who function in a change-agent capacity. The agencies and organizations may be public, private not-for-profit, private proprietary, or a mix of these three forms.

Discussions of delivery systems from a social policy perspective have been biased toward the formal support system, a system which gained momentum under the provisions of the Social Security Act of 1935 wherein the federal government acknowledged and acted on its responsibility to the collective well-being of society. However, with the current emphasis on a social systems perspective of the helping process, the social work mission articulated as being concerned with the "transactions between people and their environments" (Council on Social Work Education, 1982, p. 4), the present scarcity of formal resources, and the trend toward more community control within the context of the New Federalism, discussion more frequently includes the dimensions of an informal helping network as a policy alternative in the delivery of services.

The informal service network, sometimes identified in the literature as "natural" helpers or the natural network, is usually identified as family, friends, neighbors, co-workers, storekeepers, clergy, volunteers, and mutual aid and self-help groups (Collins & Pancoast, 1976; Froland, 1979; Johnson, 1980). According to Johnson, this informal network usually has little or no linkage with the more formal service network. Furthermore, it is most often available as needed on an unplanned and unorganized basis, although an organizational structure may later develop. For the most part, the informal helping networks are linked with individuals. However, groups formed around commonly held problems are identified as mutual aid or self-help groups (Katz & Bender, 1976) and serve many of the functions of an informal or natural network. From the literature of social anthropology, the natural network is identified as based on kinship which may become transformed into a friendship system. The natural or informal system develops from the bottom up as people reach out in their immediate environments for assistance with the most simple or the most complex tasks.

Whatever the scope of public and private expenditures for social welfare through the formal service or income security system, a vast amount of help is supplied by the informal system, primarily the family. Although this may seem incongruous at a time when so much is heard and read about the dissolution of the family, Shanas (1979), in a study of the family as a support system in old age reports: "In contemporary society, the family persists as a major source of help to the elderly even in those areas where the assistance of outside agencies is undoubtedly necessary and useful" (p. 170). Another study (Krishef & Yoelin, 1981) found that rural elderly, both black and white, used the formal system for health care and income maintenance. Both groups, however, relied heavily on informal supports for transportation and, when not available informally, they simply did without the transportation. Blacks use of informal systems was significantly greater than that of whites. It is speculated by Krishef and Yoelin that this difference might be due to the "multiperson composition of rural black households" with an available informal network and the poverty of the black rural elderly which forces them into inexpensive housing with a closeknit social structure.

The attractiveness of the informal service network is based on several assumptions not entirely tested empirically. It is assumed, for example, that services provided informally are less costly, more responsive to individual uniqueness, and more humane than those traditionally provided through bureaucratic formal organizations. However attractive these views are to the proponents of local control and management of human services, it is historically correct that the formal system of services and income security was established in part as a response to an overburdened informal (and private) system that was unable to meet the pressing social and economic problems that resulted from the Great Depression of the 1930s. In addition, changing patterns in family structure, employment, and housing, all have realistic impacts on the abilities of the informal system to respond in the same way it may have done in the past.

Those policy analysts who raise concern about total reliance on the informal system acknowledge also the shortcomings of formal helping networks. In addition, however, they point out some realities attendant to the informal system which admonish caution in exercising this policy choice. Froland (1980) suggests the following: (1) not all people have ties to an informal helping network; (2) the informal network can be exclusive and discriminatory; (3) the network is not always reliable and continuous; (4) the caregiving capacity of the informal network is often inhibited by a lack of knowledge and resources; (5) requests for help can, over time, be seen as burdensome; (6) group efforts lack the impetus to continue over a long period of time, particularly as the membership changes; and (7) power issues arise as informal groups compete for scarce resources.

Whatever the questions raised about the failures of the formal service network, that is, they may be impersonal, costly, inefficient, ineffective, and destructive of the informal helping response, the formal system is often, but not always, designed with a focus on equity and justice. It provides an avenue through which society expresses a collective concern for the well-being of its members. This, according to Froland (1980) establishes programs designed to

> . . . promote the transfer and diffusion of risks to relieve the burden of chronic and catastrophic situations, and technical knowledge and resources can be developed and used to alleviate difficulties. Systems of accountability and electoral representation are attempts to provide for the responsiveness and accessibility of power. (p. 577)

Having examined the advantages of formal and informal service networks in a general sense, the policy question to emerge is not whether one should be implemented at the expense of the other, but how the two systems can, in the words of Froland, Pancoast, Chapman, & Kimboko (1979), "interact synergistically rather than destructively" (p. 1). The basic questions relate to: (1)

how the formal system can support and interact with the informal network; and (2) how the formal system can create an informal network supportive of its target population. The latter question suggests a "top-down" approach which is counter to the prevailing "bottom-up" development of natural networks.

Both Shanas (1979) and E. Brody (1979), writing about the elderly population and the needs for long-term care, point to the fact that substantial numbers of elderly people are cared for primarily by their families. Brody states that families continue to express that the care of an elderly family member is a family responsibility. Those elderly people who are institutionalized have a family status that is quite different from those who remain in the community; they are less likely to have a living spouse and generally have no or fewer living adult children. With the family as a major informal support in old age, E. Brody takes the position that formal services must focus on the family to strengthen its caregiving capacity. This same perspective is equally applicable to younger families with children.

Two issues emerge from this discussion. First is the fear that formal, organized support of the family may undermine the structure and function of the family. To this issue, E. Brody suggests the following question ". . . at what point does the expectation of filial responsibility become social irresponsibility?" (p. 1830). Kammerman (1981) and E. Brody point to a second issue; the traditional caregivers in the informal network, particularly the family, have been women. In the case of caring for the elderly these women are, in the words of Brody, "women in the middle" (p. 1832). They are middle-aged, subject to multiple demands of spouse, parent, grandparent, filial caregiver, and worker. Even when they are employed full- or part-time outside of the home, they continue to express the responsibility of caring for an elderly parent or parent-in-law. With the ever-changing roles of women, the family system is benefited rather than destroyed by the support of other informal networks and formal helping services. Cantor (1977) found that with the coordination between formal and informal service networks, the quality of family care provided the elderly family member was enhanced because stress on the family was relieved.

The interaction between formal and informal systems has recently been the subject of investigation by Froland (1980) and Froland and colleagues (1979). Froland (1980) suggests that the contributions of the formal and informal caregiving networks are complementary yet contradictory in the sense of which network should do what and in what manner. On the one hand, the strength of the formal network is in its professional staff with technical knowledge, information, and an objectivity based in expertise. On the other hand, the informal network contributes substantially in supporting needs requiring long-term attention. At the macro level of intervention, informal networks provide the avenues for participation in local affairs while the formal support system provides the mandate and vehicle for insuring representation and a balance among competing interests.

The interface between the formal and informal systems is characterized by several types of interaction; conflict, competition, cooptation, coexistence, and collaboration (Froland, 1980). Although collaboration is a preferred strategy for social work intervention because of the value base of the profession, dilemmas arise out of the collaborative interaction of formal and informal service networks. These most frequently relate to legal and ethical issues, status and responsibility, and identity and credibility (Froland, 1980).

This discussion would be incomplete without a brief discussion of the self-help movement as a policy alternative or supplement to the formal network. The self-help movement derives from the traditional American value of mutual aid. Self-help, according to Butler, Gertman, Oberlander, & Schindler (1979–80) "refers to clusters of like-minded or like-afflicted individuals who share experience and offer one another mutual support and aid (p. 96). Such self-help groups as Alcoholics Anonymous (AA), Parents Anonymous, groups consisting of previously hospitalized mental patients, support groups for parents of mentally retarded children, and women recovering from mastectomies, to name but a few, are burgeoning in many communities. These groups have as their primary purpose to provide social support, education, and secondary prevention, that is, preventing disability from an already existing condition. They very often serve the need for extended or long-term support.

The Candlelighters, a nationwide self-help group with a primary membership of parents with children who have cancer serves as an example of the interface of formal and informal systems. The oncology social worker in a large regional medical center serving a predominately rural population initiated the development of the parent support group with several clients. These parents had found their experiences to be psychologically debilitating and the contacts with the social worker not frequent enough to meet their support needs. Transportation, child care, and job responsibilities all served as barriers to the formal support system.

Through the social worker's contacts with a branch office of a community mental health center (CMHC) consultation and education unit, a facility was procured in a town of closer proximity to the clients, and a community educator from the CMHC was able to allocate time to initially facilitate the group. Over the initial two-month period during which the parents met four times, leadership emerged and they decided to begin a newsletter, set up an outreach service to other parents, and develop a series of programs addressing their mutual concerns. The parents then went back to the oncology social worker with clearly defined requests for assistance in typing and distributing the newsletter, linkage to other parents, and help in contacting "experts" for program presentations.

In the example of the Candlelighters, two formal systems interacted in a top-down approach to provide support and assistance requested by the developing informal system. This allowed the parent group to chart its own direction and serve an unmet need—that of continued support because of their rural location and the inability of the medical setting to respond with a sufficient quantity of social work services.

The very existence of self-help groups raises questions about the effectiveness of our formal service networks. Nevertheless, as pointed out by Froland (1980), formal agencies can and do work collaboratively with some of these groups. Although the self-help movement is viewed as a positive force, as a catalyst in promoting the development of social policy directed, at least in the health care field, toward prevention and health promotion, some authors (Green, Werlin, Schauffler, & Avery 1977; Hess, 1976) have suggested that the self-help and self-care movements become the means of justifying less governmental responsibility in developing a more equitable health care system. Currently, we see such developments with the federal emphasis on mutual aid and voluntarism coinciding with massive cuts in social/health program expenditures.

In an earlier chapter of this book, the shortage of formal

helping services in rural communities was recognized. The literature on rural values and attitudes also recognizes the strong traditions of community and family as sources of social support in rural
communities. Nevertheless, an adequate policy response to rural
areas must not emphasize the development of one network (formal or informal) at the expense of the other. Although strong
traditions exist, rural America is diverse and constantly changing.
Social policy must allow for and stimulate this diversity.

According to Johnson (1980) the informal systems are most
important in communities where there is a sense of concern for
the problems of others. Persons can be identified in such communities by their availability and interest in other persons. They
are usually a visible part of the community and understand its
life and pulse. The extended family is frequently, but not always, a part of rural life and functions to benefit and support its
members in a variety of ways. Our policies must acknowledge
the strengths of the family to provide continued support over a
long period of time but must supplement that support with formal service networks.

When one examines the phenomenon of the rurally located
energy boom towns (Griffiths, 1981; McLeod, 1981), it is apparent that many problems of isolation and alienation exist that
could be addressed by a top-down approach to the development
and stimulation of informal contact among community members.
In the words of McLeod ". . . depression, suicide, homicide,
substance abuse, etc., reflect coping responses to deprived, inadequate social structures" (p. 16). Social policy directed toward
supporting interaction in isolated communities could, in part,
ameliorate these conditions.

In viewing the diversity of rural populations, social workers
must advocate for policies supportive of cultural and ethnic diversity. For example, the American Indian family consists of an
extended kinship network that participates in the child rearing
functions. Without this knowledge, or more importantly, the
incorporation of it into child welfare policies, Indian children
were removed from their immediate families on the basis of
neglect and placed in non-Indian foster homes, adoptive homes,
and institutions, at rates which far exceeded those for non-Indian
children (Miller, Hoffman, & Turner, 1980). In actuality many of
these children were being cared for by a tightly interlocking
extended family system. Child welfare policies, however, prior
to the Indian Child Welfare Act of 1979 failed among other

things to recognize and support cultural differences and, as reflected in the title of one monograph, contributed to the *Destruction of American Indian Families* (Unger, 1977).

In summary, the viability of the informal network in rural areas is dependent in large measure on the type of support it is afforded through policy mechanisms. For example, will reimbursement and/or tax credits for relatives caring for an elderly family member become accepted policy realities designed to add legitimacy and support to functions now carried out by many families? Will mental health policies, in the tradition of community mental health, stimulate the advancement of prevention by addressing the concerns raised in reference to the energy boom towns—concerns of equal importance to economically depressed rural areas? A policy focus supportive of the informal helping network holds substantial promise for rural areas, but only when there exists an equal commitment to quality formal services of sufficient quantity to address problems in the rural environment. The movement toward informal, self-care, and self-help delivery structures cannot be used as the justification for less government social responsibility. To do so ignores the complexities of the advanced industrial society and the vulnerability of substantial numbers of rural, poor, and underserved people.

Deinstitutionalization/Community-Based Services

Permeating many fields of social work practice and mandated under numerous pieces of legislation is the concept of deinstitutionalization. The recent history of the concept stems from the early 1960s at a time when increased concern was expressed about the inhumane and debilitating characteristics of institutional environments with particular reference to the mentally retarded and the mentally ill.

The purpose of this section is to examine the concept of deinstitutionalization as a policy theme and look at the corollary concept, that of community-based services. This examination will draw on the history, development, and current status of the concept, primarily using legislation from the fields of mental health, mental retardation, and aging. It is in the former two areas where the greatest efforts have occurred. The field of aging, more recently promoting social policy responses in this area, has targeted efforts toward alternatives to institutionalization—meaning alternatives to nursing home care, something which was discussed earlier in the examination of continuum of care.

The discussion of community-based services is included in this section since it is widely accepted that deinstitutionalization can achieve its goals only when there is a sufficient quantity and range of quality services available in the community to provide the necessary support for maintenance of independent functioning (Horejsi, 1978). However, as pointed out by Clarke (1979), community-based services or community care, as it is often referred to, is not a synonym for deinstitutionalization. In addition, more radical perspectives suggest that to include in the view of deinstitutionalization community-based services (a services ideology), only defines the problems of the target group as a lack of services. According to critics, the services ideology fails to address the income, social, and political factors that tend to isolate and stigmatize the vulnerable populations, whether they be elderly, mentally retarded, mentally ill, or inmates of correctional institutions (Estes & Harrington, 1981).

An historical review of deinstitutionalization reveals complex and often conflicting explanations about the precipitating factors, purpose, and effectiveness of the movement. However, unlike continuum of care, about which definitions are diverse, the definitional task around deinstitutionalization is much less problematic. This, however, is not meant to imply that an analysis of deinstitutionalization is simple.

Deinstitutionalization, in a straightforward way, is defined as a purposeful, planned movement of patients or residents out of large-scale institutional facilities. This is viewed by Horejsi as including several overlapping processes: returning to communities, in the broadest sense, those persons who have been properly prepared for appropriate functioning in settings that are "least restrictive" to personal freedom and autonomous decision making; preventing the growth of institutions by cutting down on the numbers of people needing such care and therefore requiring the development of appropriate community-based service networks and informal supports; humanization of the institutional environment so human and civil rights are protected and confinement in the institution is minimized; and educating the general public toward community acceptance of previously institutionalized populations.

The deinstitutionalization movement which gained momentum by the passage of several pieces of federal legislation in the early to mid-1960s seems to have developed from a confluence of social, economic, political, and medical factors. Socially, human and civil rights were a rallying point for constituencies newly included in the governing process by a liberal federal administration. In *Action for Mental Health* (1961), the Joint Commission on Mental Illness and Health, stated that the "incarceration" of psychiatric patients was less than helpful, producing institutionalized behavior and the development of chronic, long-term disability. Furthermore, the same report indicated that such care was custodial in nature and extremely costly to the public sector. With these glaring deficiencies in mind, the Commission recommended a clear concentration of efforts directed toward preventing hospitalization, shorter stays when hospitalization was necessary, and the return of incarcerated patients to the community for care and rehabilitative treatment.

> The objective of modern treatment of persons with major mental illness is to enable the patient to maintain himself in the community in a normal manner. To do so, it is necessary (1) to save the patient from the debilitating effects of institutionalization as much as possible, (2) if the patient requires hospitalization, to return him to home and community life as soon as possible, and (3) thereafter to maintain him in the community as long as possible. Therefore, aftercare and rehabilitation are essential parts of all service to mental patients (Joint Commission on Mental Illness and Health, 1961:XVII).

With the above statement of basic goals, social reform targeted those state mental institutions that were publicly funded as the focal point for substantial change.

The philosophical underpinning of the deinstitutionalization movement as articulated by the Commission is the principle of normalization. This principle, although applied most often to the mentally retarded population, but applicable to a much broader range of human conditions, calls for ". . . making available to all mentally retarded people patterns and conditions of everyday living which are as close as possible to the regular circumstances and ways of life of society" (Nirje, 1976, p. 231). A chief proponent of the principle of normalization, Wolfensberger (1972) defines normalization as ". . . utilization of means which are as culturally normative as possible in order to maintain personal behaviors and characteristics which are as culturally normative as possible" (p. 28).

Although the principle of normalization has demonstrated its potential and usefulness, it is not without its limitations. As noted by Mesibov (1976),

> . . . the principle is not verifiable and is geared to organizational instead of individual need. Furthermore, those aspects of the principle that appear to be testable have not been supported and the practices of using "normal" as a criterion and denying that retarded individuals are indeed different are highly questionable. (p. 30)

A competing argument for the deinstitutionalization movement is that the policy is reliant upon economic and political developments. The mental institutions, and more generally those institutions housing criminals and the mentally retarded, were asylums with little effectiveness and requiring monumental public expenditures. The fiscal pressures were acutely felt because of increased patient populations and court decisions resulting in pressure to upgrade facilities and treatment (Dix, 1976).

Whereas the large state institutions had been almost totally supported by state funds before the passage of Community Mental Health Centers (CMHC) legislation, states could now draw down other funds from the federal government that would cover expenses of care outside the institution. Most notably this included Titles XVIII and IXX of the Social Security Act (Medicare and Medicaid) which provided funds for inpatient treatment, for skilled nursing home care in private, proprietary facilities as well as inpatient psychiatric treatment in general purpose hospitals and outpatient psychiatric care. In addition, The Community Mental Health Centers Act of 1963 and the 1965 Amendments to the Act supported construction and staffing of community-based facilities.[2] Thus, the movement out of institutions was supported by federal dollars for alternatives. This trend in federal support was continued in the 1972 Amendments to the Social Security Act which created the Supplemental Security Income program implemented in 1974.[3] Several evaluations of cost savings have been done (Comptroller General, 1977; Murphy & Datel, 1976; Sheehan & Atkinson, 1974). According to Sheehan and Atkinson, in-

---

[2] Community Mental Health Centers Act of 1963, § 303, 42 U.S.C. § 2681 (1975), and § 2(b), 42 U.S.C. §§ 2688 et seq., (1975).
[3] Social Security Act of 1935, Title XVI, Supplemental Security Income for the Aged, Blind, and Disabled, § 301, 42 U.S.C. §§ 1381, 1382, 1383.

patient care in a state hospital was found to be more costly than having inpatient care available in the community with the state hospital available as a backup service.

From an economic perspective deinstitutionalization is explained by a policy that allows states to shift the burden of caring for the mentally ill, mentally retarded, elderly, and others to the federal government and from public facilities to private nursing homes, foster care, boarding homes, and other arrangements (Estes & Harrington, 1981). In examining this policy, Rose (1979) suggests that it represents how, in a capitalist society, "social deviants" are turned into profit that benefits the state on the one hand and, on the other hand, the competitive sectors of the economy as seen in burgeoning numbers of nursing homes, foster and boarding homes, one room hotels, and so on. Through this ideology, as stated by Estes and Harrington, "programs and funding are shifted, but the underlying value system goes unchallenged: the social order is maintained by providing treatment to individuals through the provision of services—feeding a service economy" (p. 824).

Another important variable in the deinstitutionalization process has been the widespread use of psychotropic drugs, but their use has not gone unchallenged. In one important study, no differences were found between a group of psychiatric patients discharged between 1947 and 1952, before the use of psychotropic drugs, and a similar group discharged between 1967 and 1972 (Bockoven & Solomon, 1975). Once hailed as a panacea, the many dangers of overuse and abuse of psychotropic medication—drug dependence, social dependence, and irreversible neurological damage—are now documented (Scull, 1976).

With an understanding of deinstitutionalization and its precipitating events, it is appropriate to examine several legislative mandates that have served to focus this effort and to assess the impact of deinstitutionalization in the areas of mental health and mental retardation.

As an outgrowth of the report *Action for Mental Health* (Joint Commission on Mental Illness and Health, 1961) and the personal commitment of President Kennedy to better social conditions, the Community Mental Health Centers Act of 1963 (P.L. 88–164) was passed by the Congress. Under this act, federal grants were authorized for the construction of public and nonprofit community mental health centers (CMHC). In 1965 the passage of P.L. 89–105 provided staffing grants to CMHCs and in 1975 the

CMHC legislation was rewritten in Title III of the Health Services and Nurse Training Act (P.L. 94–63). This particular piece of legislation retained the thrust toward deinstitutionalization and encouraged less dependence on federal categorical grant funds. A further move toward community control and responsibility for mental health programs was embodied in this Act as well as the Community Mental Health Systems Act, P.L. 96–398.

For the group of people defined as mentally retarded, the concept of deinstitutionalization follows a similar development as that for the mentally ill. Historically, the mentally retarded and the mentally ill have been viewed, treated, and housed similarly in long-term custodial care institutions. Under P.L. 88–164 discussed above in relation to mental health centers, the needs of the mentally retarded were also addressed; the impetus came from the findings of the President's Panel to combat Mental Retardation of October 1962. Under P.L. 91–517, Developmental Disabilities Services and Facilities Construction Act, later amended in 1975 as P.L. 94–103, and in 1978 as P.L. 95–602, a legal definition was given to the term developmental disability, and new directions were charted for a comprehensive continuum of care in the community for such persons. For the handicapped population in rural areas, the most crucial problems in securing general community-based services were identified as lack of facilities and services; lack of trained personnel; lack of organizational structure for identification, treatment, and referral; and the general lack of understanding and awareness of the needs of disabled persons (Popp, 1974).

The numbers of mentally retarded persons in institutions peaked at 200,000 in 1967 according to Sigelman, Roeder, & Sigelman (1981), and since that time have continually declined. It is estimated that a further reduction in institutionalization by one-third is possible. For the mentally retarded as for the mentally ill the growth of community-based providers of care and services has been in the private, nonprofit sector (54%), and proprietary organizations (38%) (Bruininks, Hauber & Kudla, 1980).

The recent development of Community Support Systems (CSS) programs has been cited as a response to the failures of deinstitutionalization and the community care concept (Rose, 1979). The CSS programs are, in part, a result of the *President's Commission on Mental Health* (1978). That report pointed to the need to encourage programs for the chronically mentally ill that would develop and strengthen the relationships between community support networks and the formal mental health system. As with coordinated care for the elderly, case management has become a primary strategy for maintaining the chronically mentally ill in the community.

Historically, institutional care has meant that people were removed from the familiarity of their surroundings. In the case of rural people there are two dimensions to this issue. First, such institutions as mental hospitals, correctional facilities, and residences for the mentally retarded, have often been located in rural, less populated areas. The specific intent of this locational choice was to remove "deviant" people from the rest of the population; that is, to protect the general population and incarcerate those people thought to be different and perhaps harmful to themselves or others. Rationale also included the restful peace and quiet of the idyllic rural setting to be healing to the disturbed mind. In addition, rural settings afforded inmates of correctional institutions and mental hospitals the opportunity to work the land, contributing primarily to the self-sufficiency of the institution, and secondly, in the moralistic tradition, to the rehabilitation of the inmate.

The second important dimension impacting rural locations was the employment of local residents. Institutions are labor intensive, requiring 24-hour staffing and large numbers of maintenance personnel. While large-scale institutions have provided employment opportunities for local people, the reduction of resident populations has meant a loss of jobs for rural people and a negative impact on the local economy (Moore, 1981). Contrary to the fact that many institutions are located in rural areas, the institutionalization of people from rural areas has meant increased isolation of the institutionalized person. Distances for families to travel have proven extremely burdensome. The elderly person needing nursing home care because a home health agency does not serve the area may be forced to go to a neighboring (or distant) community and relinquish friendships and familiarity so important to general well-being.

The discharge of Sharon S., age 61, from a large, distantly located mental hospital exemplifies the processes involved in deinstitutionalization.

Sharon S. had been institutionalized at age 40, at which time her behavior was destructive to herself and her parents with whom she lived. Her parents are now both deceased, but some cousins still live in Sharon's home town. Sharon needs assistance in following through in taking her medication as well as in meal preparation and self-care.

Under the auspice of a CMHC, a group home is being planned for Sharon's home town. However, local opposition to the group home has been mounted by several powerful individuals in the community who fear what they perceive is a danger to their children. In the meantime, Sharon is being placed in a boarding home where she will have maximum independence with some supervision. The CSS social worker will see Sharon weekly and continue to draw community resources together in her support. This will include the local church, to which Sharon once had some ties, and the local Grange which has assisted with another former mental hospital resident. The CSS worker will also urge Sharon to continue in an outpatient group that meets twice weekly. However, transportation will be a problem unless members of the Grange assist, since the consolidated social service transportation system recently cancelled its service to Sharon's community because the town felt it could no longer make a cash contribution to the system.

Successful deinstitutionalization, alluded to earlier, is premised on the assumption that sufficient community-based service and support resources exist. This assumption is problematic not only in rural but also in urban settings. The review of federal expenditures in rural areas (see Chapter 3) showed a deficiency in the area of human resources and thus provides some evidence of the service deficiencies. In addition, several reports have shown that nursing homes, boarding homes, and one-room hotels are becoming the new "backwards" of the community (Schmidt, Reinhardt, Kane, & Olsen, 1977). The CSS focus is appropriate in stimulating informal supports as well as linkages to formal supports in rural areas.

Rural populations, beset by more disability and fewer resources, will continue to be at a disadvantage under policies of deinstitutionalization unless the establishment and access to community-based services is equally emphasized as a policy alternative. Despite reservations expressed about the continuum of care, it does have relevance for deinstitutionalization as an organizing concept for the design of community-based services. The strategy of case management is likewise helpful to rural populations, both in terms of assuring client access to the delivery system and in stimulating program development for cases in which service gaps exist.

Services Coordination and Integration

Coordination is frequently proposed as a reform strategy for dealing with the problems of the social service delivery system. The history of services coordination can be documented from the development of the early Charity Organization Societies (COS) and "scientific" social work. The COS movement of the latter half of the 19th Century had as its primary concern the prevention of the duplication of cash assistance to needy individuals. This concern, based in the moralistic tradition, viewed duplication as evil in that it eroded the incentive to work and to be self-reliant, and further that it weakened the character of the recipient; weakness was viewed as the result of personal character flaws (Axinn & Levin, 1982). This problem, it was thought, could be solved by organizing charitable giving, and as pointed out by Rein (1970), assigning the distribution of *relief* to the public sector and *charity* to the private sector. With the public sector taking over more and more of the cash benefit responsibility, the concern about duplication subsided. However, concern has recently been expressed about "double-dipping" that is, receiving payment from two or more public social insurance programs, for example, military retirement and receipt of a government pension. This concern in the area of disability coverage has been addressed through the "mega-cap" provision on disability coverage (See Chapter 3, Social Insurance).

A second form of duplication which further stimulated interest in coordination was that of services duplication. In Britain, case examples pointed to clients being inundated by professionals from a number of social agencies. The use of the case conference became popular as a way of protecting the client from what many viewed as agency abuse. In the U.S. the term "multiproblem family" became the label given to families having contacts with many agencies. Contrary to the British view in which the duplication problem was viewed as belonging to the service organizations, the U.S. view focused the duplication problem on the clients, that is, multiple agency contacts meant multiple family problems (Rein, 1970).

With the rediscovery of poverty in America in the 1960s came the observation that services were being underused. This contributed to a heightened sensitivity of service providers to protect clients, afford appropriate outreach and access services, and decentralize the service network. In this way concern about duplication and overuse of services shifted to concerns about inaccessibility and underutilization (Rein, 1970). Among the strategies to address these concerns has been that of coordination and a variety of mechanisms by which to achieve a coordinated effort; namely, case conference, case sorting, coordinating councils, multipurpose centers, and most recently coordinated care and case management strategies.

Characteristic of the advanced industrial society, the interdependence of organizations as an outgrowth of the complexity of the problem-solving process has influenced the current development of coordination strategies. The need for comprehensive solutions to problems of unemployment, health status, and the environmental concerns of air and water pollution, land-use planning, and energy self-sufficiency has further stimulated the interest in comprehensive, coordinated planning and interaction.

Another potent force for coordination has been the general reluctance of policy decision makers to establish new organizations to solve complex problems. Rather, the trend has been toward funding of planning and coordinating efforts based in existing agency and organizational structures. Excellent examples of this recently prevailing philosophy are seen in the development of Health Systems Agencies (P.L. 93–641), Developmental Disabilities Councils, and the planning and coordination of alcoholism treatment efforts.

Coordination as a concept is not easily defined, nor is there unanimity about what constitutes a coordinated activity. On the one hand, the literature on this topic points to coordination as a strategy which may occur in the planning process as two or more service organizations mutually plan and make decisions. On the other hand, it may occur in the actual delivery of services wherein the activities of several organizations are integrated in their impact on client systems (Davidson, 1976). This latter type of coordination refers to the operating functions of an organization and is best exemplified in previous discussions by the case management strategy.

According to Aiken, Dewar, DiTomaso, Hage, & Zeitz (1975) ". . . the overriding requirement for adequate service delivery is coordination, an idea that is overworked, underachieved, and seldom defined" (p. 6). However, Aiken and colleagues proceed to define coordination as a process that targets on programs and services, resources, clients, and information, as service system elements in such a way ". . . that comprehensiveness of, compatibility among, and cooperation among the elements are maximized" (p. 9). A further look at this definition suggests that coordination involves the negotiation of combinations and relationships of different services across agency and program boundaries. At a level of greater complexity this involves identifying common goals and objectives among organizations, and devising services mixes or packages designed to achieve the commonly held goals with varying degrees of sacrifice in organization autonomy. Under a viable coordination effort, the intended benefit is accessibility and maximum benefit for the client system and cost-effective output for the agency (Jones, 1975).

Coordination as a form of interorganizational relationship serves to redistribute the decision-making power among a group of organizations. Applicable to this discussion is horizontal coordination occurring among a number of organizations in a community or at a particular level of government. Likewise, vertical coordination occurs to a greater or lesser extent among the levels of federal, state, regional, and local government.

Coordination occurs as a matter of degree among social service organizations. As discussed in the form of a typology with most applicability to coordination as a planning function, Davidson (1976) has suggested the following: (1) communication, whereby two or more organizations are talking and sharing ideas and information; (2) cooperation, which involves working jointly on a project of limited scope with informality and vagueness as primary characteristics; (3) confederation, in which agreements and tasks become more formalized but formal sanctions for non-participation do not exist; (4) federation, in which the participating organizations relinquish some autonomy to the structure and define in relatively precise terms the goals, functions, and tasks; and (5) merger, in which individual organizational identities are relinquished and a new formal organization is established. According to Davidson it is in the area of confederation that the majority of activities viewed as coordination take place.

Coordination in the function of direct service delivery can be viewed, as suggested by Tucker (1980) as "different types of cooperative interactions" (p. 17) to include the following: (1) loaning of staff; (2) collocation; (3) joint delivery; (4) combined delivery; (5) outstationing; and (6) consultation. Cooperative activities most appropriate to rural areas are discussed later in this chapter.

The concept of coordination is clearly stated in the Older Americans Act (OAA) of 1965 as amended. Title III of the OAA has as its purpose to "encourage and assist State and local agencies to concentrate resources in order to develop greater capacity and foster the development of comprehensive and coordinated service systems to serve older persons. . . ." [Older Americans Act of 1965, § 101 42 U.S.C. § 3001. (1978)]. Furthermore, a comprehensive and coordinated system is one in which all necessary social services are provided in a way that will:

1. facilitate accessibility to, and utilization of, all social services provided within the geographical area served by such system by any public or private agency or organization;
2. develop and make most efficient use of social services in meeting the needs of older persons; and
3. use available resources efficiently and with a minimum of duplication.

The Channeling Demonstration Program funded recently (1980) by the Department of Health and Human Services is viewed as an effort in the coordination and management of a comprehensive system of long-term services primarily to the elderly but to include other age groups as well. As outlined by DHHS, the channeling model includes client services but also involves an "altered set of relationships among health, mental health and social services agencies" (DHEW, 1980) as they assist the client to access a broad range of services. This activity includes the following components: case finding and screening, comprehensive needs assessment, case management, and services audit and program review.

As a policy theme in either services for the aging, children and youth, or the mentally retarded, coordination is more likely to occur under some conditions than others. Of utmost importance is the legitimacy given the coordination effort by funding sources. In other words, when funding from the state is dependent on showing the extent of coordination efforts, either in planning or direct service, coordination will more likely occur. Another variable, when a primary coordinator or lead agency is designated, is the influence on funds and community power structures which the coordinator possesses and the level of skill and expertise focused in coalescing organizations around common goals, need assessment, and fostering ongoing communication. Finally, the organizations involved in coordination must view the effort as a legitimate way in which to foster change in the delivery system and must, at the same time, view the process as one which will not unacceptably undermine their own autonomy or objectives.

It is well recognized among social work practitioners that higher degrees of specialization and agency isolation occur in urban areas as compared to rural settings. Specialization increases the importance of coordination. Under the rural generalist—practitioner, coordination is more easily accomplished around client-centered issues. However, this frequently means that the generalist simply performs more functions, not that she/he serves only as a case manager. However, the use of a social systems framework for service delivery which includes greater recognition of informal supports and nontraditional service providers is highly supportive of coordination efforts in small, rural communities.

One frequently sees in the literature the reference to informality in rural areas characterized by face-to-face interaction. If this is in fact true, coordination, according to the Davidson (1976) typology, would occur more frequently as communication and cooperation. Of the types of cooperative activity suggested by Tucker (1980), collocation, outstationing, and consultation are strategies of particular value in rural settings. Using Tucker's definitions (p. 17), the following serve as examples of cooperative activity in the rural setting:

Collocation occurs as service providers from differing agencies locate jointly and provide services from a location that is not a facility of any of the involved agencies. This occurs, for example, when the state department of human services, the office of employment security, the rural pediatric health service, and the family planning agency, all use space provided in the town hall of a small community. Although not imperative to service operations, connections among these agencies will increase service effectiveness by addressing delivery issues of inaccessibility and fragmentation.

Outstationing is a cooperative activity in which one agency places its direct service staff in the facility of another agency yet provides its own services. This is particularly useful when one agency has a facility and is well-established in a community but unable to address fully the needs of its target population. An example of this is the outstationing of home energy assistance staff in a local health clinic or the local office of the Cooperative Extension Service (CES). As a strategy, outstationing addresses issues of inaccessibility and discontinuity in service provision.

With the known isolation experienced by many social workers in rural areas, consultation provides professional support and knowledge building as a cooperative venture between two agencies. This occurs, for example, as a community education specialist from a regionally based family planning agency consults with an outstationed youth services social worker who is attempting to initiate a program of sex education in the local consolidated school district.

One of the major difficulties confronting rural service providers in their coordination efforts is at the planning level. Lacking expertise in planning and development functions holds the potential of increased tension in meeting federal and state planning requirements before funds are allocated. Another potential difficulty resides in seeking planning and development consultation from urban-based practitioners whose understanding of the rural community is limited to generalizations gleaned from the urban experience.

Summary

Through an examination of the policy themes of continuum of care, formal/informal networks, deinstitutionalization, and services coordination, the reader has been introduced to major policy responses impacting the organization and delivery of services and benefits. The themes, although contemporary in their application, have historical antecedents which have been described in this chapter in order to develop a more specific understanding of the context from which social policy is derived.

It has been shown that each theme, while viewed as a discrete concept, is, in application, interdependent with other themes. For example, the continuum of care provides a unifying function for the service system which is advantageous when service planners and social work practitioners are implementing a deinstitutionalization program in a particular community.

Finally, this chapter has attempted to bring into focus the

potential advantages and disadvantages of each theme relative to the rural setting. The characteristics of rural environments discussed in Chapters 1 and 3 draw us to conclude that urban based models of the policy themes will prove problematic to implementation in rural communities. The smallness of size, the sparsity of locally based traditional services, and the relatively lower economic status of rural residents, on the one hand, serve as opportunities to be seized, while on the other hand they increase liabilities under the present thrust toward services consolidation, retrenchment, and threatened and actual cutbacks in income transfer programs. In Chapter 5 policy themes with a greater impact on fiscal and management issues of social policy will be discussed.

References

Aiken, Michael, Dewar, Robert, Di Tomaso, Nancy, Hage, Jerald, and Zeitz, Gerald. *Coordinating Human Services*. San Francisco: Jossey-Bass, 1975.

Axinn, June and Levin, Herman. *Social Welfare—A History of the American Response to Need*. New York: Harper and Row, 1982.

Benedict, Robert C., "AOA's Approach to Long Term Care." Unpublished paper, Administration on Aging, Department of Health and Human Services, 1980.

Benedict, Robert C. "Emerging Trends in Social Policy for Older People." Paper presented at the 1977 National Round Table Conference, American Public Welfare Association, Washington, D.C., Dec. 9, 1977.

Benedict, Robert C. "Trends in the Development of Services for the Aging Under the Older American's Act" in Herzog, Barbara Rieman (Ed.), *Aging and Income*. New York: Human Sciences Press, 1978, 280–306.

Benedict, Robert C. and Hoke, Richard R. "Developing Community Services for the Aging: A State Agency Perspective" in Maddox, George L. and Karasik, Robert R. (Eds.), *Planning Services for Older People*. Proceedings of a workshop held at Duke University, 1975. North Carolina: Center for the Study of Aging and Human Development, 1976, 124–144.

Bockoven, J.S. and Solomon, H.C. "Comparison of Two Five-Year Follow-Up Studies: 1947–1952 and 1967–1972," *American Journal of Psychiatry*, 1975, 132(8):796–801.

Brody, Elaine M. "Women's Changing Roles, The Aging Family and Long-Term Care of Older People," *National Journal*, 1979, 11(43):1828–1833.

Brody, Stanley J. "The Thirty-To-One-Paradox: Health Needs of the Aged and Medical Solutions," *National Journal*, 1979, 11(44):1869–1873.

Bruininks, Robert H., Hauber, Florence A., and Kudla, Mary J. "National Survey of Community Residential Facilities: A Profile of Facilities and Residents in 1977," *American Journal of Mental Deficiency*, 1980, 84(5):470–478.

Burns, Eveline M. *Social Security and Public Policy*. New York: McGraw Hill Book Co., 1956.

Butler, Robert N., Gertman, Jessie S., Oberlander, Dewayne L., and Schindler, Lydia. "Self-Care, Self-Help, and the Elderly," *International Journal on Aging and Human Development*, 1979–80, 10(1):95–117.

Cantor, Marjorie H. "Neighbors and Friends: An Overlooked Resource in the Informal Support System." Paper presented at the 30th Annual Meeting of the Gerontological Society of America, San Francisco, Calif., 1977.

Clarke, Gary J. "In Defense of Deinstitutionalization," *Milbank Memorial Fund Quarterly/Health and Society*, 1979, 57(4):461–479.

Collins, Alice and Pancoast, Diane. *Natural Helping Networks*. Washington, D.C.: National Association of Social Workers, 1976.

Comptroller General of the United States. *Returning the Mentally Disabled to the Community: Government Needs to Do More*. Washington, D.C.: U.S. Government Accounting Office, 1977.

Council on Social Work Education. *Curriculum Policy Statement*. New York: Council on Social Work Education, 1982.

Davidson, Stephen M. "Planning and Coordination of Social Services in Multiorganizational Contexts," *Social Service Review*, 1976, 50(1):117–137.

Department of Health, Education and Welfare, Division of Contract and Grant Operations, Request for Proposal, "National Long-Term Care Channeling Demonstration," April 25, 1980.

Dix, George E. "The Alabama Right to Treatment Case," *Community Mental Health Journal*, 1976, 12(2):161–167.

Ecosometrics, Inc. "Discussion paper on the Development of an Analytic Framework for the Identification of Cross-Cutting and Program-Specific Issues Which Relate to the OHDS Mission." (Contract #105-78-7406), 1978.

Estes, Carroll L. *The Aging Enterprise*. San Francisco: Jossey-Bass, 1979.

Estes, Carroll L. and Harrington, Charlene A. "Fiscal Crisis, Deinstitutionalization, and the Elderly," *American Behavioral Scientist*, 1981, 24(6):811–826.

Froland, Charles, Pancoast, Diane L., Chapman, Nancy J., and Kimboko, Priscilla J. "Professional Partnerships with Informal Helpers: Emerging Forms." Paper presented to the Annual Convention of the American Psychological Association, New York, N.Y., Sept. 4, 1979.

Froland, Charles. "Formal and Informal Care: Discontinuities in a Continuum," *Social Service Review*, 1980, 54(4):572–587.

Gilbert, Neil and Specht, Harry. *Dimensions of Social Welfare Policy*. Englewood Cliffs, N.J.: Prentice-Hall, 1974.

Golant, Stephen M. and McCaslin, Rosemary. "A Functional Classification of Services for Older People," *Journal of Gerontological Social Work*, 1979, 1(2):1–31.

Green, Lawrence W., Werlin, Stanley, H., Schauffler, Helen H., and Avery, Charles H. "Research and Demonstration Issues in Self-Care: Measuring the Decline of Medicocentrism," *Health Education Monographs*, 1977, 5(2):161–189.

Griffiths, Kenneth A. "Social Work Education: Issues and Approaches as Related to Rapid Growth in Rural Areas" in Griffiths, K.A. (Ed.), *Rapid Growth Development in Rural Areas: Implications for Social Work*. Salt Lake City, Utah: Graduate School of Social Work, University of Utah, 1981, 29–38.

Hess, Beth B. "Self-Help Among the Aged," *Social Policy*, 1976, 7(3):55–62.

Horejsi, Charles R. "Rural Community-Based Services for Persons Who are Mentally Retarded," in Green, Ronald K. and Webster, Stephen A. (Eds.), *Social Work in Rural Areas: Preparation and Practice*. Knoxville, Tn.: University of Tennessee, School of Social Work, 1978, 368–380.

Johnson, Louise. "Human Service Delivery Patterns in Nonmetropolitan Communities," in Johnson, Wayne (Ed.), *Rural Human Services*. Itasca, Ill.: Peacock Publishers, 1980, 65–74.

Joint Commission on Mental Illness and Health, 1961. *Action for Mental Health*. New York: Basic Books, 1961.

Jones, Terry. "Some Thoughts on Coordination of Services," *Social Work*, 1975, 20(5):375–378.

Kammerman, Sheila. "Public Policy for the Elderly: The Dilemmas in a Family Policy Perspective" in *Strengthening Informal Supports for the Aging*. New York: Community Service Society of New York, 1981, 12–18.

Katz, A.H. and Bender, E.I. *The Strength in Us: Self-Help Groups in the Modern World*. New York: New Viewpoints, Franklin Watts, 1976.

Krishef, Curtin H. and Yoelin, Michael L. "Differential Use of Informal and Formal Helping Networks Among Rural Elderly Black and White Floridians," *Journal of Gerontological Social Work*, 1981, 3(3):45–59.

Martinez, Arabella. "Relating Human Services to a Continuum of Need," *The Social Welfare Forum, 1979*. The National Conference on Social Welfare. New York: Columbia University Press, 1980, 39–44.

McLeod, Katherine. "A Feminist Perspective on Energy Development" in Griffiths, K.A. (Ed.), *Rapid Growth Development in Rural Areas: Implications for Social Work*. Salt Lake City, Utah: Graduate School of Social Work, University of Utah, 1981, 11–19.

Mesibov, Gary B. "Alternatives to the Principle of Normalization," *Mental Retardation*, 1976, 14(5):30–32.

Miller, Dorothy L., Hoffman, Fred, and Turner, Denis. "A Perspective on the Indian Child Welfare Act," *Social Casework*, 1980, 61(8):468–475.

Moore, Gary A. "Mental Health Deinstitutionalization and the Regional Economy: A Model and Case Study," *Social Science and Medicine*, 1981, 15c:175–189.

Murphy, Jane G. and Datel, William E. "A Cost Benefit Analysis of Community versus Institutional Living," *Health and Community Psychiatry*, 1976, 25(March):165–170.

National Commission on Neighborhoods. *People, Building Neighborhoods*. Final Report to the President and the Congress of the United States. Washington, D.C.: United States Government Printing Office, 1979.

Nirje, Bengt. "The Normalization Principle and Its Human Management Implications," in Kugel, Robert B. and Shearer, Ann W. (Eds.). *Changing Patterns in Residential Services for the Mentally Retarded*. Washington, D.C.: President's Committee on Mental Retardation, 1976, 231–240.

Popp, Dennis. "Service Delivery in Rural Areas" in Charington, Carolyn and Dybwad, Gunnar (eds.), *New Neighbors: The Retarded Citizen in Quest of a Home*. Washington, D.C.: President's Committee on Mental Retardation, 1974, 129–130.

President's Commission on Mental Health, Report to the President. Washington, D.C.: United States Government Printing Office, 1978.

President's Panel to Combat Mental Retardation. *A Proposed Program for National Action to Combat Mental Retardation*, Washington, D.C.: U.S. Government Printing Office, 1962.

Rein, Martin. *Social Policy: Issues of Choice and Change*. New York: Random House, 1970.

Rose, Stephen M. "Deciphering Deinstitutionalization: Complexities in Policy and Program Analysis," *Milbank Memorial Fund Quarterly/ Health and Society*, 1979, 57(4):429–460.

Scull, A.T. "Decarceration of the Mentally Ill: A Critical View," *Politics and Society*, 1976, 6(2):173–212.

Schmidt, Leonard J., Reinhardt, Adina M., Kane, Robert L., and Olsen, Donna. "The Mentally Ill in Nursing Homes," *Archives of General Psychiatry*, 1977, 34(6):687–691.

Shanas, Ethel. "The Family as a Social Support System in Old Age," *The Gerontologist*, 1979, 19(2):169–174.

Sheehan, D.N. and Atkinson, J. "Comparative Costs of State Hospitals and Community Based In-Patient Care in Texas," *Hospital and Community Psychiatry*, 1974, 25(4):242–244.

Sigelman, Lee, Roeder, Phillip W., and Sigelman, Carol K. "Social Service Innovation in the American States: Deinstitutionalization of the Mentally Retarded," *Social Science Quarterly*, 1981, 62(3):503–515.

Tucker, David J. "Coordination and Citizen Participation," *Social Service Review*, 1980, 54(1):13–30.

Unger, Steven (Ed.). *The Destruction of American Indian Families*. New York: Association of American Indian Affairs, 1977.

Watkins, Dennis A. and Watkins, Julia M. *Toward a Continuum of Care Policy Framework for Decision Making by State Units on Aging and Area Agencies on Aging: Issues and Opportunities in Rural Service Provision*. Final Report submitted to the Administration on Aging, Grant #90-AR-2073/01, July 1981.

Wingspread Report. *Strengthening Families through Informal Support Systems*. Racine, Wis.: The Johnson Foundation, 1978.

Wolfensberger, W. *The Principle of Normalization in Human Services*. Toronto: National Institute of Mental Retardation, 1972.

5 Contemporary Policy Themes: Fiscal Development and Services Management

Introduction

In Chapter 4, four policy themes closely related to the organization and delivery of services were examined. Complementary to the organization and delivery themes are several themes related more specifically to fiscal and management concerns: accountability, public/private partnership, and block grant funding. These themes provide the substance for the present chapter and represent responses in a broader sense to the question raised by Burns (1956) and Gilbert and Specht (1974) about the funding of income and service provisions. As in Chapter 4, discussion of the themes will overlap at some points. However, the themes are viewed separately in order to chart a clearer understanding for the reader.

The themes presented in this chapter are those thought to dominate the present social policy arena and to have implications for rural settings. Each theme will be examined first by placing it in an historical context and second by showing its relevance through social policy legislation and then reviewing the implications for rural areas.

Accountability

The clamor for increased accountability in social services, health care services, and income maintenance programs has intensified over the past decade as the result of an increasing portion of public funding directed toward public social and health care programs, and the trend toward resource scarcity in a period of economic recession. Program efforts once assumed to be good, effective, and socially valuable by a majority of political actors are being tested and questioned from all political persuasions, including the most liberal and the most conservative. Although this section focuses on accountability in the social policy arena, the authors recognize that the nature of the topic permeates most facets of public and private economic activities.

Accountability is a concept that implies answerability for behavior and actions. For the social work practitioner this involves a combination of value-based practice, ethical response to situations, and goal-directed action that ultimately involves self-evaluation as well as assessment of client system goal attainment and agency focus. According to Bjorkman and Altenstetter (1979), "Accountability provides a set of constraints on actions or omissions because someone is held responsible, and thus accountability implies a set of criteria against which comparisons are made and then sanctions (penalties or rewards) are applied" (p. 360). In this sense, accountability goes beyond the concept of responsibility and implies a sense of control over actions taken in carrying out a service intent (goal). Lipsky (1981) suggests that workers are held more accountable by the actions of management that "control," that is, reduce the amount of worker discretion and alternatives in a given situation. Thus, accountability is related directly to the effectiveness of the social worker as a change agent. In addition, accountability raises questions about the effectiveness of programs, that is, to what extent a given program is accomplishing its intent, and the efficiency of programs, that is, is the intent accomplished with the least expenditure of resources?

These general statements can be operationalized by delineating four basic types of accountability having relevance for social policy decisions (Bjorkman & Altenstetter, 1979). Political accountability is that which occurs when elected officials submit their actions to the scrutiny of the electorate. The criteria for measuring political performance are frequently the campaign promises and the subsequent actions taken toward their achievement. For example, the local politician elected on the campaign promise to develop a rural health center and attract a physician to the community would be politically remiss in not acting on that promise. For a number of complex reasons external to the politician—for example federal funding cuts, fewer physicians being trained, or the opposition of a regional medical center—the goal may not be achieved. Nonetheless, the local politician may remain in office because a range of inputs—for example, grant possibilities from the private and the public sector, alternative personnel arrangements to include physicians' assistants and nurse practitioners, and a mobile or satellite clinic from a larger medical facility—was explored.

Bureaucratic accountability is that which social workers experience in answering to their supervisors in large-scale bureaucratic organizations. A rurally based support enforcement unit that fails to collect a specified amount of dollars from absent fathers is ultimately responsible to the state agency, which in turn is accountable to an elected official (in this case a governor) who has espoused a policy of cutting state expeditures for AFDC by retrieving a certain percent of court-ordered support payments. At another level, the federal and state bureaucracies are accountable to the Congress through the oversight function of the General Accounting Office (GAO). The GAO oversees the implementation of Congressional action in an investigatory way with published reports of its findings. However, a shortcoming of the process is that the GAO functions at the request of Congressional committees and has no power to enforce the law.

A third type of accountability, professional accountability, is that provided by the peer review process in which professionals with similar training and expertise judge the performance of their colleagues. In social work practice professional accountability is facilitated by the supervisory process, peer interaction, licensure and certification mechanisms, and professional grievance, and inquiry processes. Although not impossible to implement, the relative isolation of many social workers in rural areas presents constraints to professional peer review not found in urban areas. The function of self-evaluation takes on additional importance as an accountability measure to ensure effectiveness of service outcome provided by the rurally based social worker.

According to Bjorkman and Altenstetter, economic accountability refers to the relationship between service consumers and the products of the professional providers. In the market economy this relates to supply and demand. However, social programs do not respond in supply and demand terms which characterize much of the economy. As noted by Somers and Somers (1977) and Ahearn (1979), contrary to usual economic market principles, supply creates demand in the health care sector as seen in the evidence that physicians create the demand for their services and furthermore, that demand has little to do with the location of physicians. Although rural areas have great demand for physician services, this has not dramatically increased the overall supply. A further difficulty in applying economic supply and demand analysis to the social and health care services is the point noted earlier wherein service availability (supply) often defines need (demand) (Golant & McCaslin, 1979). Furthermore, the basis of exchange frequently lacks reciprocity and is viewed as unilateral (Boulding, 1967). An additional caution is in order since the service consumer is not always clearly defined. Is the consumer the client or direct recipient of services or a more generally identifiable group of taxpayers? The relationship of one consumer group or another (demand) to the service (supply) has the potential to determine the parameters of social policy in very different ways. Nevertheless, consumer involvement or citizen participation as it is frequently referenced, is an accountability mechanism important in both services and income strategies and warrants further discussion at a later point in this section.

Accountability in the social policy arena has particular relevance and at the same time is particularly problematic when applied to the social services (Rossi, 1978). The 1962 Amendments to the Social Security Act emphasized services intervention by trained professionals directed toward the rehabilitation of public assistance recipients. This emphasis was supported by vast, open-ended federal expenditures. Moving individuals off the public assistance (welfare) roles into economically productive roles was the criterion of success and made rehabilitative service efforts rather easily measurable (Hoshino, 1973). However, throughout the 1960s, despite vast expenditures of service dollars (vast in comparison to all previous efforts), the numbers of people receiving public assistance increased dramatically. This left both the welfare (income) and the service systems open to the criticism of large public expenditures with questionable impact as measured by the single criterion of reduced welfare participation (Hoshino, 1973).

More conclusive evidence suggests that the expansion of public assistance during the 1960s was in part the result of more inclusive eligibility criteria, the political and economic struggles represented by the Civil Rights Movement, the Anti-Poverty Programs, and National Welfare Rights Organization, high levels of unemployment, population increases, and basic inadequacies of the Social Security system. Nevertheless, the services strategy of the 1960s was viewed by the Congress as a failure in social policy and replaced in 1967 with what Hoshino described as a work-and-training strategy, with the development of the Work Incentive Program (WIN). Subsequent work programs such as Comprehensive Employment and Training Act of 1974 (CETA) served to intensify the accountability issue around rehabilitation for employment as a measurable criterion for program success.

In 1973 the action of Congress which imposed a ceiling of $2.5 billion on the open-ended federal expenditures for social services and greater restrictions on the target group served to further highlight the "crisis of accountability" (Newman & Turem, 1974). Eventually, this action resulted in the 1974 passage of Title XX of the Social Security Act, the social services block grant to the states. Through the Title XX legislation, accountability was thought to be enhanced with a fixed level of funds going to the states which in turn had increased responsibility for defining priorities and services to meet needs. Second, the mandate for a goal-oriented planning and reporting process open to citizen participation shifted the accountability of programs from the federal government to the various public interest groups participating in the development of service plans (McKay & Baxter, 1980). This basic process continues under the present federal policies but with a 25 percent reduction in funding and a debatable commitment to public input in the planning process.

Traditionally speaking, social work has been accountable as a profession in terms of input or process evaluation. This form of accountability documents such process considerations as numbers of clients served, numbers of interviews (or contact hours) held, and the result of the intervention as measured against some rather vague set of criteria. At the agency level, records document the size of waiting lists, client characteristics, and types of activities of the agency. This type of accountability further assumes that with those workers with the best credentials, the outcome of social work intervention, however measured, is effective and thus a justifiable expenditure of funds.

Two examples of mandated accountability are appropriate to mention as having substantial influence on social work practice. The establishment of Professional Standards Review Organizations (PSROs) in the health care delivery arena was legislatively provided for in the Social Security Amendments of 1972 (P.L. 92–603). This accountability mechanism includes the development of utilization review plans to monitor the reasons for hospital admission and continued hospitalization as well as to develop discharge plans. According to Constable and Black (1980), PSRO legislation as well as such legislation as the Education of all Handicapped Children Act (P.L. 94–142), have stimulated increased professional accountability directed toward assessing specified and agreed upon outcomes with the client as an active, collaborating participant. As pointed out by Constable and Black, these policy mandates have broad implications for social work practice: (1) specific client participation is mandated as an entitlement; (2) explicit outcomes are specified and contracts for their achievement negotiated; (3) recording and documentation skills are more important; and (4) a full evaluation of the degree to which outcomes are achieved is expected.

The present thrust toward accountability focuses not only on inputs at the level of the individual worker but has an ever increasing concern about program outcome and the delivery system (Rossi, 1978). Outcome is the end product measured against program goals and objectives. Adding complexity to the desirability of using outcome measures is the need for cost-effectiveness and the cost-benefit analysis of one program as compared to alternative programs. The questions are formidable and complex, particularly when one recognizes that the goals and objectives set forth in most legislation or program policies lack detail and specificity and in some instances are clearly contradictory of one another.

Mechanisms of Accountability

The mechanisms for measuring and evaluating outcome and documenting program and worker accountability are many. Since the state of the art is relatively underdeveloped, there are many questions for which answers are insufficiently developed. However, to carry out the purpose of examining policy themes two mechanisms are thought appropriate for discussion at this point: citizen participation and program evaluation as exemplified by cost analysis procedures.

Citizen Participation

Within the democratic framework of United States history, citizen participation, from the early town meetings to presentday Congressional hearings, has been a time-honored tradition. As coordination is a way of changing power relationships among organizations, citizen participation is viewed as a mechanism for redistributing power between providers and consumers of social and health care services. Furthermore, it is the process by which consumers (clients) can impact administrative decisions about services and programs that will ultimately affect their well-being. The former view is that of citizen participation as an avenue toward social reform, and the latter as a way of overcoming ". . . the problematic nature of overcentralized decision making" (Gulati, 1982, p. 73).

Citizen participation in social policy decisions as a social reform movement was given strong support in the 1960s with the enactment of the antipoverty programs and has subsequently continued in one form or another in many pieces of social legislation. Milbrath (1981) points out that citizen participation is a fairly new "social invention" which is increasingly prominent in policy making, having been mandated by Congressional action and executive orders.

Conceptually, citizen participation has been arrayed on a continuum from that of tokenism—going though a ritualistic process—to that having substantial power or influence over the outcome (Arnstein, 1969). The latter involves a real transfer of power to citizens, a process through which programs and institutions become responsive to the views and opinions and ultimately the needs of a previously unempowered group. The former—tokenism—represents, in the words of Arnstein, "manipulation, therapy, informing, consultation, and placation, all processes through which citizens participate but have no power to insure an impact" (p. 217).

The forms of citizen participation are many and varied. Several, however, are more commonly recognized in current social legislation and included here for discussion purposes. Citizen committees and citizen representatives on agency boards constitute well-known and much used forms of participation. In such instances citizens are usually appointed by public officials and hence subject to manipulation and cooptation. Unless specified in legislation or regulations promulgated by a federal agency, citizens are seldom selected from powerless, vulnerable groups of people. Rather, as a political constituency, appointed citizens represent the same class and political interests as do the politicians. The administrators of social agencies frequently work with citizens as board members. As participants in the policy making process, these citizens are, on the one hand, potentially subject to the same manipulation as a politically appointed citizen advisory committee. On the other hand, they may be full participants in the policy making process, thereby lending legitimacy and support for decisions that impact a larger agency or program constituency group. The following example shows both the pitfalls and the power of citizen participation.

Alarmed over the high percentage of youth not completing high school, high rates of teenage pregnancy, and substantial use of alcohol and drugs, the town manager of one small community appointed a citizens advisory committee to examine the problem and its causes and to recommend action to curb the problem. This blue-ribbon committee of 14 people represented a broad cross-section of the community. However, it was dominated by middle-aged white males and a vociferously vocal Chief of Police. The solutions proposed by the committee to the town council were for tougher law enforcement of illegal possession of alcohol by a minor and truancy from school. This would be accomplished by hiring a part-time police officer and the purchase of an additional police cruiser.

At a public hearing on the proposal, the town council heard a very different analysis of the problem and possible solutions. Several teenagers pointed to the isolation they felt from the rest of the community and the lack of any recreational or job opportunities for them in the community. Several parents of teenagers suggested that tough law enforcement was not the answer and that any resources available ought to be directed toward developing a teen recreation center. After vigorous lobbying by parents during and after the public hearing, the police chief resigned from the committee and a new proposal was developed. As a result, a purchase-of-service contract was negotiated with a YMCA in a neighboring, larger community for personnel to develop and staff a teen center. Through the foresight of one town resident, low-cost space was made available in a vacant main street building. Four months after the center was opened, three other service agencies had inquired about space in the building for collocation of their services.

Another common form of citizen participation is through the public hearing process. This participation can be in the form of oral or written presentations, but is often viewed as a process to fulfill a regulatory requirement after the major policy decisions have been reached (Checkoway, 1981; Milbrath, 1981). This suggests that the public hearing as a mechanism for citizen participation is seldom influential in policy decision making. Obstacles to full citizen involvement include the scheduling of hearings with short public notice at hours inconvenient to the public, the use of technical language requiring great effort for the nonspecialist to understand, and the domination of hearings by people with a large economic stake in the decisions (Checkoway, 1981). Nevertheless, public hearings have been a prominent feature of the New Federalism as a way of increasing citizen action at the local level. At this writing, there seems to be a diminished interest at the federal level in promoting public hearings as a part of block grant funding. What importance and level of effort states will assign to the hearing process as a way of fostering citizen participation as they move into the second and subsequent years of block grant funding is yet unknown.

Two remaining avenues for citizen input are important from a policy perspective and mentioned briefly here: the citizen survey and the community development corporation. The citizen survey has most commonly been referred to as a needs assessment technique designed to collect data on citizens' perceptions of service and community issues and possible solutions. One of the primary assets of the citizen survey is that through the sampling process and survey technique (telephone, face-to-face, mail, or a combination of these), a representative view is generated. Like other forms of citizen participation, however, there is no guarantee that agency and public officials will utilize the data in formulating policy decisions as the following demonstrates.

In a small coastal community known for its beauty as a vacation and resort town, a survey of community needs and preferences was conducted. The survey was mailed to all persons on the voter registration list. Seventy-six percent of the questionnaires were completed and returned to the town office. The questionnaire covered a wide range of topics and the results showed clearly that those people responding wanted to follow a "no growth" policy, in spite of a depressed economy.

Six months later, an out-of-state developer proposed to the town manager and town council that a part of the town's harborside be developed into condominiums. Through debate and public hearings, those townspeople with the greatest economic stake in such a development prevailed. The town now boasts 25 partly completed condominium units, a bankrupt developer, and an obstructed view of the harbor.

The community development corporation is a mechanism wherein control is vested in the citizens of the community and the corporation provides needed services to the community. Such corporations are generally engaged in community revitalization and economic activity. Their source of investment funding is derived from a network of community development banks. Profits generated in economic activities are used to finance needed community services. This type of participation has had most impact in urban areas with high concentrations of minority populations. Its ultimate goal is to foster minority participation in the economic sector.

The use of citizen participation as a mechanism fostering accountability in the service arena is valuable first in the setting of social policy, particularly at the local level, and second in performing an oversight function as policy mandates are implemented. Within an open system which is continually interacting with its environment, citizen participation performs the function of accountability as discussed by Gruber (1974), that is, the involvement of those to whom the system, be it agency, program, or larger organization, is accountable (Glisson, 1975). It is shortsighted, however, to suggest that democratic principles embodied in the participatory process totally justify utilization of any methods reviewed. The real value of their use is in the impact they have, something about which we have little information upon which to base substantive conclusions (Buck & Stone, 1981; Gulati, 1982).

Some of the basic constraints to citizen participation achieving its goals have been identified. It has been pointed out that those who participate seldom represent a constituency to which they are accountable. Furthermore, it is difficult to engage participants and to sustain their interest over a long enough period of time to develop knowledge and insights helpful in the policy making process (Buck & Stone, 1981; Checkoway, 1981). In spite of the obvious defects of citizen participation, it remains a viable mechanism for counteracting the bureaucratic, centralized decision-making process characteristic of the advanced industrial society.

Cost Analysis

As contrasted with citizen participation, cost analysis is an accountability mechanism less dependent on the process of involvement and more dependent on controlling the process—its input, throughput, and output—so that predictability is established and the results of social programs can be related to cost functions (Turem, 1974).

Cost-benefit and cost-effectiveness analysis are two techniques used to examine the potential benefits of alternative policies. Cost-benefit analysis has been used extensively by the government in weighing the benefits of a program relative to its costs, the conclusion being that unless the benefits outweigh the costs, the program cannot be justified and an alternative should be considered. The basic assumption of cost-benefit analysis is that the benefits can be assigned a monetary value (an economic indicator) that can then be compared with the costs. Not only is it difficult to assign a monetary value to policy results that are often intangible, it is equally difficult to determine which alternative is best because of the value and cultural dimensions to such decisions. For example, as pointed out by Sorkin (1975), "No amount of analysis is going to tell us whether the nation benefits more from sending a slum child to school, providing medical care to an old man or enabling a disabled housewife to resume her normal activities" (p. 103).

Cost-effectiveness analysis, evolving from the research activities in the area of national defense, is a technique like cost-benefit analysis used ". . . for assessing and comparing the costs and effectiveness of alternative systems or programs; it is designed to assist decision-makers in identifying a preferred choice or choices" (Doherty & Hicks, 1977, p. 191). Unlike cost-benefit analysis, it does not require reducing effectiveness to a monetary value. In the case of social program accountability this has particular relevance; the program frequently cannot be assigned a market counterpart. In other words, ". . . the effectiveness of an alternative is expressed in terms of its actual physical or psychological outcomes rather than monetary value" (McKay & Baxter, 1980, p. 24). In such cases, the impact of policies and resulting programs can be compared but a monetary value need not be assigned to the impact.

As an analytic technique facilitating the accountability process, it is felt by Doherty and Hicks that cost-effectiveness analysis has taken on meaning which ascribes more emphasis to cost than to effectiveness. From such a perspective, efficiency of effort, doing more with less, and showing how a given program will save money, become the primary criteria of accountability. This leads Doherty and Hicks to conclude that ". . . effectiveness is discussed impressionistically at best, or, at worst ignored" (p. 190).

As one examines the delivery system literature one finds great debate over the cost-effectiveness of community-based versus institutionally delivered services for a variety of target groups—juvenile offenders, the elderly, the mentally ill, and the mentally retarded. With the soaring costs of health care, primarily hospital and nursing home care of which 55 percent is reimbursed by Medicaid and Medicare, recent attention has focused on alternative care settings—in-home care, health clinics, ambulatory care centers, and day care for elderly individuals.

Acknowledging that the motivation behind the thrust toward noninstitutional care arrangements is in large part cost motivated, two economic questions prevail. As stated by Doherty, Segal, & Hicks (1978) the questions are first, "What, if any, would be the saving if people were deinstitutionalized and provided with alternatives such as home care?" and second, "What would be the impact on aggregate demand for care and expenditures of making alternative services more available?" (p. 10). Although one might assume that alternatives are more cost-effective, the research evidence is not so clear and exemplifies the dilemmas of cost analysis.

In one study examining the costs of adult day care and nursing home care the combined costs of day care and the expenses of living at home were found to result in savings of 12–35 percent over the annual costs of nursing home care (Weissert, 1978). The saving is dependent on the number of days (2.5 to 4) that the elderly person was in day care. However, the savings were present only when day care was used as a full substitute for nursing home care.

Weissert's study also reported that in terms of median costs, day care was more costly than was nursing home care ($21.32 and $19.22 per day, respectively). Thus, actual savings resulted from coverage that was 2.5 to 4.0 days per week rather than continuous. Day care costs are higher for several reasons:

1. heavy reliance on highly skilled, expensive personnel and a higher number of administrators than for nursing homes;

2.   costly transportation to and from the day center;
3.   inefficiencies in staff and facility allocation; and
4.   the small numbers of participants (median 28.5 in the
     Weissert study) which could not compete for economies
     of scale found in nursing homes with a median of 75
     residents (Weissert, 1978).

Another research effort by Weissert, Wan, Livieratos, &
Katz (1980) showed no substantial health benefits to a group of
elderly people participating in adult day care. The use of homemaker services by randomly matched groups seemed to result in
more contentment and slightly longer longevity, yet the rate of
hospitalization increased. It is speculated that early detection of
health problems by the homemaker is the reason for this finding,
and furthermore, that the hospitalization rather than the homemaker service effected greater contentment and longevity.

Another study (Quinn, 1979) focused on day care and nursing
home utilization, reporting low rates of nursing home usage by
experimental and control groups. Such findings only add complexity to the issue of alternatives. With more accessible noninstitutional care options, more persons are drawn into the service
system while some people are moving from institutional to the
same noninstitutional services. Thus, the overall costs show little,
if any, decrease. A recent evaluation report on the Triage project
confirmed the increased costs of health care, due primarily to
increased utilization (Hicks, Raisz, Segal, & Doherty, 1981).

Home health care is discussed as a viable alternative to institutionalization. It is felt by many authors (Demkovich, 1979;
Plass, 1978; Widmer, Brill, & Schlosser, 1978) that home care
and particularly home health care is appropriate for many individuals, can reduce the costs of long-term care, and can reduce
the number of persons who would otherwise enter an institution.
In spite of the growing commitment to home health services, a
report by the General Accounting Office (1979) was highly critical
of the "excessive" cost of home health care and the wide variance
found in Medicare reimbursement for such services. Changes in
reimbursement toward tighter fiscal controls were recommended.

The move toward tighter fiscal controls, an enormously complex topic, is exemplified by recent initiatives to change the
Medicare reimbursement for hospital care services which in fiscal
year 1983 are anticipated to exceed $35.5 billion. Rather than
reimbursing for "reasonable costs" it has been proposed that pay-

ment be made at a fixed rate according to the type of diagnosis and established prospectively. The incentive to the provider is that if care is provided for less than the agreed-upon figure, the hospital would share in the savings (Demkovich, 1982). While seemingly simple in concept, issues of quality of care, hospital admissions skewed toward more profitable diagnoses, accounting for inflation, and the inclusion of Commercial and Blue Cross/Blue Shield health insurance plans all raise substantive issues of great importance to social policy.

To summarize, accountability is an increasingly important issue in the provision of public and private social services and public income security programs. Accountability is stressed at all levels of government and raises questions about program alternatives, professional expertise, and the general effectiveness of the results of social policy mandates.

Citizen participation as a mechanism of accountability is perhaps enhanced at the local level at which face-to-face interaction predominates. An example is small communities. One must, however, be cautioned about the representativeness of those who participate. In highly dispersed population areas, travel time may be an excessive barrier to the public hearing and the citizens' committee as forms of participation. In addition, for undereducated and poverty populations, the confidence to participate, apathy engendered by a number of past failures to influence, and the lack of technical expertise raise special barriers to participation. The successful use of citizen survey techniques in rural areas is tied in part, depending on the form of the survey, to phone availability, alternatives to census tract sampling procedures, the factors of respondent motivation, and understanding of the questionnaire.

Social work practice in rural areas in which linkage with the informal network is commonplace may place special constraints on accountability since adequate mechanisms have not been developed by which dollar amounts can be assigned to the support provided by neighbors and friends. Likewise, documentation of the social work process in the usual ways (number of interviews, phone calls, and so on) will not convey an accountability of what actually occurs in practice in rural areas; travel time, development time, and so forth.

Mandates to agencies at the local level to implement a form of cost-analysis as good management practice require little justification. However, it must be recognized that the small scale in rurally located agencies probably means that the level and type of expertise are not readily available to implement sophisticated models. Furthermore, in a time of retrenchment, little if any funds exist for external consultation. These considerations place the rural community and its social agencies in a particularly vulnerable position vis-à-vis the currently espoused accountability mechanisms.

Public/Private Partnership

Recent policy pronouncements at the federal level have espoused the benefits of including the private sector as a resource for human and community betterment. The message comes at a time of greatly diminished public resources for human services with decreases in the federal budget through a series of perceived cost-cutting moves directed at nondefense spending (Clark, 1982). However, to understand the recent thrust toward a public/private partnership in the provision of human services, or more broadly speaking, promoting human and community betterment, one must retrace briefly the earlier development of this movement.

In the history of social welfare, the private sector has stood for the voluntary, nonprofit service provider, the very essence of which has been the American propensity to align oneself with voluntary membership organizations in the spirit of democracy and freedom. According to Levin, (1977), "Voluntary social welfare embodies the right of free people to assemble peaceably to express their will in regard to social problems" (p. 1573). Certain commitments or purposes, albeit often only philosophical, are cited as the reasons supporting the voluntary sector. The following predominates: Individuals organize to promote and/or provide a service related to their interests or values, the Grange being one example. Many persons in the organization volunteer time and expertise without monetary reimbursement in such capacity as boards of directors and volunteer staff personnel. Furthermore, the organization is funded by voluntary contributions of the membership and solicitation of other voluntary contributions from nonmember sources. Without financial or legislative accountability to a general public (through the collection and expenditure of public funds) the organization represents freedom of choice and avenues for innovation, criticism, and reform (O'Connell, 1981).

The history of the voluntary agency through which the majority of social needs were met took a dramatic turn with the advent of the Great Depression. Unable to meet the growing needs precipitated by the social and economic order of industrial depression, the voluntary agencies themselves pressed for public intervention. The Social Security Act of 1935 represented the major commitmént of public monies and acknowledgement of government responsibility for ameliorating the human economic condition. This continues today as voluntary, nonprofit organizations advocate for stronger government support of the arts, humanities, sciences, and social welfare.

Since the Depression critics of public expansion into human services have suggested that it has contributed to the demise of the voluntary organization. To the contrary, O'Connell (1981) states that, "Americans are organizing to influence every conceivable aspect of the human condition" (p. 41). Recent polls have shown increasing numbers of Americans serving in volunteer capacities. Furthermore, and highly encouraging is the trend toward participation of all economic groups. However, voluntarism through some of the traditionally strong community organizations, churches, and hospitals has decreased. Equally troublesome to the voluntary sector is the fact that voluntary contributions are decreasing both as a percent of GNP and of disposable personal income (O'Connell, 1981). Under the Reagan administration a 44-member panel has been formed to explore the potential for and to stimulate partnerships between the public and private sectors. This panel has suggested that corporate and individual (private sector) giving in the next four years be doubled (Kirschten, 1982).

One might begin to think that the voluntary, nonprofit sector exists entirely on its own merit and source of income in American democratic society. However, a policy perspective leads us to a more complex analysis in which a very early history of public support was evidenced for voluntary organizations and continues today through the contracting mechanism. This developing partnership is examined along with a discussion of some contemporary manifestations of public/private partnerships. This will show the development of a private sector to be far more inclusive than the voluntary, nonprofit organization or agency.

Partnerships exist when there is an agreement between two parties. Public services have usually been delivered by a public entity, but not exclusively so. As pointed out by Terrell (1979), "Elected officials enact statutes, provide for their funding, and designate organizations to carry out the services authorized. For the most part, these organizations are public agencies—whether federal, state, or local. Their employees are civil servants—the bureaucracy of today's welfare state" (p. 58). Prior to the growth of the public role in service delivery, the public sector provided assistance, particularly at the state and local level, to private charities as they helped and assisted persons designated as wards of the state, that is, such dependent populations as the blind, destitute, insane, and wards of the court system (Terrell, 1979). Begun early in the 19th Century, this pattern continues today and has shown unparalleled growth during the past 15 years, with public funds now accounting for more than 90 percent of the financing for community social service programs.

The rapid growth of governmental funding in the past 20 years has led to a number of concerns about effective service delivery and how it is best accomplished. The purchase-of-service contract is the cornerstone of the present public/private partnership. This contract results in a partnership in which each party to the contract performs the part for which they are best equipped. The public sector sets forth policies and goals as well as accountability mechanisms and then contracts with a voluntary nonprofit agency to provide the direct service. The following serves as an illustration.

> Under the policies and goals of the Adoption Assistance and Child Welfare Act of 1980 (P.L. 96–272), the public agency in one state has contracted with a regional medical center, department of psychiatry, to provide assessment services of families referred for child abuse or neglect as well as therapeutic social services to selected families living in the surrounding rural communities. Services designed to hold the family together are provided by circuit-riding social workers who spend two days each week in several outlying communities. These social workers also provide consultation to locally based providers around issues related to such preventive services as day care, foster care, and substance abuse treatment.

Most recently, the public support for the delivery of social services through the private sector was stimulated by the enactment in 1967 of Title IV (A) of the Social Security Act and later by Title XX in 1974. In addition, Title I of the Comprehensive Employment and Training Act of 1973 (CETA), General Revenue Sharing of 1972, and Title I of the Housing and Community Development Act of 1974, further allow local governments to contract with private providers for a wide variety of services. Terrell

(1979) reports a substantially high percentage of local governments did use the contract mechanism with community-based nonprofit service providers in the expenditure of human services funds under the latter three programs. With such contractual agreements commonplace it is difficult to equate public services with public administration and implementation. Likewise, it is difficult to locate a private, voluntary agency that receives no governmental funds to support its basic service delivery mission.

Critics who view governmental bureaucracies as unresponsive and ineffective in service delivery also advocate for the pluralism of community-based providers as the most effective way of insuring a responsive, efficient, and innovative system that is open to citizen and wider consumer input. This approach, based on competitive market pressures, has been suggested as a way of reducing governmental expenditures in the purchase of services.

The discussion thus far has focused on the public contract with private, nonprofit providers. Another part of the private sector emerging more strongly today than in the past is the private, for-profit (proprietary) agency or organization. In today's political environment, social policy reflects the capitalist belief in the profit motive as a way of addressing service delivery issues of efficiency and effectiveness. In this environment, for-profit providers are no longer excluded from social policy mandates. In fact, their participation is encouraged, as was evidenced in a request for proposals from the Office of Health and Human Services, Office of Human Development Services (*Federal Register*, Monday, November 16, 1981, 56364-56378).

In the past two decades the for-profit nursing home sector has become a major contractee for governmentally funded long-term care expenditures through Medicaid. Increasingly, proprietary (for-profit) hospitals are capturing a share of the Medicare funds. A basic question raised is: Can the for-profit sector carry out a program for the general social welfare without sacrificing quality for the competitive edge in the market? The full answer to this question is not known (Fottler, Smith, & James, 1981).

An equally important question pertaining to the nonprofit sector, built on the premise of autonomy, is the extent to which the nonprofit agency or organization maintains sufficient autonomy in the face of governmental oversight and accountability to claim its historic role as stimulating participation, innovation, and social action in reform of unacceptable practices? The reality of this question was demonstrated in December 1981, when the

Office of Personnel Management proposed to exclude "activist" organizations from receipt of funds collected through the Combined Federal Campaign, the federal government employees' payroll deduction plan for charitable giving (Kirschten, 1982).

The current emphasis on the private sector also includes, in a more vigorous way than in the past, the private foundation and the corporate sector with its growing interest in what has become known as corporate social responsibility. Historically speaking, a foundation has been a way for private individuals to contribute to the public good. However, aside from the purely altruistic and philanthropic purposes has been the tax advantage to the individual or corporation. Large sums of money placed in the foundation during years of high profits and/or high taxes reduced the tax responsibilities of the individual or the corporation. Foundations may be set up either as a trust or as a corporation with either trustees or a board of directors to oversee the expenditure of funds.

According to figures released by the Foundation Center in 1977 to 1978, the following is a percent of grants awarded by the major foundations by field: education, 23 percent; health, 15 percent; science and technology, 18 percent; welfare, 23 percent; international activities, 7 percent; humanities, 11 percent; religion, 3 percent. For the welfare category the dollars granted in 1977 to 1978 are shown in Table 5.1 (*The Foundation Directory*, 1979).

A newer type of foundation with implications for social policy is the community trust or foundation. The first of this type was the Cleveland Trust established in 1916. At present, there are approximately 295 community foundations across the country. A community foundation is locally organized as an endowment fund with a specific geographical area as its target for expenditure of funds. It allows individuals who do not have the massive wealth needed for establishing a private foundation to contribute funds with some specificity about their expenditure, for example, to the arts, social agencies, and so on. Community foundations generally view their efforts as appropriate for smaller scale, one-time projects or needs. They are not to be viewed as a source of ongoing funds for any organization. However, they may contribute funds to voluntary social agencies to be spent on innovative projects which would not receive public contracts for service.

The third element comprising the private sector is that of the business or corporate community, often referred to as the productive sector. In a capitalist, industrial society the primary initiator of corporate activity is the profit motive. Social work as a profes-

Table 5.1.   Foundation Grants to the Welfare Sector: 1977–1978

Welfare Area	Amount (thousands)	Percent
Youth Agencies	$37,738	16
Community development	34,788	15
Community funds	34,419	15
Child welfare	27,243	12
Aged	19,038	8
Recreation and conservation	18,552	8
Handicapped	17,768	8
Social agencies	17,491	8
Delinquency and crime	11,565	5
Housing and transportation	10,326	4
Race relations	3,426	2
Total	$232,354	101*

Source: The Foundation Directory, 1979, p. xx.
*Percent does not equal 100 due to rounding error.

sion and its advocates for social responsibility very early came in contact with corporate bodies through the works of the settlement houses and the development of trade unions in efforts to mitigate the exploitive tendencies of American business and industry.

At this point in time the tremendous complexity of corporate structures and the increased political power they exert across geographic boundaries bring them into a more central position to address in a collaborative way the critical social problems beleaguering American society. In addition, corporate America has at its disposal vast monetary and human resources and skills that can be directed toward the general welfare. Expectations that business and industry will move beyond self-interest of the profit motive is evidenced in the shift in public opinion that social improvements are not a particular government responsibility but a moral responsibility of those organizations (business and industry) which effect substantial influence on the quality of life and well-being of communities and individuals.

The topic title of this section suggests the importance of partnerships in defining and implementing what has been described as corporate social responsibility. The corporation, according to its critics, must in its own operations reflect the values of the larger society ". . . by promoting safety and honesty; by minimizing or preventing disruptions to society and its environments; and by creating conditions of nondiscrimination" (Brown, 1981, p. 40).

Partnerships between the public sector and the private corporate sector or between corporations and voluntary agencies are becoming increasingly familiar. This is seen in policies directed toward the development of employee assistance programs involving issues of quality of life and provision of social work services, increasingly negotiated as part of the union contract. Corporations are also moving to provide business expertise to community advocacy, planning, and service organizations.

The public sector has been the focus for services in rural America with mandated statewide geographic coverage in order to participate in the federal grants-in-aid programs under the Social Security Act. In many rural communities the public agency (branch office, toll-free number, circuit riding, or outstationed social worker) has been the focus of, and in fact the only point of access to, existing services. Such services as the Cooperative Extension Service and Farmers Home Administration have also existed to serve the rural population. Voluntary, formally organized agencies, with the exception of the church and sometimes a community hospital, have been lacking. Without the industrial base of urban areas, the corporate social sector is difficult to see as a major influence in rural areas. Nevertheless, it does exist in the form of agribusiness, energy-related companies (coal, oil, gas), wood and wood products, and manufacturing activity.

Does this reliance on the public sector for formally organized service provision render the policy shift toward a public/private partnership impossible in the rural setting? Perhaps it is not impossible, but certainly it is more complex to develop than within the urban infrastructure.

Under a service system based on partnerships and the principles of a competitive market, both urban and rural consumers face problems in accessing the system. However, to the rural service consumer the economic structures are differentially applied. First, competition requires a substantial number of buyers and sellers interacting in unrestrained exchange (Roemer & Roemer, 1982). Without substantial numbers rural areas do not meet this criterion. Furthermore, consumer choice is constrained by the nature of the problems calling for intervention, for example, the severely depressed young mother in an isolated mountain village has little opportunity to shop around for some help. Other misapplications of the competitive market in social and health services are examined in Chapter 6.

Extractive industries (mining, wood products) are located primarily in rural areas. In the emerging boom town areas where energy resources are being tapped, corporate responsibility can and should include a commitment to human resources. Griffiths (1981) and McLeod (1981) underscore the psychological depression resulting from isolation and alienation in new, demographically fluctuating communities. The rapidly expanding need for health, mental health, recreation, and educational services places unprecedented burdens on existing local communities. The public/private partnership takes the form of industrial or corporate interaction with local governments to restore a sense of equilibrium and ensure the full participation of the local population and newer community residents. In rural areas where extractive or manufacturing plants close, creating depression rather than boom, a similar corporate responsibility exists to ease the burden of depression by retraining, reemployment, and social service support during transitions. Likewise, a similar responsibility exists when a corporation comes under new ownership with differing policies toward the community than those held by its predecessor.

Much of what corporations have done in discharging their social responsibility has been in urban areas (Pierce & Troup, 1982). The newest proposal for revitalizing economically depressed areas is the creation of new enterprise zones. Should the proposal pass the Congress, these zones, of which 75 would be designated in the next three years by the Department of Housing and Urban Development (HUD), will be designed to "stimulate business activity and employment in depressed areas by using federal tax and regulatory relief to entice new businesses to locate in those areas" (Brenne, 1982, p. 3).

However attractive the appeal of the enterprise zone concept, there appear to be some major disadvantages for rural areas in its implementation. First, small communities and rural areas will be competing with urban areas; there are no special provisions for rural areas. However, a rural enterprise zone bill (HR 4576) was recently introduced to provide incentives to small businesses to locate in rural areas. Second, with small populations, the technical support and creative talent may not be available to ensure viability of the concept. Third, growth and change may be constrained by a more conservative value stance. Fourth, the rural infrastructure may need considerable improvement before its services can be sufficiently attractive to bring new businesses to the area. This disadvantage is only exacerbated at a time when federal funding of the Farmers Home Administration and the Economic Development Administration—a primary source of funds for infrastructure and rural communities—has been reduced by 40 to 50 percent.

An example of rural interest by the private sector was expressed by Control Data Corporation which set up Rural Ventures, Inc. to help small farmers and rebuild rural economies. Rural Ventures, Inc. is "a nonprofit consortium of corporations, religious organizations, and the Midwest's two largest farm co-ops, with projects in Minnesota, Oklahoma, the Connecticut River Valley and Alaska" (Pierce & Troup, 1982, p. 909). The question remains unanswered: Will new governmental initiatives further stimulate the private sector to increase its share of community support over the next decade and to focus a substantial portion of that support in rural areas?

Block Grant Funding/The New Federalism

Important characteristics of the post-industrial society as discussed in Chapter 1 are the growing interdependence of social, political, and economic institutions and the development of large-scale, bureaucratic organizations with highly centralized decision-making structures. These characteristics have stimulated, in part, the development of what has been labeled the New Federalism and the block grant funding mechanism as a way of operationalizing the New Federalism. However, let us back up momentarily to define our terms and articulate an historical perspective.

The concept of federalism is defined by delineating the division of authority and function between federal and state government as set forth in the Constitution. This states-rights model, according to Reagan and Sanzone (1981), presents federalism as a static concept with mutual independence as a chief characteristic. The present reality of federalism, according to these authors is that of the *inter*dependence of federal and state governments wherein cooperation, not subordination becomes a cornerstone. The embodiment of a more contemporary view of federalism is found in the grant-in-aid system of cooperation between federal and state government. Grants-in-aid are those payments made by a higher level government to a lower level government with various degrees of specificity regarding purpose and conditions of receipt and expenditure, including in many instances a percent of matching funds put up at the state and/or local level. The grant-in-aid mechanism has a long history and addresses a wide range of functions, from highway beautification to agricultural experiment stations created in 1887. It received a decided boost with the enactment of the Social Security Act of 1935 and the funding of public assistance, unemployment programs, and public housing loans to state and local housing authorities.

Grants-in-aid to the states are distinguished first by the criteria for distribution (formula versus project grants) and second by the degree of discretion allowed at the state and local level in expenditure of the grant (categorical versus block grants) (Reagan & Sanzone, 1981). Since these distinctions have great importance for rural areas, they necessitate a closer look; the block grant in particular because it represents the dominant trend in the present political environment.

First, however, the criteria for distribution of the grant-in-aid will be discussed. The formula grant is distributed among all eligible grantees according to a predetermined set of criteria (for example, per capita income, numbers of elderly) with no discretionary powers exercised by the granting agency relative to who receives how much. Programs with such criteria are known as entitlements and distributed to the grantee as a right. The federal government exercises its influence through administrative requirements attached to the grant. An example of such distribution is found in the Community Development Block Grant. Examples of entitlement programs for individuals are Social Security retirement benefits and veterans' benefits. A major shortcoming of the formula grant is that it is not necessarily responsive to need in the establishment of criteria with the formulae often reflective of political compromise.

Project grants are those distributed to address specific problems on a competitive basis. That is, the amount of grant monies is limited and rather than distributed proportionately to all potential participants according to a set of criteria, the number of participants is limited to those whose grant proposals most clearly and appropriately address the specific needs for which the funding was designated (Reagan & Sanzone, 1981). An example of project funding is that found in mental health research, and until recently community mental health centers' funding. Project funding is that found in the area of human capital expenditures as discussed in Chapter 3.

A second distinction made of the grant-in-aid system is that of categorical and block grants (Reagan & Sanzone, 1981). Categorical grants characteristically are very narrow in purpose and scope with little or no discretion left to the local or state government in using the funds. Examples of such grants-in-aid are AFDC and Medicaid. Even though some discretion exists (as noted in Chapter 3), the federal government determines the basic purpose and intent and, within guidelines, establishes the target population and range of services appropriate to the grant.

The block grant mechanism is broader in defining the target population but usually restricts the use of funds within a sector, that is, health, housing, social services. The point of decision making is at the state and local level, in contrast to categorical funding with its vast federal control. Under the block grant concept funds are generally allocated by a formula to general purpose governments and represent a consolidation of previously categorical programs. The block grant represents a midpoint, conceptually, between prescriptive categorical grants and totally permissive revenue sharing programs.

Turning to a historical context, several important pieces of legislation elucidate the trend from federal control through categorical grants to state and local control with block grant funding. Title XX of the Social Security Act (P.L. 93–647) known as the Social Services Amendments of 1974, ushered in a new era for the previously categorical, noncash service programs, as a block grant formula program consolidating the previously categorical programs into one and placing a cap of $2.5 billion on the amount of federal money to be expended. This was in large part a Congressional response to a federal expenditure for social services that had increased between 1963 and 1971 from $194 million to $740 million. An even greater increase of approximately one billion dollars occurred in the two years between 1971 and 1973 (Derthick, 1975). The increase of expenditures was to be expected as the federal government, over the decade of the 1960s, sought to assume more responsibility and relieve the states of the fiscal pressures from the social services sector (Gilbert, 1977).

Throughout the period (1960–1980) other pieces of legislation indicated a hastening pace toward the devolution of broad policy making powers back to the states by way of the "New Federalism." First, with the Partnership for Health Act [Section 314(d) of the Public Health Service Act], nine categorical grant programs were combined into one block grant with the intent of encourag-

ing innovation in community health programs by decreasing federal requirements. This legislation, although unsuccessful in
meeting its goals, was seen as working in concurrent fashion with
Section 314(b), the substate, regional health planning agencies.
The planning [314(b)] agencies were later to be replaced by the
Health Systems Agencies (HSA) under P.L. 93–641 (Greenberg,
1981).

The Revenue Sharing Act of 1972 (P.L. 95–512) represented
another step in the trend toward block grant funding and, as
discussed by Reagan and Sanzone, is a more permissive grant
mechanism than is the block grant. Passed during the Nixon administration, general revenue sharing became the mechanism
used to pass federal dollars back to the states and municipalities
with very broad discretionary powers for their expenditure at the
local level. The Comprehensive Employment and Training Act of
1973 (CETA), and the Housing and Community Development
Act of 1974, both represent a further expansion of the block grant
approach.

The basic purpose of block grant funding is to divest the
federal government of its broad influence and authority and to
allow for increased policy decision making at the state level. It has
also been suggested that, at least in the current situation, it is a
way of ultimately passing on to the states the responsibility of
funding the various programs under growing constraints of substantially reduced federal dollars (Morell, 1982).

As with all policy decisions, there are relative advantages and
disadvantages to the block grant mechanism, and these may not
always be mutually exclusive. According to Hudson (1981) the
advantages of block grants fall roughly into three broad categories:
(1) improved coordination at the point of service delivery; (2)
building the capacity of state institutions in policy and planning
arenas; and (3) encouraging greater citizen participation and sensitivity to state and substate issues.

Each of these categories is examined briefly at this point.
Coordination, a theme dealt with in Chapter 4, is facilitated when
many or several previously categorical programs are grouped
under a single structure. Rather than several planning processes
and the accumulation and expenditure of funds in a fairly autonomous way, the block grant brings together resources, client systems, and service agencies through which more appropriate targeting of resources with increased efficiency and effectiveness can
occur. Thus, in the words of Reagan and Sanzone, "When local

directors of programs previously funded independently all receive their resources from a single point and have their activities planned and reported jointly, there is a strong incentive for more effective program cooperation and integration" (p. 152).

By redefining and broadening the role of the individual states, institutions are strengthened with a subsequent strengthening in "the policy performance of state level actors" (Hudson, 1981, p. 15). The general purpose government in which most authority lies at the state level, has under its power and authority the block grant, that is, funding with a more inclusive purpose and target group. A major asset of this power realignment is in the responsibility and accountability of government to the electorate closer to the point of implementation. The distant federal bureaucracy can no longer serve as the scapegoat when programs fail or are costly and ineffective. This represents a good political compromise from the standpoint of the Congress.

Being more responsive to local needs is reflected in the attempts by state and local governments to respond to the voice of the local electorate. Although not essential to the block grant approach but certainly a premise of decentralized decision making, many such grants include the mandate for citizen participation in the planning process, through either advisory board functions or public hearing and review processes. It is assumed that negotiation of differences may occur with the expectation of reasonable compromise that reflects local need (Hudson, 1981; Reagan & Sanzone, 1981).

From another perspective, a number of real and potential disadvantages have been identified with block grants. From one perspective, the mechanism serves to weaken the state level agency responsible for implementing programs under its block grant mandate. This occurs, aside from the perceived strengthening through additional authority, in that the state agency does not have the same level of support of the federal agency and is thus positioned defensively with client and citizen groups as well as elected public officials to justify its actions or inactions.

Additional support to the state agency may be eroded in that local/state governments have not traditionally championed the causes of vulnerable and stigmatized populations. One only needs to look at the Civil Rights movement, including activities for women's rights, to see that state and local government had to be pushed and even coerced by the federal government to increase their guarantee and protection of human and civil rights (Reagan

& Sanzone, 1981). On the part of the federal government, action included a vast array of legislation covering voting rights, equal employment opportunity for women, minorities and the elderly, education and accessibility of institutions to the handicapped, and protection from the destructive forces of domestic violence. Additionally, as suggested by Hudson (1981) provider/client support under the earlier categorical programs may be eroded as groups compete for funding under the broader aegis of the block grant, particularly when fewer funds are available.

Although increased citizen and provider participation in decision making is viewed as an advantage of block grant funding, the issues raised previously about citizen participation persist. The carryover strengths of groups served under categorical programs may now come to dominate the block grant structure as well. As an example Hudson, in a discussion of long-term care, suggests that institutional care providers which have gained strength through the reimbursement mechanisms of Medicare and Medicaid would be able to gain a disproportionate advantage in block grant funding also. If the Title XX program can serve as an example, it was found that some states under Title XX simply continued to distribute program monies in the same way they had under the categorical programs (*The Age Discrimination Study*, 1978).

Entering into the block grant discussion as a disadvantage is the observation, backed by some empirical evidence and contrary to observations made earlier about universal eligibility criteria, that "have nots" fare less well in more universally available programs. Under Title XX, groups of "non-poor" were made eligible for services for the first time. This, according to Gilbert (1977) was a movement toward "universalism." Such universal inclusion serves to further the disparities, at least in the case of young and old (Schram, 1979).

Although there is risk that special interest groups stand to lose under the block grant approach, some scholars believe that the argument for a universalistic approach to public policy is compelling, in that policies must be designed to impact problems, and similar problems are shared by many groups of people. For example, low-income and poor health status are not characteristic of only the elderly but many young and middle-aged individuals as well. Nevertheless, this compelling logic does not hold up when groups become competitive for the shrinking availability of money (Schram, 1979). Particularistic policies have served the elderly well

(Binstock, 1978) even though this is viewed as adding to the stigma and isolation of the group (Estes, 1979; Etzioni, 1976).

Prior to 1981, Title XX was the major block grant affecting social service delivery. With the passage of the Omnibus Budget Reconciliation Act of 1981, the Congress consolidated 25 health and human service programs into seven blocks of funding: energy assistance; community services; primary care; maternal and child health; health prevention and services; alcohol abuse; drug abuse; mental health; and social services. Two previously existing block grants were reauthorized: community development (CDBG) and comprehensive employment and training program (CETA).

The Community Services Block Grant of 1974 as reauthorized terminated the Community Services Administration, the successor of the Office of Economic Opportunity that administered the antipoverty programs of the 1960s. The programs contained in the block grant are nutrition, health, housing, and employment-related services designed to assist low-income people toward an improved standard of living.

The social services block grant consolidates three Title XX programs—social services, day care, and state and local personnel training. The formula for allocation of funds to each state is based on the ratio of the states' population to the total population of the U.S. and is authorized at $2.45 billion in fiscal year 1983 and $2.5 billion in fiscal year 1984 (NASW NEWS, 1981).

It comes as no surprise that rural areas stand both to gain and to lose under the New Federalism and its block grant funding mechanism. First, the positive side. If by decentralization, decisions do reflect local need, then rural areas stand to gain in the often frustrating counterattack against urban-based policies. This, however, will necessitate a responsiveness on the part of the state government to its rural populations, many of which are found in highly urbanized states, for example, New York, Pennsylvania, and Ohio. The degree of local government participation in decisions will be decided by the states. This will differ from one state to another depending upon the state–local structure (Beyle & Dusenbury, 1982).

Other characteristics of the block grant have more clearly arguable and detrimental implications for rural areas. First, grants based on formulae of population rather than need will clearly place states with small, and usually impoverished populations, at a clear disadvantage, for example, South Dakota and Maine. Second, local decision makers, as pointed out many times throughout this book, are often not strong advocates for minority and disadvantaged people. Third, block grants incorporating mechanisms for citizen participation are subject to the concerns expressed under our discussion of accountability. Fourth, at the same time the block grant may be viewed as facilitating the development of a local policy and planning infrastructure, the rural areas struggle with a lack of technical expertise to meet the grant requirements and appropriately define community needs in a documented way. Fifth, it is possible that the competition among service providers for scarce resources will be shifted to the state level where the leverage of provider coalitions will be lessened and state governments will assume tremendous power.

Summary

The purpose of this chapter has been to introduce the reader to several contemporary policy themes characteristic of funding and management issues as reflected in social policy decisions. Accountability, public/private partnerships, and the block grants as a service funding mechanism, represent ways in which policy decision makers have attempted to address the characteristics of the advanced industrial society; namely, resource scarcity, turbulence in the environment, centralization of decision making, and the interdependence of social, political, and economic institutions.

The link between the policy themes and the rural environment has been shown. Although each theme, as developed in this chapter, has the potential for positive impact on both depressed and growth areas, there are also problematic aspects of which the social worker should be aware. These cluster around the lack of an appropriate infrastructure and adequate personnel to carry out decentralized policy and at the same time to ensure a rural voice in the decision making processes.

References

Ahearn, Mary C. "Health Care in Rural America," U.S. Department of Agriculture, Washington, D.C., Pub. No. 428, 1979.

Arnstein, Sherry R. "A Ladder of Citizen Participation," *American Institute of Planners*, 1969, 35(4):216–224.

Beyle, Thad L. and Dusenbury, Patricia J. "Health and Human Services Block Grants: The State and Local Dimension," *State Government*, 1982, 55(1):2–13.

Binstock, Robert H. "Federal Policy Toward the Aging," *National Journal*, 1978, 19(45):1838–1845.

Bjorkman, James W. and Altenstetter, Christa. "Accountability in Health Care: An Essay on Mechanisms, Muddles, and Mires," *Journal of Health Politics, Policy and Law*, 1979, 4(3):360–379.

Boulding, Kenneth, "The Boundaries of Social Policy," *Social Work*, 1967, 12(1):3–11.

Brenne, M.J. "Can Enterprise Zones Work in Small Towns?" *Reporter*, published by the National Association of Towns and Townships, No. 24, 1982.

Brown, Edwin G. "Corporate Social Responsibility: The Boom Town and Rapid Growth Perspective" in Griffiths, Kenneth A. (Ed.), *Rapid Growth Development in Rural Areas: Implications for Social Work*. Salt Lake City, Utah: Graduate School of Social Work, University of Utah, 1981, 39–47.

Buck, J. Vincent and Stone, Barbara S. "Citizen Involvement in Federal Planning: Myth and Reality," *The Journal of Applied Behavioral Science*, 1981, 14(4):550–565.

Burns, Eveline M. *Social Security and Public Policy*. New York: McGraw Hill Book Co., 1956.

Checkoway, Barry. "The Politics of Public Hearings," *The Journal of Applied Behavioral Science*, 1981, 14(4):566–582.

Clark, Timothy. "Reagan's Budget: Economic Political Gambles," *National Journal*, 1982, 14(7):268–285.

Constable, Robert and Black, Rita Beck. "Mandates for a Changing Practice: PSRO and P.L. 92–142," *Social Service Review*, 1980, 54(2):273–281.

Demkovich, Linda E. "Devising New Medicare Payment Plan May Prove Much Easier Than Selling It," *National Journal*, 1982, 14(47):1981–1985.

Demkovich, Linda E. "In Treating the Problems of the Elderly, There May Be No Place Like Home," *National Journal*, 1979, 11(51-52):2154–2158

Derthick, Martha. *Uncontrollable Spending for Social Service Grants*. Washington, D.C.: Brookings Institute, 1975.

Doherty, Neville, and Hicks, Barbara. "Cost-Effectiveness Analysis and Alternative Health Care Programs for the Elderly," *Health Sciences Research*, 1977, 12(2):190–203.

Doherty, Neville, Segal, Joan, and Hicks, Barbara. "Alternatives to Institutionalization for the Aged: Viability and Cost Effectiveness," *Aged Care and Services Review*, 1978, 1(1):2–16.

Estes, Carroll. *The Aging Enterprise*. San Francisco: Jossey Bass, 1979.

Etzioni, Amitai. "Old People and Public Policy," *Social Policy*, 1976, 7(1):21–29.

Federal Register. Part IV, Department of Health and Human Services, Office of Human Development Services, Discretionary Funds Programs: Availability of Funds and Requests for Preapplications, Monday, Nov. 16, 1981, 46(220):56364–56378.

Fottler, Myron D., Smith, Howard L., and James, William L. "Profits and Patient Care Quality in Nursing Homes: Are They Compatible?," *The Gerontologist*, 1981, 21(5):532–538.

General Accounting Office. "Home Health Care Services—Tighter Fiscal Controls Needed." Washington, D.C.: U.S. Government Printing Office, 1979.

Gilbert, Neil. "The Transformation of Social Services," *Social Service Review*, 1977, 51(3):624–641.

Gilbert, Neil and Specht, Harry. *Dimensions of Social Welfare Policy*. Englewood Cliffs: Prentice-Hall, 1974.

Glisson, Charles A. "The Accountability Controversy," *Social Work*, 1975, 20(5):417–419.

Golant, Stephen M. and McCaslin, Rosemary. "A Functional Classification of Services for Older People," *Journal of Gerontological Social Work*, 1979, 1(2):1–31.

Greenberg, George D. "Block Grants and State Discretion: A Study of the Implementation of the Partnership for Health Act in Three States," *Policy Sciences*, 1981, 13:153–181.

Griffiths, Kenneth A. "Social Work Education: Issues and Approaches as Related to Rapid Growth in Rural Areas," in Griffiths, K.A. (Ed.), *Rapid Growth Development in Rural Areas: Implications for Social Work*. Salt Lake City, Utah: Graduate School of Social Work, University of Utah, 1981, 29–38.

Gruber, Murray. "Total Administration," *Social Work*, 1974, 19(6): 625–636.

Gulati, Padi. "Consumer Participation in Administrative Decision Making," *Social Service Review*, 1982, 56(1):72–84.

Hicks, Barbara, Raisz, Helen, Segal, Joan, and Doherty, Neville. "The Triage Experiment in Coordinated Care for The Elderly," *American Journal of Public Health*, 1981, 71(9):991–1003.

Hoshino, George. "Social Services: The Problem of Accountability," *Social Services Review*, 1973, 47(3):373–383.

Hudson, Robert B. "A Block Grant to the States for Long-Term Care," *Journal of Health Politics, Policy, and Law*, 1981, 6(1):9–28.

Kirschten, Dick. "Even if Charity Does Begin at Home, Government May Still Play a Key Role," *National Journal*, 1982, 14(21):902–909.

Levin, Herman. "Voluntary Organizations in Social Welfare," in Turner, John B. (Ed.), *Encyclopedia of Social Work*, 17, Vol. II. Washington, D.C.: National Association of Social Workers, 1977, 1573–1582.

Lipsky, Michael. "The Assault on Human Services: Street-Level Bureaucrats, Accountability, and the Fiscal Crisis," in Gruber, Murray L. (Ed.), *Management Systems in the Human Services*. Philadelphia: Temple University Press, 1981, 342–356.

McLeod, Katherine. "A Feminist Perspective on Energy Development," in Griffiths, K.A. (Ed.), *Rapid Growth in Rural Areas: Implications for Social Work*. Salt Lake City, Utah: Graduate School of Social Work, University of Utah, 1981, 11–19.

Milbrath, Lester W. "Citizen Surveys as Citizen Participation Mechanisms," *Journal of Applied Behavioral Science*, 1981, 17(4):478–496.

McKay, Alec and Baxter, E.H. "Title XIX, Title XX, and Catch XXII: Cost Analysis in Social Program Evaluation," *Administration in Social Work*, 1980, 4(3):23–30.

Morell, Bonnie Brown. "ABC's of Block Grants," *Social Work*, 1982, 27(2):126–127.

NASW NEWS. "Big Reagan Victories in Congress Signify Reversal of Federal Role," September, 1981, 26(8):6.

Newman, Edward and Turem, Jerry. "The Crisis of Accountability," *Social Work*, 1974, 19(1):5–16.

O'Connell, Brian. "The Independent Sector and Voluntary Action," *The Social Welfare Forum, 1980*. The National Conference on Social Welfare. New York: Columbia University Press, 1981, 39–52.

Pierce, Neil R. and Troup, Calvin L. "What Companies Can Do," *National Journal*, 1982, (21):905–909.

Plass, Penelope. "Home-Care Services: How Many Can They Help?," *Health and Social Work*, 1978, 1(3):182–189.

Quinn, Joan L. "Triage: Coordinated Care for the Elderly," *The Journal of Continuing Education in Nursing*, 1979, 10(4):50–57.

Reagan, Michael D. and Sanzone, John G. *The New Federalism*. New York: Oxford University Press, 1981.

Roemer, Milton I. and Roemer, John E. "The Social Consequences of Free Trade in Health Care: A Public Health Response to Orthodox Economics," *International Journal of Health Services*, 1982, 12(1):111–129.

Rossi, Peter H. "Issues in the Evaluation of Human Services Delivery," *Evaluation Quarterly*, 1978, 2(4):573–599.

Schram, Sanford F. "Elderly Policy Particularism and the New Social Services," *Social Service Review*, 1979, 53(1):75–91.

Somers, Anne R. and Somers, Herman M. "A Proposed Framework for Health and Health Care Policies," *Inquiry*, 1977, 14:115–170.

Sorkin, Alan L. *Health Economics*. Lexington, Mass.: Lexington Books, 1975.

Terrell, Paul. "Private Alternatives to Public Human Services Administration," *Social Service Review*, 1979, 53(1):56–74.

The Age Discrimination Study, A Report of the U.S. Commission on

Civil Rights. Washington, D.C.: U.S. Government Printing Office, 1978.

The Foundation Directory, 7th edition, Lewis, Marianna O. (Ed.). New York: The Foundation Center, 1979.

Turem, Jerry. "The Call for a Management Stance," *Social Work,* 1974, 19(5):625–636.

Weissert, William G. "Costs of Adult Day Care: A Comparison to Nursing Homes," *Inquiry,* 1978, 15(1):10–19.

Weissert, William G., Wan, T.T.H., Livieratos, B.B., and Katz, S. "Cost Effectiveness of Day Care Services for the Chronically Ill: A Randomized Experiment," *Medical Care,* 1980, 18(6):567–584.

Widmer, Geraldine, Brill, Roberta, and Schlosser, Adele. "Home Health Care: Services and Cost," *Nursing Outlook,* 1978, 26(8):488–493.

6 Social Policy Applications in the Rural Environment

Introduction

The purpose of this chapter is to articulate the connection between social policy formulation and social work practice in the rural environment. The context in which the formulation of social policy and social work practice are linked is the advanced industrial society. The characteristics of turbulence, resource scarcity, and the growing interdependence of the social, economic, and political spheres of activity which permeate the advanced industrial society serve as the anchor point of practice skills and expertise. The overarching theme which unites practice and policy is that of quality of life referring both to individuals as members of families or in interaction with significant others and to communities as the focal points of interaction, around which, as suggested by Boulding (1967), the individual builds an identity.

The purpose of this chapter will be accomplished by examining the prevailing practice modalities in rural settings and by suggesting a framework within which such practice occurs and the conceptual underpinning for that practice. The use of a strategic perspective will be developed as an approach to link social work practice and social policy in rural areas. The components of strategy are reflected in the continuum of care concept and the life transitions of individuals, families, and communities. At a macro level of practice, the strategic perspective brings together the goals and aspirations of the community and assesses their viability against a turbulent, resource-scarce environment. At a micro level of practice the strategic perspective facilitates congruity of short-term and long-term interventions and supports policy formulation and program development reflective of human need.

Social Work Practice: The Generalist

While the literature base for social work practice in rural areas has
grown substantially in the past few years, there is still not a clear
consensus about the nature of rural practice and how it differs from
urban-based practice. Munson (1980) even questions the productivity of placing an emphasis on such definitional issues. The position taken in this book has articulated the following: (1) rural environments, even in their diversity, differ from urban environments
and therefore place differing demands on the service and income
security systems; and (2) the majority of social policies enacted at
the federal level embody a predominately urban view of problems
and their solutions—a comprehensive policy directed toward rural
America does not exist.[1] These points have been addressed in
preceding chapters. A third point, namely, that social work practice in rural areas is perceived as being different from that in urban
areas, a perception shared both by the social work professional and
by the community, provides the basis for the subsequent discussion. At the very least, rural settings provide for differing practice
foci than do urban areas. The reader is reminded, however, that it
is not the intent of this chapter to look at rurally based practice in
its entirety. Substantial work has been done by other authors
(Farley, Griffiths, Skidmore, & Thackeray, 1982). Rather, the components of rural practice most closely tied to the policy formulation
process will be examined.

Despite the lack of consensus about rurally based social work
practice, there seems to be widespread agreement on one point: a
generalist practice perspective is most useful in rural areas. The
generalist perspective is reinforced in the social work mission as
described by Minahan and Pincus (1977), and the focus of professional practice more recently articulated in by the Council on
Social Work Education (1982), as ". . . the transactions between
people and their environments that affect their ability to accomplish life tasks, alleviate distress, and realize individual and collective aspirations" (p. 4).

According to Minahan and Pincus, the generalist is

[1] For a discussion of various responses by the federal government to stimulate
the development of a comprehensive rural policy perspective the reader is re-
ferred to the work of Ronald C. Powers and Edward O. Moe, "The Policy
Context for Rural-Oriented Research" in Dillman, Don A. and Hobbs, Daryl J.
(Eds.), *Rural Society in the U.S.: Issues for the 1980s*. Boulder, Colorado:
Westview Press, Inc., 1982, pp. 10–20.

... defined as a person with a broad view who can look at the entire social situation, analyze the interactions between people and all the resource systems connected to that situation, intervene in those interactions, determine which specialists are needed from a variety of disciplines, and coordinate and mobilize the knowledge and skill of many disciplines—this worker is a generalist." (p.352)

This definition implies that social work intervention occurs in various settings (for example, mental health, child welfare), with various populations (for example, children, adults, elderly), and using a variety of methodologies, tasks, and roles as appropriate to an intervention plan and the problem-solving process. In the words of Mermelstein and Sundet (1976), "The generalist social worker assesses social phenomena in all of their systemic ramifications and identifies and intervenes at whatever level is efficient and effective to bring about the desired social changes" (p. 16).

Within the generalist model of social work practice and the rural setting the clearest and perhaps most productive link with policy formulation occurs in the area that has been variously referred to as indirect or macro level practice. Although work with individuals and families in the direct service roles of caregiver, educator, and member of a treatment team is impacted by policy and often (or should) stimulates policy development, this is not the point at which formulation of broad social policy occurs. The macro or indirect focus includes planning and development activities that respond with sensitivity to the community, involve the community, and take into account the changes occurring in the larger environment.

The characteristics of contemporary rural environments which make indirect practice particularly applicable have been discussed by both Wylie (1976) and Mermelstein and Sundet (1976). The points having greatest relevance for discussion of planning and development activities as discussed in this chapter are the following: (1) smallness of scale that translates to policy formulation and a more viable setting for policy and program innovation; (2) interaction based on face-to-face communication and relatively stable relationships through which community leadership capacity may be developed; (3) community awareness of both problems and resources through the transactions with informal networks and a relatively stable core population group; and (4) transitions occurring in rural areas that give planning and development activities great promise to achieve desired outcomes.

It is from the generalist perspective with a focus on indirect practice activities that the adoption of a strategic perspective facilitates an appropriate policy response to rural America in an advanced industrial society. However, the generalist perspective is linked with the policy-making process by a more broadly articulated theme, quality of life, and underpinned by the components of strategy reflected in the continuum of care. The bridge between strategy formulation and its application to social work practice is articulated by reviewing the concepts of quality of life and social need in the next section.

Quality of Life

Guiding the policy-making process is the overarching conceptual theme of quality of life. For discussion purposes, quality of life is a measure or series of measures that define levels below or above which a community or, more broadly speaking, a society does not desire to deviate (House, Livingston & Swinburn, 1975). According to Watkins and Watkins (1976), quality of life definitions must focus on the objective conditions of life as well as on how those conditions are perceived by individuals. For example, social programs for income security which appear to be effective from a reading of goals and objectives often fail to meet the needs of beneficiaries to advance beyond the poverty level. The resulting ". . . gap between expectations and performance represents areas of discontent which can perhaps be attacked at the local level if decision makers have access to relevant information assessing these dichotomies" (Watkins & Watkins, 1976, p. 2).

Within the boundaries of social policy, quality of life is concerned with the involvement and participation of people in the broader structures of societal activity, that is, social, economic, and political. More specifically, involvement requires reciprocal communication between those affected by circumstances and those who plan, develop, and set priority objectives. Improved quality of life is viewed as the outcome of responsive decision making wherein participation in the fullest sense of choice and self-determination are valued inputs to the policy process. Given the population characteristics and interaction patterns in rural areas, participation is an important opportunity to develop as social workers seek to enhance the quality of life in the rural community.

Social Need

A clear understanding of the definition of need is essential to the planning and development process. Need is also viewed as a component of strategy and as such is discussed under the section headed Components of Strategy in this chapter. The identification of a problem or a statement of goals is not the same as defining need, even though they are often used synonymously. From a social systems perspective, need is viewed as the inputs necessary to address a problem or to achieve a given goal (Morasky & Amick, 1978). The needs assessment strategy involves the specification of the problem and the resources required to address the problem and attain the desired quality of life for the client system. As stated by Sallis and Henggeler (1980), "needs assessments should suggest the types of interventions needed to ameliorate identified community problems" (p. 200).

The concept of quality of life recognizes the interdependence of the conditions of life in a given environment and how those conditions are perceived by various population subgroups. In order to arrive at meaningful decisions about quality of life and later in the problem-solving process, decisions about appropriate interventions, both subjective and objective data about the condition of society are useful (Campbell, Converse, & Rogers, 1972). As indicators of social need, subjective data rely on the reported perceptions of people and their demands for a service or social program. Bradshaw (1974) has described these measures as felt need and expressed need or demand. Objective indicators of social need are derived from normative and comparative definitions according to Bradshaw.

Eliciting responses from the population about their perceptions of need is the most frequent way of determining felt need. Examples are community need assessments and surveys by social service agencies. Although community and agency surveys provide an avenue for obtaining a representative sample, the observations of individuals are at risk of being limited by their perceptions of what is available (needed) to address problems and their reluctance to admit that they themselves may be in need of a service (Bradshaw, 1974).

As reflected earlier, when rural people are asked about conditions of life, their responses are not congruent with objective conditions (Lee & Lassey, 1980). On the one hand, this may be the result of a lack of awareness or the unavailability of services. On the other hand, it may be reflective of the independent nature of rural people (for example, attachment to the workforce at substandard wages) and their reluctance to cast aside existing ways of interacting with larger systems for the yet unanticipated consequences of new ways.

The preference expressed by many Americans to live in smaller communities and the rural in-migration of the 1970s is an example of felt need turned to expressed need or demand. Based on subjective perceptions of felt need, people act on their interpretation that less-populated areas have a better quality of life. These beliefs are based somewhat on the prevailing but stereotypic views of rural America. However, confusing the overall needs-assessment process are the existing objective criteria which show lower crime rates, lower housing costs, and greater recreational opportunities than are found in many urban areas. Although these indicators are changing, they are persuasive to many people wishing to leave the urban environment. Demand for social services is usually not expressed in a market environment. The service recipient does not pay for the service according to the usual transaction expectations of the marketplace, that is, buyers and sellers. However, in those situations in which economic demand has relevance, demand can be estimated according to a cross-classification relationship where the observed outcome of two variables is noted. As an illustration, Patton (1979) has applied this analysis to rural public transportation. For example, demand could be estimated by examining households according to such characteristics as size, income, and auto ownership.

The objective indicators of social need are derived from normative and comparative definitions (Bradshaw, 1974). Normative criteria are those specified by experts as desirable. Families determined eligible for AFDC benefits are declared in need, since a gap exists between their income levels and the normative standard of need as determined by the policy experts and professionals at the state level. Children are thought to be in need of foster care or home-based intervention when their living arrangements do not meet certain normative standards of health, protection, and nurturance. Representing standards based on middle-class and/or professional biases, normative definitions of need risk patronizing and stigmatizing people or population subgroups whose own definition of standards may differ as was shown with American Indian children (see Chapter 4). Furthermore, standards change over time as reflected, for example, in the way family planning and abortion services are viewed by many policy decision makers.

Comparative need is based on the assessment of one group of people receiving a service (inputs to achieve a specified level of quality of life) and comparing this group to another with similar characteristics not receiving that service. According to this definition, it might be suggested that rural areas are in need of expanded adult protective services or health services for women when compared with similar population groups in urban areas where such services are available. In comparisons with urban populations the ratio of the rural adult population with similar characteristics (that is, vulnerability to abuse and neglect or lacking in gynecologic and obstetric care) to services, is higher than in urban areas. Thus, in a comparative sense, there is a need for services to achieve a comparable quality of life.

Assessing need is basic to social work practice. At all levels of practice it serves to guide intervention activities—the inputs needed to attain a specified goal or outcome. At the macro level this means policy formulation as a guide to action, that is, planning and program development activities. Caution must be exercised, however, in the ways by which need is determined. For example, rural residents may be less disposed to use services that are provided. Assuming that a population is receptive ignores the complexity of attitudinal and value components which may preclude the use of services even though they are thought to be needed. More particularly, perceptions about relative well-being, distrust of outsiders, and a general conservative posture may be strong forces mitigating against service utilization. In addition, low levels of felt need and expressed need as stated by rural people may serve to reinforce the urban perspective that rural residents are less in need of social programs than are urban people.

In spite of the growing tendency of policy and program decision makers to utilize a variety of needs-assessment techniques, questions have been raised about the effectiveness and the real intent of the processes used. Focusing on the needed responsiveness of community mental health centers (CMHC) to the community, Sallis and Henggeler (1980) state that ". . . needs assessments are frequently used more to meet CMHC needs than community needs" (p. 200). In a pointedly critical review, Kimmel (1977) suggests that most needs assessments ". . . will have only a small chance of impacting on policy and resource allocation decisions" (p. 60). Rather than developing needs assessment techniques, Kimmel points to the potential utility ". . . of a problem-oriented and problem-specific issue or policy analysis as a major alternative to or method of needs assessment" (p. 66). However, needs assessment, to be most effective in addressing issues and problems in the rural setting, will go beyond the problem definition to include an analysis of resources. This is stated by Morasky and Amick (1978) as follows: ". . . the task or objective of the needs assessment strategy is twofold: (1) to identify specific problems in the system network according to type, extent, location and nature; and (2) to identify the inputs required in order to alleviate the problems identified in (1) above" (p. 48).

The Strategic Perspective

Through the previous chapters and the themes presented, it is concluded that compared with the decade of the 1970s the following needs will dominate social work practice in the 1980s:

1. The need to respond to population diversity in rural settings, and in many cases, the growing constituency base that will be more demanding of quality and comprehensive services;
2. The need for increased attention to the mix of services and income programs appropriate to the needs of the rural population and rural communities in transition;
3. The need for increased contingency planning as a response to long-run mandated program responsibilities and short-term and unpredictable funding cycles;
4. The need for public/private development strategies to leverage a shrinking and at best constant level of public funds for social programs;
5. The need to respond with an appropriate planning posture to increasing autonomy in the expenditures of funds;
6. The increasing need to respond to cost containment measures and public accountability.

Responsiveness on the part of the social work practitioner necessitates a basic familiarity with the policy-making process and an ability to articulate policy within a planning posture that reflects the setting of a post-industrial society. It is to these requirements that the strategic perspective is directed.

Planning, including the policy-making aspects of the process, when viewed from a strategic perspective is based on the fundamental assumption that environmental change is taking place with relevance to the well-being of an entity. In this case, well-being is equated with quality of life as the overarching theme and underpins interventions directed toward the rural community. The strategic perspective involves "the task of choosing future directions and areas of concentration for an organization" (Radford, 1980, p. ix). In turbulent environments specific interventions follow systematic identification of future opportunities and threats in such a manner as to exploit opportunities and minimize threats. From Steiner's (1979) perspective this is interpreted as designing a future as one would like it to be and identifying ways and processes by which the design may be implemented. This same theme was articulated by Minahan (1981) when she suggested that social work participate in shaping the future.

A strategic perspective highlights planning and development as a continuous activity. This is accomplished by responding to significant changes in the environment by setting overarching philosophies and aims, defining strategies and policies, and implementing decisions. Appropriate change in the content of the plan is a function of the degree of turbulence in the environment.

According to Steiner, strategic planning has four defining characteristics: (1) current decisions are anchored in the implications they have for the future; (2) planning is a process distinct from the output or product; (3) it performs an overall coordination function by linking the three major types of plans: strategic plans, medium-range plans, and short-range budgets and operating plans; and (4) strategy formulation is systematically planned and managed in strategic planning. In view of Golant and McCaslin's (1979) criticism of service directed planning in which there is no difference between the service system and the plan, systematic strategy formulation is especially relevant. By assuming a strategic perspective, the capriciousness of funding and political ideology become formal issues to be addressed (Ansoff, 1979).

Organizational Constraints

For social work, the majority of intervention activities are carried out within an organizational context. One characteristic of that context that is particularly relevant to the policy process is how organizations interact with and remain responsive to the larger environment.

All organizations through time have a tendency to ossify or develop what Argyris (1970) more pointedly describes as "dry rot." That is, they become increasingly unresponsive to their environments. From Argyris' perspective, all organizations must grapple with the same tendency, be they public or private, for-profit or nonprofit. How visible dry rot becomes is, in part, a function of environmental turbulence. In an extremely stable environment, organizations with few mechanisms for change might well survive and in some cases prosper. However, in turbulent environments there is a need for mechanisms that can deal aggressively with change and enhance the ability of the organization to remain responsive to its environment. On the one hand, the discipline of the competitive market is no guarantee of appropriate organizational response to environmental turbulence. On the other hand, large monopolistic agencies in the public sector with poorly articulated mechanisms for accountability can skillfully defend dry rot and remain unresponsive to environmental turbulence.

Two examples will show the relevance of the foregoing discussion.

Adoption agencies in the early 1960s faced an environment of extreme turbulence. The introduction of the widespread use of oral contraceptives resulted in a greatly diminished number of infants available for adoption. In addition, the legalization of abortion (Roe vs. Wade) in 1973, and greater social acceptance of out-of-wedlock pregnancy and parenthood, further exacerbated the situation. Faced with fewer and fewer numbers of infants available for adoption, agencies were forced to change their focus in order to survive in a turbulent environment. Change included an emphasis on older, hard-to-place children and providing a wide range of support services for unmarried, pregnant women, many of them teenagers.

The network of services for the elderly placed considerable emphasis on the development of transportation services during the past decade. This commitment of resources to transportation services assumed a population that was somewhat mobile. During the past few years a significant increase in the numbers of "frail" elderly (those age 85 and over) has occurred, and now necessitates a commitment of resources to home-based services. This shift in the organizational environment requires a new development posture to ensure agency vitality and responsiveness.

Not being responsive to change would result in the demise of agencies if clear accountability mechanisms are present. Likewise, the agencies represented by the examples above could continue to function in a stable environment or in a turbulent environment devoid of accountability mechanisms; that is, they could continue to operate and yet be ineffective in performing their service mission.

The goal of the strategic perspective is to maintain congruency between the environment and the response of the organization. To unravel this process, the concept of strategic change is elaborated for the reader. According to Hofer and Schendel (1978), strategic change occurs in an organization's environmental domain that alters the conditions needed for effectively attaining the organizational mission or purpose. Effectiveness is altered by changes that affect the relationship of the organization to its environment. Efficiency, not to be confused with effectiveness, is affected by changes in the internal operating structure of the organization. A strategic change is one that articulates a significant environmental change.

Strategy is a concept that relates the deployment, expenditure, and acquisition of resources to changing needs and opportunities in the environment. Examples of generalized strategies are presented in a subsequent section. For Hofer and Schendel, the basic characteristics of this "match" between organizations and environment is called a strategy. Even though an organization does not have an explicit strategy, it has an implicit strategy. As long as a strategy remains implicit, the management of an organization's strategy remains a chance occurrence and the organization fails to benefit from a proactive planning posture (Hofer & Schendel, 1978).

The rural environment presents many opportunities for the importance of developing a strategic perspective. For example, changes are occurring in rural areas in the form of population in-migration and may have strategic relevance for certain agencies. Strategies are necessary for agencies to maintain congruence between the expenditure and acquisition of resources and the changing service demands of an expanding and more diverse population base. Relative to an agency's planning and development posture the question of resource commitment must be confronted. Given a particular agency, what proportion of its planning and managerial resources will it commit to strategic concerns (effectiveness) versus day-to-day management of the agency's operations (efficiency)? This commitment of agency resources will vary depending upon the service focus identified by the agency as its domain. Two examples demonstrate this point.

The Community Mental Health Center (CMHC) with a catchment area that includes a small, stable Western community has been providing professional out-patient services through an outstationed social worker. The prospect of rapid growth in the community with the development of energy resources will necessitate a different response by the CMHC. The agency, if it responds to the fast-paced community change precipitated by a population influx with different sociodemographic characteristics from the existing population and needs resulting from rapid growth, will need to commit an expanded agency resource base to planning and program development. This situation is a strategic change that alters the effectiveness of the CMHC in this community. Moving from one outposted social worker to a full planning unit that considers various strategies and their implementation requires a significant shift in resource allocation.

The Community Action Program (CAP) in a northern midwestern town is faced with the need to reallocate planning resources as the federal government moves closer to a policy of deregulation of the natural gas industry. The turbulence created by deregulation is thought to mean higher consumer prices for home heating and increased vulnerability of a substantial elderly population on low fixed incomes. The CAP agency is looking toward developing strategies to deal with the situation (strategic change) in ways similar to the fuel crisis in the Northeast when oil prices escalated and placed a significant strain on many households. Strategies might include rationing or maximization (discussed later in this chapter). Whatever the strategies, however, a changed pattern of resource allocation to planning and development will be needed in order to maintain agency effectiveness as an advocacy and service organization.

Components of Strategy

The defining characteristic of a strategy is maximization of congruence between the objectives of an organization and changing environmental opportunities, or the minimization of environmental threats to agency obsolescence and ineffectiveness. There are two critical elements to any strategy statement: the concepts of environment and resource development and deployment (Hofer & Schendel, 1978; Radford, 1980; Steiner, 1979). In order to achieve goals, any organization must interact with the most critical aspects of its environment while concomitantly acquiring and deploying resources. Continuum of care is the larger framework which integrates the assumptions of quality of life with the components of strategy development. For the purposes of social policy development in a rural setting, an agency's strategy is identified as the fundamental pattern of resource development and deployment and how the agency will achieve its goals and objectives as it interacts with the environment (Radford, 1980; Hofer & Schendel, 1978).

Four explicit components of an agency's strategy can be identified:

1. Need: Central to the environmental aspect of quality of life is the concept of need. The assessment of needs attempts to unmask the priority aspects of domain and note changes in the composition of domain. Congruence requires as a necessary condition a sense of domain as agreed upon in agency goals and objectives. This allows for detection of shifts in need within a fixed domain as well as the detection of emergent needs in an expanded or contracted domain.

2. Resources: In the pursuit of goals and objectives any agency must find resources, organize them in the most efficient manner possible and deploy them in a way consistent with the purposes and aims of the agency and expend them in a manner consistent with policy. In rural

settings much effort will be focused on the development and coordination of resources.

3. Transitions: The focus of strategy development should be on those environmental changes which emphasize transitions in the human experience. There are fundamentally two types of transitions: abrupt transitions, as illustrated through divorce, death of a spouse, domestic violence, the closing of an industry in a small community, or the growth of energy boom towns; and longer-run changes, as illustrated by the aging process, the maturational process of adolescence, and the gradual demise of family owned farms with an attendant economic decline in the community.

4. Accountability: It is important that an agency's strategy be constructed in such a manner as to allow multiple decision points to give input and evaluation—particularly to agencies performing public service. Isolation and inaccessibility are not in the public interest.

Implementation

Many agencies are disturbed and disappointed about the performance of their management and planning systems. Those agencies contemplating the adoption of a system are often discouraged by the planning experiences of other agencies. Systems created with the purpose of enhancing flexibility and efficiencies often behave in an opposite manner—contributing to the rigidity of the organization and adding yet another layer of bureaucracy and interest group to the agency. In rural areas the question of usefulness and antiplanning attitudes are additional factors to be considered.

Recent research addressing the issue of planning system relevance to the reality of organizational settings has found that the implementation process should be an integral part of the strategy development process (Quinn, 1980). This requires a continual recycling of efforts among various points in the planning process. This implies that planning models based on discrete analytic phases which move progressively through a series of steps are grossly inadequate in describing the organizational and behavioral realities of most agencies.

For Quinn, commitment to specifics too early in the development process will impair the flexibility and commitment needed to exploit further information or new opportunities. This places special emphasis on the ability of decision makers to tolerate prolonged periods of ambiguity during the planning and development process. Since the testing of assumptions and reaction to viewpoints of others is critical to the growth of a relevant perspective, reserving commitment to the latest moment possible allows the utilization of emergent information and the learning process to take place. Moreover, this process allows political commitment to be generated through the involvement process. Commitment becomes a significant component in advancing the development of the process. During the evolution of this process, periodic projections of its implications for the total organization stimulates questions, support and feedback. For Quinn this perspective represents a synthesis of information-analysis, power-politics and organizational/psychological processes in ways appropriate to different phases in the process.

The literature on strategy development reflects the centrality of the competitive position of an organization. Furthermore, it is heavily derived from the private sector where competition is a major environmental component. The applicability of competition to the provision of social services in a rural area is an issue needing further examination.

Four assumptions of competitive environments have been identified by Roemer and Roemer (1982):

1. an abundance of consumers and sellers in unconstrained exchange;
2. knowledgeable and informed consumers exercising choices in the purchase of a product;
3. low transaction costs for the item being purchased; and
4. insubstantial economies of scale.

While perhaps applicable to urban settings (although questionable) these assumptions fail to meet the realities of rural environments.

Lacking a sufficiently developed service infrastructure, rural areas have few sellers and the service consumers are often widely dispersed. Large monopolistic agencies, often public entities, provide services as outposting of central state agencies. The fundamental benefits that accrue from competitive contracting through the purchase-of-service mechanism fail to materialize because of the lack of potential contractors in the local area. Moreover, contracts with outside agencies risk the availability and provision of services lacking in sensitivity to the local environment.

Although individuals are becoming increasingly knowledgeable about health and social services, a substantial knowledge gap exists which precludes the exercise of informed choice in the purchase of a service. Institutional barriers in the form of professional ethics mitigate against second opinions and shopping around. In addition, the conditions leading to the need for a service are often precipitated by a crisis event which obviates the luxury of taking one's time to reach a decision.

Because of the tendency of large monopolistic agencies to serve rural areas, economies of scale are possible, as exemplified in nursing home and hospital chains acquiring small, community services. A final point is that a competitive posture in the services sector will only exacerbate and reinforce the already existing inequalities of income and access to resources which have been documented as characteristic of the rural environment.

Framework for Strategy Components

With the overarching theme, quality of life, the strategic perspective directs the development of policy decisions. The components of strategy elaborated in the previous section are bound together by the continuum of care concept. The continuum of care, discussed in Chapter 4 as a policy theme, is used in this context in an expanded way, i.e., beyond the use of only needs and resources as components and now to include transitions over time. However, let us move beyond the earlier discussion of need and by building on the work of Ecosometrics (1978), Martinez (1980), and Benedict (1977), view need based on subjective and objective indicators as several continua rather than a single continuum. Resources become the interventions (available or developed) that are applied through a variety of strategies at various points on a continuum of need to support a desired quality of life.

Using the continuum of care, viewed as several continua elaborated in Chapter 4, a boundary is formed for strategic policy decisions which addresses several concerns expressed about service planning processes. From a review of service plans and typologies, planning emerges primarily as a process of classifying services by sector, that is, health, housing, and social, and arranging service packages to meet individual deficits of functioning.

The problems inherent in this approach are several with (1) planning as a static function unresponsive to the larger environment; (2) the service or output not distinguished from the underlying planning process; in other words, the service is the plan; and (3) service classification based on an inductive approach in which existing services define need (Golant & McCaslin, 1979; Kimmel, 1977). This results in a service bias with increased uncertainty about the "fit" between services and needs (Estes, 1979, p. 137). To avoid the service bias and account for environmental dynamics in the policy and planning processes, the continuum of care provides the framework for a strategic perspective that is directed toward insuring congruency between resources and needs.

Transitions

The several continua interact with one another and contribute to the environmental conditions with significance for a community and its individual members. The elements of the community environment, when viewed as continua, form predictable ranges of conditions (needs) to which social policy decisions can respond. On each continuum transition points exist at which social systems (families, individuals, or communities) move from an environment characterized by independence to one in which dependence dominates. These points of transition in any given continuum of need have the least amount of formal or societal resource systems to draw upon and pose significant dilemmas for the caregiving and resource capacity of the informal and local system, particularly as the care and resource demands increase and/or become less predictable. Thus, over time resources change in their adequacy to meet the needs of a defined population at risk. Moreover, dimensions of choice in policy decisions (Gilbert & Specht, 1974) can be analyzed through time in an attempt to arrive at an appropriate use of resources. The following discussion shows how the dimensions of choice in policy decisions may be viewed relative to transitions (see Figure 6.1).

As a dimension of choice service delivery alternatives represent the interventions over time and their relative adequacy or inadequacy in meeting a continuum of need. Policy questions have been raised, for example, around the issue of community-based services and the institutionalization of the elderly or mentally retarded. As discussed earlier, service delivery technology as

Figure 6.1. Dimensions of Choice/Transitions
in the Promotion of Quality of Life

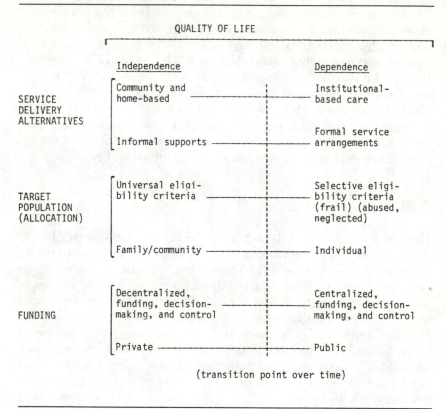

QUALITY OF LIFE

| | Independence | | Dependence |

SERVICE DELIVERY ALTERNATIVES

Community and home-based ——————— Institutional-based care

Informal supports ——————— Formal service arrangements

TARGET POPULATION (ALLOCATION)

Universal eligibility criteria ——————— Selective eligibility criteria (frail) (abused, neglected)

Family/community ——————— Individual

FUNDING

Decentralized, funding, decision-making, and control ——————— Centralized, funding, decision-making, and control

Private ——————— Public

(transition point over time)

currently operationalized with the elderly population is clearly biased toward institutional arrangements (Butler, 1979). The observations are similar but less conclusive at present relative to such other target populations as the mentally retarded, mentally ill, and children in need of substitute care.

Although far from conclusive, cost data suggest that community and home-based care is more cost-effective for the less impaired (Lawton, 1978; Taietz, 1979). As pointed out by E. Brody (1979), it is a myth that ". . . severely impaired older people can actually be maintained more cheaply in the community than in institutions" (p. 1828). As the level of impairment increases or multiple impairments develop through time a point is reached at

which institutional care is more cost-effective than is community-
and home-based care (E. Brody, 1979). A current dilemma raised
by Weissert (1980) is the extent to which community-based services are used as alternatives within a system of long-term care.
The type of utilization pattern has far-reaching implications for
cost-effectiveness. Moreover, informal supports which currently
constitute the bulk of service support when an impaired person
lives in the community are more appropriate as a response to the
less-impaired given the present absence of accessible, supplementary, formal community-based arrangements (Brody, Poul-
schock, & Masciocchi, 1978). As level of impairment increases
through time, the informal supports are frequently strained beyond their capacity and reluctantly, reliance is placed on such
formal care arrangements as institutional care (E. Brody, 1979)
(Figure 6.1).

In the present view of target population (allocation) the
greater the inclusion of persons with less impairment, the more
the benefit allocation will meet universal criteria. This shift is
seen in the discussion of Title XX eligibility presented by Gilbert
(1977). With fewer people needing highly specialized formal support services as level of impairment increases, the target population becomes selectively smaller. As reflected, for example, in the
original Older Americans Act of 1965, a broad group of elderly
persons was targeted. Subsequent amendments have focused concern on a more selective group within the elderly population,
most recently the vulnerable elderly. Moreover, the family and
community become less of a force as the individual's level of
impairment increases to the point at which responses are focused
almost entirely on the individual to the relative exclusion of the
surrounding environment. An examination of the family status
and characteristics of institutionalized versus noninstitutionalized
elderly persons substantiates the trend in social isolation as impairment increases (E. Brody, 1979). A similar analysis is applicable to the mentally retarded.

This argument assumes that institutionalized elderly are
more impaired than are persons in the community. However,
best estimates suggest at least an equal number of similarly impaired individuals reside in the community, usually because of
caregiving relatives (E. Brody, 1979; S. Brody and colleagues,
1978; Kane & Kane, 1979). Productive policy interventions will
be a function of appropriate identification of characteristics differentiating those elderly who remain in the community from those

requiring institutional care. This is generalized in the view of Wylie (1976):

> The core of quality planning is the problem analysis stage of the process. From this all else flows. Thus a social planner would not recommend—based on an observation that many older people in a community are being institutionalized in other parts of country or state—that the problem is a lack of institutional facilities in the community. (p. 48)

The focus on funding as a dimension of choice as decentralized (block grant) and/or private, parallels the two previous dimensions at the level of less impairment, or in the case of social agencies and communities, greater autonomy. The less impaired individual is able to exercise more control in the decision-making process, usually at a local or community level and to purchase services from the private sector. The child having adjustment problems is more likely to be seen by a social worker in a private not-for-profit setting, where the parent or insurance company reimburses the provider. Over time, if impairment increases, the shift to centralized decision making and public auspice takes precedence. As pointed out by Winn and McCaffree (1979), government rather than the individual is the primary purchaser of long-term, institutionally based care. The individual, as resources are depleted, can no longer purchase services from the private sector with private (personal) funds. Furthermore, the individual exercises increasingly less personal control in decision making (Lawton, 1978), as personal assets are liquidated to cover the increasing costs of care, and in cases of severe incapacity, the transfer of decision-making powers to a court appointed conservator (see Figure 6.1). In a similar way, private, nonprofit, or proprietary agencies are thought to exercise more control in internal policy decisions and in their interactions with the larger environment, whereas the large-scale bureaucratic organizations exercise relatively less control in the process.

Figure 6.1 shows three dimensions of choice requiring policy attention in the promotion of an agreed-upon quality of life. A key element in a policy decision is the transition point between independence and dependence. The goal of social policy decisions is to promote an acceptable quality of life for a maximum amount of time and to prevent at the individual level premature institutionalization and economic dependence, thus postponing the transition from independence to dependence, or at the community level preventing decline from an economically viable to an economically depressed community.

Adding to the complexity of policy decisions is the need to promote movement back to a previous independent or viable status, not just postponing the transition from independence to dependence. At the individual level present policies are designed for one-way movement, for example, reimbursement for nursing home care with extremely limited reimbursement of home-based care (Butler, 1979; Demkovich, 1979). In spite of the continued emphasis on maintaining the stability of the family unit exemplified in legislation such as The Adoption Assistance and Child Welfare Act of 1980 (P.L. 96–272), the realities of child welfare practice frequently fail to facilitate movement of the child back to the family once he/she has been placed in foster care. Under conditions of scarce resources, the efforts of social workers are all too often directed toward the routine maintenance of difficult cases in foster care rather than restoration of the family unit.

It is possible to evaluate the relative adequacy or inadequacy of interventions over time. Two basic types of shifts in independence to dependence can occur. With respect to time-oriented chronicity of a situation which is of a progressive or gradual nature, the greatest inadequacy of interventions is at the point of transition from independence to dependence and the greatest relative adequacy exists at the fully dependent state, that is, institutional care. Adequacy in this sense does not necessarily imply quality or the best choice. For example, the Community Support Systems (CSS) programs for the chronically mentally ill are an attempt to bridge the transition from institution back to community and to prevent further institutionalization. The reader will remember from previous discussion in Chapter 4, the CSS programs were initiated to address the failures of CMHC programs. It might be interpreted that the CMHC adequately served the less-impaired but was not designed (or had insufficient resources) to address the transitional needs of those people with greater levels of impairment. However reluctant the social worker is to suggest institutionalization, for the rural individual it may be the only choice available given the paucity of community mental health services in many areas. This situation is in large part due to reimbursement mechanisms biased toward institutional care and conservative community attitudes which have opposed the development of community alternatives.

As distinct from a gradual shift in a person's life situation are instances when a change occurs very suddenly, for example, a catastrophic illness, sudden unemployment, the death of a spouse, or the death of one or both parents. It is often found that the formal and informal systems respond to an emergency but fail to provide rehabilitation, occupational retraining for other employment, or social support for extended periods of time. The demands become increasingly burdensome (Froland, 1980). Furthermore, few resources are allocated to preventive activities designed to postpone movement toward dependence.

Generalized Strategy

Whereas the probelm-solving process guides generalist social work practice with client and target systems, it is the strategic perspective that directs the policy response of agencies in interaction with their larger environments. Strategic change takes place in that environment in part as the result of state and federal policy decisions. This section details generalist practice applications using a strategic perspective and building on the planning and development activities of social work practice in a rural setting.

Rationing

Related most closely to fiscal and management themes, services rationing is a strategy which responds to environment scarcity and turbulence. It is a way of maximizing the fit or congruity between needs and resources in response to state and federal level policies of scarcity in the human services arena. According to Coulton, Rosenberg, & Yankey (1981), "Rationing is a means of allocating limited resources according to specific rules" (p. 16). The purpose of a rationing strategy is to decide in an explicit way which needs will be addressed by services that are in scarce supply and have great demand.

As a strategy, rationing becomes an explicit, planned way of addressing the issue in the larger environment of scarce service provisions. It differs from eligibility (allocation) decisions in that it is a more specific allocation among those individual or community needs that are eligible for a particular service or benefit. By this is meant individuals needing out-patient mental health services or community neighborhoods as sites for low-income housing units. Coulton and colleagues discuss several ways by which benefits are rationed: queuing; hidden and hard-to-get benefits; creaming; equal rationing; rationing to protect society; the preferred recipients; market rationing; and triage.

Using as an example services for battered women in a rural setting, the practice implications of rationing are examined.

> The battered woman presents a situation of immediate need. Furthermore, the social agency may have a broader profile of need from a community assessment or from state and federal social indicators. The resources of the rural community are sparse both in terms of formal organizations and professional social workers. Nevertheless, need defined as the continuum of well-being indicates immediate intervention is necessary. The agency, however, has faced severe funding cutbacks from the state and seems unable to meet the needs related to increased levels of domestic violence surfacing in an economically depressed community. In addition, the agency, using the continuum framework to formulate its service strategy, views the battered woman as in transition. The most recent battering episode and contact with the agency has meant a break with her family and friends; the informal resource system upon which she has relied in the past.
>
> The overarching goal of the service agency, in this case, is to promote the independent functioning of the woman. This may involve a number of service interventions, for example, job training, assertiveness training, and building of self-confidence.

Rationing according to "creaming" would involve accepting the battered woman for services only if it was thought that services would be effective—that success was possible with expenditure of fewer resources. "Market" rationing would follow the policy of accepting the woman only if she could pay for the needed services or the agency would be reimbursed through Title XX funds. Both of these forms of rationing risk leaving many vulnerable people without services and only postpone the need for services later on with more of a remedial and less of a preventive focus.

In the rural setting, rationing is a strategy that inflicts heavy social costs on the community since services are not found in abundant supply and populations at risk are great in number. However, if any of the several forms of rationing are used as an explicit strategy, the agency may be in a better position to document expressed need and advocate for greater resources from the environment or to examine more closely its internal deployment of resources to increase maximum effective utilization.

Maximization

As a strategy maximization seeks to utilize all of the entitlements and benefits available under federal law that will enhance the quality of life of a target population (Copeland & Iversen, 1981). This population is defined from a generalist perspective to broadly include individuals and communities. The strategy has the purpose of enhancing the service fit between state and local levels and the program allocations at the federal level.

To accomplish a maximization strategy, that is, shift a higher portion of funding for community services to the federal level, Copeland and Iversen suggest the following techniques: (1) upgrading eligibility by monitoring eligibility for multiple programs, particularly those with high levels of federal matching funds; (2) upgrading pricing practices by assuring that costs of care to be reimbursed by the Federal Government are real costs for the service; and (3) encouraging intertitle transfers by transferring cases from a lower match federal program to one which has a higher match and if possible open-ended federal funding.

At the level of one local agency in a rural community it was found that a particular client who was mentally retarded was drawing from the charity resources of a community health clinic for repeated out-patient medical treatment. A maximization strategy was pursued that involved upgrading of eligibility. The particular client was found eligible for SSI and hence Medicaid, much to the amazement of his uninformed parents. This strategy pursues funding such as Medicaid payment of the Medicare Part B premium as was seen in the earlier example of Ms. S. in Chapter 3.

An illustration of the maximization strategy applied in the community economic development area is the recent interagency agreement between HUD and the Small Business Administration to create up to 300,000 new permanent, private sector jobs through the joint investment of $5 billion in small businesses in 21 states. This program allows the combining of federal economic development tools with state resources for economic development and job creation.

From the perspective of rural service agencies, maximization may be a difficult strategy to implement because it requires a high degree of budget and management expertise at the agency level. Nevertheless, with large public agencies serving rural populations, there is a direct link to the state level agencies where maximization can have decidedly positive effects on state service budgets and ultimately result in better services for client populations.

System Development

The third generalized strategy to be discussed is that of system development. As a strategy system development seeks to develop a system of care based on the continuum of care concept whereby a relatively homogeneous client group is served by similar services linked by the movement of clients in and out of the continuum components (Copeland & Iversen, 1981). The purpose of system development is to address the incongruities between an agency attempting to serve a client holistically and the federally mandated environment of categorical programs (excluding the block grant) with little coordination of purpose.

Drawing upon the recent child welfare legislation, P.L. 96–272, the Adoption Assistance and Child Welfare Act of 1980, this strategy is clearly exemplified. The Act specifies the child welfare priorities of the federal government to: (1) maintain the child with her/his own family if possible; (2) place the child with an adoptive family; (3) develop a long-term foster care arrangement; and (4) place the child in an institutional arrangement only if one of the previous priorities is not possible. Underpinning these priorities is the concept of permanency planning which is interpreted to mean a commitment to stable placements for children and continuity in child care (Rooney, 1982). The federal priorities support certain types of services which, when viewed as a continuum of well-being, range from those preventive and supplementary to those remedial and substitutive of the family functioning.

To interact effectively with the Federal Act, P.L. 96–272, the social worker adopts a strategy that is system oriented, that is, responds to the needs of families and children with rationality and predictability and views their needs holistically. If the needs of a family are viewed as acute and transient, services that are preventive and/or crisis-oriented are the most appropriate in addressing the priority of P.L. 96–272. Problems associated with a more chronic, long-occurring situation may require intervention (resources) that will either hold the family together or move toward placement of the child in another environment (Copeland & Iversen, 1981).

Whether the needs are derived from acute or chronic situations, the family is in transition. The task of the social worker is to develop a system that will help maintain independence and allow movement back to a previous, more independent state. System development in the rural setting requires a meshing of formal and informal resources and the assessment of need that is not biased by "a lack of awareness of and education about the incidence and impact of child abuse/neglect and its spin-off problems in the community (truancy, juvenile delinquency, crime, etc.) . . ." (Sefcik & Ormsby, 1980, p. 98). The systems development strategy serves to mitigate the adverse characteristics that engulf the social worker in the rural setting—loneliness, isolation, the lack of specialized resources—as well as the general attitudes cited by Sefcik and Ormsby of conservatism, protection of parental rights, and privacy of the family.

Summary

In this, the concluding chapter of the book, social policy impacts on a rural setting have been linked with generalist social work practice. More specifically, a strategic perspective has been presented as the way of linking policy and practice and contributing to enhancing the quality of life in rural communities.

The debate continues about the nature of practice in rural settings and how or even if it differs from that found in urban areas. Although not settled, the debate has suggested that enough difference exists in the focus and the delivery system to warrant special discussion. Within the setting of advanced industrial society with its characteristics of turbulence and scarcity, the formulation of social policy at all levels of government will have decided impacts on practice. In order to interact with this setting and carry out the activities which seem (at least in proportion) most applicable to practice in rural areas, that is, planning and development, a strategic perspective is particularly useful.

The components of strategy, namely needs, resources, transitions, and accountability, are anchored in the continuum of care concept. Using these components, agencies and larger organizations develop strategies to insure not only a responsiveness to the larger environment but a way of influencing that environment and shaping the future. Three generalized strategies (rationing, maximization, and system development) have been discussed to show the linkage between agency policy decisions, the policies developed at the state and federal level and social work practice in the rural setting.

References

Ansoff, H. Igor. "Strategic Issue Management," European Institute for Advanced Studies in Management. Working Paper No. 79-14, 1979.

Argyris, Chris. *Intervention Theory and Method—A Behavioral Science View*. Reading, Mass.: Addison-Wesley Publishing Co., 1970.

Benedict, Robert C. "Emerging Trends in Social Policy for Older People." Paper presented at the 1977 National Round Table Conference, American Public Welfare Association, Washington, D.C., Dec. 9, 1977.

Boulding, Kenneth. "The Boundaries of Social Policy," *Social Work*, 1967, 12(1):3–11.

Bradshaw, Jonathan. "The Concept of Social Need," *Ekistics*, 1974, 220:184–187.

Brody, Elaine M. "Women's Changing Roles, The Aging Family, and Long-Term Care of Older People," *National Journal*, 1979, 11(43):1828–1833.

Brody, Stanley J., Poulshock, Walter, and Masciocchi, Carla G. "The Family Caring Unit: A Major Consideration in the Long-Term Support System," *The Gerontologist*, 1978, 18(6):556–561.

Brody, Stanley. "The Thirty-To-One-Paradox: Health Needs of the Aged and Medical Solutions," *National Journal*, 1979, 11(44):1869–1873.

Butler, Patricia. "Financing Noninstitutional Long-Term Care Services for the Elderly and Chronically Ill: Alternatives to Nursing Homes," *Clearinghouse Review*, 1979, 13:335–376.

Campbell, Angus, Converse, Philip E., and Rogers, Willard L. *The Quality of American Life: Perceptions, Evaluations, and Satisfactions*. New York: Russell Sage Foundation, 1972.

Copeland, William C. and Iversen, Iver A. "Refinancing and Reorganizing Human Services," *Human Services*, Monograph Series No. 20, 1981.

Coulton, Claudia J., Rosenberg, Marvin L., and Yankey, John A. "Scarcity and the Rationing of Services," *Public Welfare*, 1981, 39(3):15–21.

Council on Social Work Education. *Curriculum Policy Statement*. New York: CSWE, 1982.

Demkovich, Linda E. "In Treating the Problems of the Elderly, There May Be No Place Like Home," *National Journal*, 1979, 11(51-52):2154–2158.

Ecosometrics, Inc. "Discussion paper on the Development of an Analytic Framework for the Identification of Cross-Cutting and Program-Specific Issues Which Relate to the OHDS Mission," (Contract #105-78-7406), 1978.

Estes, Carroll L. *The Aging Enterprise*. San Francisco: Jossey-Bass, 1979.

Farley, O. William, Griffiths, Kenneth A., Skidmore, Rex A., and Thackeray, Milton G. *Rural Social Work Practice*. New York: The Free Press, 1982.

Froland, Charles. "Formal and Informal Care: Discontinuities in a Continuum," *Social Service Review*, 1980, 54(4):572–587.

Gilbert, Neil. "The Transformation of Social Services," *Social Service Review*, 1977, 51(4):624–641.

Gilbert, Neil and Specht, Harry. *Dimensions of Social Welfare Policy*. Englewood Cliffs, N.J.: Prentice Hall, 1974.

Golant, Stephen M. and McCaslin, Rosemary. "A Functional Classification of Services for Older People," *Journal of Gerontological Social Work*, 1979, 1(2):1–31.

Hofer, Charles W. and Schendel, Dan. *Strategy Formulation: Analytical Concepts*. St. Paul: West Publishing Co., 1978.

House, Peter W., Livingston, Robert C., and Swinburn, Carol D. "Monitoring Mankind; The Search for Quality," *Behavioral Science*, 1975, 20:57–67.

Kane, Robert L. and Kane, Rosalie A. "Alternatives to Institutional Care of the Elderly: Beyond the Dichotomy." Santa Monica, Calif.:The Rand Corporation, 1979.

Kimmel, Wayne A. *Needs Assessment: A Critical Perspective*. Department of Health, Education, and Welfare, 1977.

Lawton, M. Powell. "Institutions and Alternatives for Older People," *Health and Social Work*, 1978, 3(2):109–134.

Lee, Gary and Lassey, Marie L. "Rural–Urban Residence and Aging: Directions for Future Research," in Lassey, William R., Lassey, Marie L., Lee, Gary R., and Lee, Naomi (Eds.), *Research and Public Service with the Rural Elderly*, WRDC Pub. No. 4, 1980, 77–87.

Martinez, Arabella. "Relating Human Services to a Continuum of Need," *The Social Welfare Forum, 1979*. The National Conference on Social Welfare. New York: Columbia University Press, 1980.

Mermelstein, Joanne and Sundet, Paul. "Social Work Education for Rural Program Development" in Ginsberg, Leon (Ed.), *Social Work in Rural Communities*. New York: Council on Social Work Education, 1976, 15–27.

Minahan, Anne. "Social Workers and the Future," (editorial), *Social Work*, 1981, 26(5):363–364.

Minahan, Anne and Pincus, Allen. "Conceptual Framework for Social Work Practice," *Social Work*, 1977, 22(5):347–352.

Morasky, Robert L. and Amick, David. "Social System Needs Assessment," *Long Range Planning*, 1978, 11(April):47–54.

Munson, Carlton E. "Supervision and Consultation in Rural Mental Health Practice" in Davenport, Joseph, III, Davenport, Judith A. and Wiebler, James R. (Eds.), *Social Work in Rural Areas: Issues and Opportunities*. Laramie: University of Wyoming, 1980, 87–93.

Patton, Carl V. "Rural Public Transportation: Problems and Possibilities," Ch. VII in Getzels, Judith and Thurow, Charles (Eds.), *Rural and Small Town Planning*. Chicago, Ill.: Planners Press, 1979, 219–250.

Powers, Ronald C. and Moe, Edward O. "The Policy Context for Rural-Oriented Research," in Dillman, Don A. and Hobbs, Darryl J. (Eds.), *Rural Society in the U.S.: Issues for the 1980s*. Boulder, CO.: Westview Press, Inc., 1982.

Quinn, James Brian. *Strategies for Change: Logical Incrementalism*. Homewood, Ill.: Richard D. Irwin, Inc., 1980.

Radford, K. J. *Strategic Planning: An Analytical Approach*. Reston, Va.: Reston Publishing Co., 1980.

Roe vs. Wade 410 U.S. 113 (1973).

Roemer, Milton I. and Roemer, John. "The Social Consequences of Free Trade in Health Care: A Public Health Response to Orthodox Economics," *International Journal of Health Services*, 1982, 12(1):111–129.

Rooney, Ronald H. "Permanency Planning: Boon for all Children?" *Social Work*, 1982, 27(2):152–158.

Sallis, James and Henggeler, Scott W. "Needs Assessment: A Critical Review," *Administration in Mental Health*, 1980, 7(3):200–209.

Sefcik, Thomas R. and Ormsby, Nancy J. "Establishing a Rural Child Abuse/Neglect Treatment Program" in Johnson, H. Wayne (Ed.), *Rural Human Services: A Book of Readings*. Itasca, Ill.: Peacock Pub., Inc., 1980, 97–105.

Steiner, George A. *Strategic Planning*. New York: The Free Press, 1979.

Taietz, Philip and Milton, Sande. "Rural-Urban Differences in the

Structure of Services for the Elderly in Upstate New York Counties," *Journal of Gerontology*, 1979, 34:429–437.

Watkins, Dennis A. and Watkins, Julia M. *Community Services Planning and the Small Municipality: A Quality of Life Framework for the Development of Rural Human Services*. University of Maine at Orono, Life Sciences and Agriculture Experiment Station Bulletin 726, 1976.

Weissert, William G. "Toward a Continuum of Care for the Elderly: A Note of Caution." Paper presented at the 108th Annual Meeting of *APHA*, Detroit, Michigan, Oct. 19–23, 1980.

Winn, Sharon and McCaffree, Kenneth M. "Issues Involved in the Development of a Prepaid Capitation Plan for Long-Term Care Services," *The Gerontologist*, 1979, 19(2):184–190.

Wylie, Mary L. "Nonmetropolitan Social Planning" in Ginsberg, Leon (ed.), *Social Work in Rural Communities*. New York: Council on Social Work Education, 1976, 47–55.

Epilogue

Nancy A. Humphreys

The authors have asked that I address issues of the future, especially future practice in social work. My thoughts reverted to George Orwell's classic book, *Nineteen Eighty-Four*, since 1984 *is* upon us. In addition to provoking unspecified Orwellian fears ("big brother is watching us"), 1984 stands as a unique milestone in the long awaited future. Now the future is here! And with it, our queries, "How can it have occurred so quickly? Why haven't we made more progress?"

In many respects, it is humbling to confront such a critical juncture in the "future." I am impressed both with how astute Orwell was and with how gradually his predicted changes have taken place. My thoughts are drawn to the future beyond 1984, while simultaneously I am reminded of how difficult it is to project the future with confidence. It is in this spirit of expectant uncertainty that I will discuss the future of social work practice in the context of issues previously raised in this book.

The authors initially raised a series of policy issues that emanate from the current conservative shifts in political philosophy, especially the emphases on state and local discretion rather than federal prescription and on increased private sector and volunteer provision of services. The authors also note an ever-decreasing commitment to the poor in favor of meeting the needs of the middle class and the rich, i.e., tax breaks for upper income people and social program cuts for those at lower levels. Questions are posed about the extent to which social services will become less diversified, producing a narrow array of services aimed at reducing the dependency of the poor. With trends to-ward in-kind provision of services and more sophisticated forms of social control, the authors raise questions about how and in what ways the social work profession will respond to these conservative social policy initiatives and the manner in which they will impact the rural environment. More specifically, they wonder whether the social work profession will turn inward and focus on issues of self interest to the neglect of its traditional foci, defining services for and meeting the needs of all citizens, especially those most vulnerable, children, the elderly, the poor and the handicapped, a disproportion of whom reside in rural areas.

There is no way to predict the future with certainty. Only as we move into the future can the authors' questions be answered. But allow me to muse first on the concern that an inward, self-interested focus will develop in the profession. There is historical evidence that suggests that social workers will not forsake their traditions. While the social work profession has always been af-fected by an environment of shifting philosophies, rarely has it mirrored society's changes. On those rare occasions when society has incorporated the values and the ideology of the profession, there has been congruence; usually, however, the interests are divergent. Accordingly, we can hope and anticipate that social workers will not necessarily become more conservative and self interested.

Self interest, as popularly defined, includes attention to so-cial status, competition at the expense of others, devotion to ma-terial security, and so forth, and is associated with individualistic thinking and acting. Self interest, when applied to social workers, tends to have an alternative definition. Perhaps the clearest ex-amples of professional social work self interest can be found in the efforts to achieve legal regulation and in the demand for pay commensurate with the education, training, skills, and responsi-bilities of social workers. These efforts and demands are not com-parable to *self* interest but are primarily oriented to achieving an ultimate goal of better service for *others*.

Social work is not alone in its pursuit of self interest for humanitarian reasons. The women's movement in this country provides a ready comparison. A tenet of the women's movement is "comparable worth." The thrust of demands for "comparable-ness" is not only to redress historical disparities in the pay rates for men and women occupying comparable jobs requiring compa-rable skills providing comparable value to organizations but also to reduce the absolute wage differences between men and women. The efforts by the women's movement to insure comparable pay for work of comparable value is not generally perceived as an inappropriate exercise in the pursuit of self interest. It is seen as a logical development in the evolution of demands by women for equity and parity in all social institutions. Likewise, the same effort pertains to equity and parity for rural residents as they participate in the larger institutions of society. I believe that the "self-interest" pursuits of social workers are, as in the women's movement, directed towards equity, parity, and equality. Should this be surprising when we recall that the social work profession is predominantly populated by women, that the services performed by social workers are akin to services performed in other predominantly male helping professions, and that the self-interest pursuits of our profession have been a part of the larger women's movement? It is therefore imperative that we in the profession critically examine the social workers' concerns for self interest knowing what it is, rather than applying traditional definitions from the larger society. One final observation on this pursuit of self interest bears repeating: the effort by social workers to be licensed is motivated by a desire to improve the quality of services delivered. The direct beneficiaries of better quality services will automatically be the client group served by social workers. To the extent that social workers are serving the disadvantaged, the disenfranchised, the vulnerable, then being serviced by better paid, better trained, more carefully regulated social workers would be in the interest of these groups of citizens.

This discussion of a "better serviced client" brings us back to a second concern voiced by the authors: will the trend toward diversification in services result in those services being delivered increasingly to an advantaged population with social workers forsaking their traditional responsibilities to disadvantaged members of society? Diversification in the provision of social services over the years has brought many more people, representing a broader span of the general population, into contact with the social service system. I do not believe that evidence would attribute this increasing diversity in the client population to social workers' preferences but rather to conditions in clients' lives. Social workers have not sought to serve more advantaged clients. More people, from all socioeconomic groups, have sought services to alleviate stresses in their lives and we now recognize that our responsibility includes the amelioration of social, physical and emotional problems as well as those caused by economic deprivation. The authors' attention to social policy in the rural environment is but one of many examples that characterize the diversification of social services. As social workers expanded their knowledge of rural experience, they were able to offer new services to new client groups. Eventually, people not previously considered disadvantaged were incorporated into the social service delivery system.

In many respects, the authors' work suggests that the diversification of services need not lead to a neglect of our profession's historical concerns for the plight of the disadvantaged. In fact, the reverse can be true. A greater diversification may lead to a more widespread understanding of the problems that traditionally were associated solely with the disadvantaged. This assertion is supported by the fact that many of our profession's fundamental concerns can be seen to involve the general population. For example, the most critical problem in our society today is unemployment, a phenomenon that touches all socioeconomic classes. Chronic unemployment will inevitably force all who experience it into the disadvantaged position. Today, the person who is unemployed is as likely to be formerly employed as never employed; as likely to be the victim of the collapse of a major American industry as the victim of chronic poverty. Social problems that now cut across the middle class and the poor have, in-and-of themselves, resulted in a greater diversification of services. Other examples of such pervasive social problems are alcohol and drug abuse, mental illness, family violence and child abuse. As social problems are less classbound, so must be the services of the social worker. The authors suggest furthermore, that a diversity of services will allow social workers to respond to the needs that differentiate rural from urban populations.

While we may applaud the greater understanding and use of social services by society in general, a warning is in order. What may become problematic is the distribution of these diversified social services. Reductions in the commitment to provide social services may redistribute social service resources in the same manner that economic resources are allocated, with more to advantaged classes and less to those who are disadvantaged. Therefore, maintaining parity and equity in the diversification process may only be possible when circumstances permit services to be readily and universally available, funded at a level that precludes competition in a social services "market place." The authors point to the urban bias in the distribution of resources and the need to formulate social policy in ways that insure adequate and equitable resource allocation to rural areas.

The third and last of the nascent future trends on which I wish to comment addresses directly the profession's commitment to social action and social reform. For those of us in social work education, the level of commitment to the profession paired with the degree of discontent with society as expressed by our current students seems greater than at any time since the 1960s. Discontent with society is a major factor that draws people toward alternatives, and in these times, social work is an alternative to the status quo. Yet, to become a social worker today, at a time of intense unpopularity for the profession, demands a high level of commitment and risk-taking, including endangering the relationship with one's own family, who may not view this as a positive career choice. Therefore, I suggest that we shall become more, not less, socially active as a result of society's intensely conservative philosophies. Our understanding of social policy and our participation in its formulation will be increasingly important. If my speculations are accurate, then I also assume that the highly committed and discontented young professionals being trained in schools of social work today will be more proactive than their earlier counterparts as they move into social work practice.

Some social workers might argue that these conclusions are invalidated by the fact that many students entering schools of social work today are also interested in preparing for private practice, perceived as the "cleanest" setting and the one that is most highly attentive to individual self interest. Several mitigating factors must be addressed. First, the growing number of social workers in private practice parallels the loss of jobs in traditional social work settings and may result primarily from the increasing lack of these positions. I am compelled to ask, "to what extent are social workers more interested in private practice because other social work jobs are not available?" I also question the assumption that social workers in private practice are more conservative or less socially active than their colleagues in other settings. To my knowledge, no research supports this view. Indeed, it must be noted that two of the seven national PACE trustees (the NASW Political Action Committee) are full-time private practitioners without current agency affiliations.

As I look to the future, I see social workers assuming active roles in elected politics as one of the most important strategies for proactive social change. As we respond in an increasingly political fashion, it will add to the evidence that social work practice will be more, not less, proactive in its challenge of current conservative philosophies.

Finally, it is easy to succumb to pessimistic fascination with Orwell's dour prophecies for our age. With 1984 upon us, our advances in meeting social deprivation are small and our resources limited. Nonetheless, I am heartened by the "other interest" of colleagues as they share their talents with persons who have been disadvantaged by Orwellian policies. The continuing social movement's aim toward reducing the disparities between the advantaged and the disadvantaged, the growing political clout of progressive social forces, the idealistic determination of our students—all suggest that Orwell may not have been predicting the future as much as goading us from our complacency. Orwell prophesied what would be, were we not to recognize the forces allied against social justice. As the authors point out, our challenge is to be ever vigilant in assuring that our social policies truly reflect our social needs.

Nancy A. Humphreys, D.S.W.
Director
School of Social Work
Michigan State University

Index

Springer publishing company

Springer Series on Social Work

Vol. 1 / **Battered Women and Their Families**
Intervention Strategies and Treatment Programs
Albert R. Roberts, *Editor*

Studies the impact of battering on all family members, and examines service delivery issues, treatment techniques, and intervention strategies. "An extremely useful contribution...essential reading." — Carolyn Needleman. 224pp / 1984

Vol. 2 / **Disability, Work, and Social Policy**
Models for Social Welfare
Aliki Coudroglou and **Dennis L. Poole**
Foreword by **Sen. Dennis DeConcini**

An in-depth overview of national disability policy, including income maintenance, health care, vocational rehabilitation, and social services. Advocates a model for bringing disabled back into society's mainstream. 160pp / 1984

Vol. 3 / **Social Policy and the Rural Setting**
Julia M. Watkins and **Dennis A. Watkins**

Vol. 4 / **Clinical Social Work in Health Settings**
A Guide to Professional Practice with Exemplars
Thomas O. Carlton

Presents the essential knowledge base for health social work. Discusses diagnosis and intervention, the role of clinical social work in the health care field, and more. Includes a selection of key readings to supplement the text. 320pp / 1984

Vol. 5 / **Social Work in the Emergency Room**
Carol W. Soskis

A state-of-the-art overview of health social work in the modern emergency room. Addresses issues ranging from psychiatric treatment and drug abuse to setting up a social work service and anticipating legal needs. 1984

Order from your bookdealer or directly from publisher.

B14

Springer Publishing Co. 200 Park Ave. S., NY, NY 10003

Springer publishing company

The Elderly in Rural Society
Raymond T. Coward and *Gary R. Lee, Editors*

This comprehensive, landmark volume represents a complete state-of-the-art overview of the situation of America's elderly population in rural areas: their problems, handicaps, special needs, and present level of services. Included in these studies are portrayals of kinship structures, housing patterns, and health services, along with problems related to alcoholism, mobility, and income maintenance. It is a work of immediate concern to professionals and students in the areas of rural studies, gerontology, sociology, and social work, as well as to policy-makers and researchers. 1984

Counseling Through Group Process
Joseph D. Anderson

Techniques for group counseling, with a solid grounding in concepts, theory, and research. The author presents an original, field-tested process model for group practice, taking the reader through each stage: trust, autonomy, closeness, interdependence, and termination. Useful for either formal classroom or skills laboratory use. 288pp / 1984

Counseling Adults in Transition
Linking Practice with Theory
Nancy K. Schlossberg

A transitional model of adult development is the basis for this new approach to counseling skills and process. The book presents an overview of research and theory, exploring the way adults experience concerns about self-identity, competency, stagnation, and goal achievement. This understanding is then applied to the real needs of counselors working with clients, including case examples. 224pp / 1984

Community Support Systems and Mental Health
Practice, Policy and Research
David E. Biegel and *Arthur J. Naparstek, Editors*
Foreword by **Gerald Caplan**

A comprehensive exploration of social support networks including those based on family, neighborhood, church, job, ethnicity, and age group. This interdisciplinary volume demonstrates practical ways in which these support systems can be linked with professional services to provide improved care and to meet the needs of underserved population groups. The book's four sections focus on intervention models, the relation between formal and informal networks, research, and the implications of public policy. 384pp / 1982

Order from your bookdealer or directly from publisher.   B13

Springer Publishing Co. 200 Park Ave. S., NY, NY 10003